F
Frau

Elder Fraud Wars

Case Histories from an Enforcement Attorney

DAVID NEIL KIRKMAN

Exposit

Jefferson, North Carolina

ISBN (print) 978-1-4766-8149-8
ISBN (ebook) 978-1-4766-3971-0

LIBRARY OF CONGRESS CATALOGUING-IN-PUBLICATION DATA
BRITISH LIBRARY CATALOGUING DATA ARE AVAILABLE

Library of Congress Control Number 2020017059

Front cover images © 2020 Shutterstock

Printed in the United States of America

Exposit is an imprint of McFarland & Company, Inc., Publishers

Exposit
Box 611, Jefferson, North Carolina 28640
www.expositbooks.com

To my wife Debra,
Will Garrett and Bill Tucker,
each of the other elder fraud warriors mentioned herein
and, most important of all,
the victims and their families

Table of Contents

Introduction:
The Elder Fraud Industry
Marches Through Town

Each spring when I was in high school, my town hosted a 20-mile char-ity walk-a-thon. Those of us who participated found ourselves walk-ing through almost every neighborhood in the community. To divert my attention from the aching and throbbing that developed in my legs, I began counting each home or street along the way where there resided a young high school beauty for whom I held an unrequited crush. One year my final tally was something like four dozen.

Now, almost five decades later, I can take you for a drive along that same walk-a-thon route and point out the homes or streets of older towns-people who have lost $10,000 to $100,000 to con artists. Their number eas-ily exceeds the four dozen high school crushes mentioned above. Several homes, in fact, belong to parents (or late parents) of old schoolmates. I can expand the route to the three large retirement communities now sit-uated on the edges of town and show you the cottages and apartments of victims who have lost $100,000 to $250,000 each.

Until recently, I could have taken you on a similar "fraud tour" in any community in the state of North Carolina. Here's how.

For three decades prior to my retirement in 2017, I was an enforce-ment attorney in the Consumer Protection Division of the North Car-olina Attorney General's Office. During the latter portion of my tenure there, I also managed a small unit known as the Elder Fraud—Prevent Re-Victimization Project. It was funded by the federal Victims of Crime Act (VOCA) and the North Carolina Governor's Crime Commission. As its name and funding sources imply, the project's task was to serve older North Carolina fraud victims and keep them from being victimized again.

The chapters you are about to read chronicle the growth of an insidious, multinational elder fraud industry whose main weapon is repeat victimization. Repeat victimization and the staggering individual losses it often inflicts set elder fraud apart from the hundreds of other types of scams we handled in the Attorney General's Office.[1]

The Elder Fraud Project worked with as many as 2000 North Carolina fraud targets and fraud victims each year. Prior to their involvement with the Project, each year's crop of new victims had lost as much as $10 million, and the scammers were pressuring them to pay millions more. On average, they had been victimized four times already, but some had been defrauded dozens of times for hundreds of thousands of dollars. The average individual losses ranged from $8,000 to $10,000, depending upon the year. The good news is that most of those victims suffered no further losses to the scammers once the Project staff started working with them. Those who continued to deal with the fraud artists, however, challenged and confounded their family members, our staff and the friends, neighbors and businesspeople who wanted to protect them from further harm.

One year, back when Canada was a hotbed of groups targeting U.S. seniors with sweepstakes, lottery and credit scams, we and our attorney general colleagues from six other states surveyed our citizens who had used one of the well-known wire service companies to send money across the border. We were trying to determine what percentage of them were victims of fraud. To our surprise around 25 percent of the transfers over $500 were fraud-induced.

Even more surprising was the fact that only 1 percent of the North Carolina victimizations had been reported to us or to our federal counterparts, the Federal Trade Commission. Our North Carolina home repair fraud cases, which saw older victims repeatedly handing huge sums of cash to their victimizers, also featured a report rate of around 1 percent. This was consistent with widely cited recent studies that put the report rate for elder financial exploitation at just over 2 percent.[2] These percentages suggest that the number of actual elder fraud victims in North Carolina dwarfs the numbers cited above and that their total financial losses are even more staggering—perhaps several hundreds of millions per year.

Judging from the average victim's losses, one would think that the elder fraud industry confines itself to the state's more affluent citizens.

The Project's statistics—and the cases described in this book—reveal that no community or income group is immune. The same holds true for education level, business acumen, political affiliation, race, national origin and gender. Our sweepstakes scam victims ranged from a pair of retired mill workers who lived in a tiny house in eastern North Carolina to a corporate executive from the west coast who had retired to an upscale retirement community in the mountains. The former almost died after a sweepstakes scammer conned them out of their January Social Security payments and left them unable to pay utility bills, buy food or purchase medicine. The latter lost over $900,000, more than any other North Carolina victim of phony sweepstakes officials.

A retired bank vice-president in a small town in the central part of the state lost $1.2 million to overseas sweetheart scammers over the course of two years. She cashed out her retirement savings, maxed out her credit card accounts and mortgaged her home so she could send cash to her on-line love interest, a supposed Texas construction company owner working in the Middle East. The payments began when the fictitious Texan suddenly sent her a series of emails claiming that he had been thrown in jail and needed money to post bail and hire attorneys. He then begged her for more money in order to pay supposed fines, back taxes and bribes to corrupt prosecutors and police officials.

Another former business executive living near Charlotte lost $3.2 million over three years to scammers in Nigeria who claimed that one of his distant relatives had died in their country and left an enormous estate. Every few days, they presented him with another huge fee or tax payment that needed to be paid, or another expensive crisis that had to be resolved, before his $50 million inheritance could be released.

Elder fraud is not just a North Carolina phenomenon. My attorney general counterparts throughout the United States reported identical problems in their states. When I attended the International Association of Financial Crime Investigators conference in August 2019, attendees from other countries spoke of how their older citizens were being targeted and defrauded in similar fashion.

As staggering as the dollar losses might seem, the non-monetary losses inflicted by the elder fraud industry are far, far greater. Those losses are not confined to the individuals who have lost their savings either. You will become painfully familiar with these other victims as you read further.

What follows are summaries of actual elder fraud cases and initiatives that my public and private sector colleagues and I handled. The criminals we targeted in these cases and initiatives were mostly organized groups—businesses, basically—that systematically targeted and defrauded seniors. The very common phenomenon of an individual relative, neighbor, caregiver, legal guardian or clergy member who insinuates himself or herself into the heart and financial affairs of a vulnerable senior is not the subject of this book, although that problem is just as severe and equally difficult to attack.

The following stories about Tommy and Carol McPhaul, the Colonel and "the Elder Orphan" are compelling, sometimes *uplifting* personal tales in and of themselves. The techniques and audacity of individual members of the elder fraud industry, such as charismatic driveway paver "Tommy C," will be explored as well. After reading these case histories, you, too, will be quite familiar with the depth and breadth of the elder fraud industry, the types of people who comprise it and the techniques that they have developed over the years to harvest the wealth of an entire generation. You will also become familiar with the various age-related vulnerabilities that elder fraud artists carefully look for in their victims and then exploit. Whether you are a banker, a law enforcement official, a medical professional or a family member, these insights should help you to spot elder fraud incidents as they occur, predict what is likely to confront the victim next and then get the victim out of harm's way.

We will also explore

1. legitimate business services that scammers depend upon to obtain their victims' savings and how separating the scammers from those services is a key tactic in fighting the frauds;

2. successes, frustrations and failures that my colleagues and I experienced as we fought different elements of the elder fraud industry;

3. the elder fraud industry's tactic of "reloading" that makes their crimes so devastating compared to other types of scams;

4. why we do not have more elder fraud prosecutions;

5. the importance of breaking a victim out of his or her cycle of fraud and some techniques for accomplishing that breakout; and

6. the importance of enlisting as many people as possible (family members, businesses, professionals, court officials, and local,

state and federal law enforcement) to spot and address each elder fraud incident.

Many Americans have older loved ones who have been taken by elements of the elder fraud industry. Many professionals have had customers, patients, parishioners or clients who have been defrauded by it. Very few people, however, have been able to witness the full breadth and depth of the elder fraud industry, the age-related vulnerabilities of its victims, and the techniques it has developed to separate those victims from their life's savings and even their beloved family members. As one of those few, I want to share these things with you.

My hope is that these cases inspire you to join the war against the elder fraud industry. It does not require a full-time commitment. Each of the professionals who worked these cases and initiatives had significant non-elder fraud duties that commanded the bulk of their daily schedules, yet they had a huge impact. Anyone can play a vital role in stopping these crimes.

PART ONE

Before We Even Called It "Elder Fraud"

1

Will Garrett's Morning Run

One morning in 1994, Will Garrett was jogging through his neighborhood in the Richmond, Virginia, area. He noticed a red truck in the driveway of an older neighbor's home, plus other trucks parked on the street in front. This was not the first time that Will had noticed the trucks, or that most of them bore North Carolina tags, or that they did not have the name of a business on their sides. It had been weeks since he had run past that home and the trucks were not there.

Will was a special agent with the FBI, about 52 years old and approaching the end of his career with the bureau. It had been a highly successful career, one filled with excitement, intellectual challenges and, from time to time, substantial danger. This particular morning run would launch one of his most meaningful and satisfying cases. He had no idea what was going on at his neighbor's home, but his professional instincts warned him the guys in the trucks were dirty. And so, as FBI special agents are wont to do, he started investigating.

Will greeted the older neighbor one morning as she retrieved the *Richmond Times-Dispatch* from her driveway. He told her that he was thinking of having some remodeling work done at his home and asked about the crew that was working so hard on her roof and under her house each day.

She replied that they had been working on her home for more than six months, fixing various problems and letting her know whenever they found new ones. Will could tell by her pronunciation of "house" ("hoose") that she was genuine Virginian, either from Richmond or points south. He also surmised that she was in her 80s.

He asked how she managed to find these fellows. She replied that they found her, that one of them knocked on the door and asked to clean the leaves out of her gutters. The man stated he had been working on another house just around the corner but was having to wait for some supplies to be delivered. Claiming he was bored and wanted something to do, he offered to clean out all of her gutters for just $25.

She told Will that once the man finished the gutter cleaning, he came down off the roof and showed her a handful of rotted wood. He warned that in several spots her roof decking was just like the material in his hand and that it was due to water leaks caused by the previous roofing contractor's poor workmanship. He warned, further, that she would suffer a series of expensive problems if she did not get the roof repaired immediately.

She then described how she had paid the man and his crew more than $40,000 during the ensuing six months for a series of jobs on the roof and throughout the house. At that moment, they were performing additional work that would take the price above $50,000. When he asked her, "What kinds of work?" she responded, "Wood rot. Attic and floor bracing. Rafter repairs. Waterproofing. Mold abatement. Mortar mites in the chimney."

Mortar mites?

The repairman claimed that mites were gnawing away the mortar between the bricks. He warned her that the chimney was about to topple onto the house next door.

The next morning, Will arrived at the woman's home before the work crews showed up. He obtained her permission to go up into the attic and onto the roof to check out their work.

Will quickly surmised that the workers had done very little real work other than lay new shingles over those that were already on the roof. In addition, they had installed unnecessary wooden braces throughout her attic and basement, covered the cinder block basement walls with new, unneeded coats of paint (expensive "water proofing"), and driven hundreds of nails into rafters and floor joists for no reason whatsoever. There was also a noticeable smell everywhere in the house, a combination of kerosene and bleach.

When he asked the homeowner about the smell, she replied that the men had gone throughout the house with a big spray jug, treating several areas for toxic mold. Apparently, they had to repeat the process several times because the mold infestation was so bad. She told Will he was smelling a fancy European manufactured fungicide, that it was very expensive but very effective.

No, it was bleach and kerosene. Will was certain of it.

Will never did find any mortar mites. The mortar between the chimney bricks appeared to be as sound as when it was applied and pointed 50 years before. As far as he could tell, the workers had simply painted the old mortar white to make the poor homeowner believe they had refurbished her chimney. The sloppiness of their paint-between-the-bricks project was not visible two stories below when she looked up at it. She proudly told Will that she had paid $5,000 for the newly mortared chimney and that it was worth every penny.

Will noticed something else that morning. As he was speaking with the homeowner in her yard, the workers pulled their trucks up to the curb in front of the house one by one. Some trucks were red, and some were white. All bore North Carolina tags. Suddenly and in unison, the drivers restarted their engines and slowly drove the trucks down the street and around the corner. During subsequent visits, he noticed similar movements. The men would drive on if they spotted Will there. If they were already present when Will arrived, each would slip out of the house or the yard without saying anything at all, then drive off.

One day during his lunch break, Will decided to drive by the woman's house. As he rounded the corner at the end of the street, he could see the red and white pickups in front of the house again. One of the men was carrying a large spray jug up the front steps and into the house.

"Must be more mortar mite spray," he thought to himself.

When he got back to his office, Will drafted a report on his visits with the elderly homeowner. He did not have an open investigation on the poor woman's dealings with the men in the red and white trucks, but he wanted to memorialize what he heard and learned. Perhaps the local law enforcement folks would be interested.

When he was done with the report, Will stuck it in a file folder. He paused for a minute. Then he grabbed a sheet of file folder labels, stuck it into the carriage of the typewriter and pecked on the keys.

"Operation Spray Jug."

2

Three Early Cases

As it turns out, I handled elder fraud cases long before I realized elder fraud even existed. Lessons learned from those cases helped me throughout my legal career. The following are summaries of two such cases from my days as a newly minted attorney working with Legal Services of Southern Piedmont, Inc. (LSSP) in Charlotte back in the early 1980s, plus one case from my early days in the North Carolina Attorney General's Office.

Early Case 1: "How can I get sued 'cause someone is crazy?"

When I worked for LSSP, all of our clients were low income individuals and all of our cases involved non-criminal matters: landlord-tenant, government benefits, bankruptcy, domestic violence, consumer transactions, etc. At that time, Legal Services eligibility guidelines still allowed some low-income homeowners to qualify for services, and that was a good thing. Scammers often targeted such homeowners in a big way. It was not the modest homes they were after but the land on which they were constructed, especially if the land was in an area being eyed for expensive, upscale development.

Such a case walked through the door one afternoon when I was working in the Concord satellite office of LSSP. It was in early 1981. The prospective client, his wife and his two elderly parents had just been sued for non-payment of a contract for home improvements which the parents had signed. The plaintiff, an aluminum siding contractor, had placed liens on the property for labor and materials and was seeking a monetary judgment against all four of them for several thousand dollars.

"That's my property," the prospective client thundered, "and I never signed any contract to do work on it! I don't even live there—it's just my elderly parents and two of my nieces. How did I get sued? Why did my wife get sued? We didn't even know work was being done."

"And the work they did?" he continued. "Somebody walled in the front and side porches with not so much as a tiny window. And they went and built plywood walls down the middle of two little bedrooms, saying they were now four bedrooms. Just crazy! Lawyer Kirkman, how can I get sued 'cause someone is crazy?"

This was something I had to go see, but the home was in neighboring Stanly County and I had other clients to meet that afternoon. The client hung around Concord as I finished up my afternoon appointments, then led me down the highway to the property. The drive took about 35 minutes.

The home was situated on a forested hillside and enjoyed a gorgeous view that was punctuated by the waters of Badin Lake in the distance. The structure was old, wooden and bore no paint whatsoever on its exterior cladding. Its raw wood siding was aged to a grayish-brown hue and seemed to be preserved only by the rays of the sun. The roof was tin and fairly new. Smoke was drifting straight up from a metal chimney near the center of the roof line. Behind the structure was a decrepit wooden privy that bore all the signs of being in service.

The client led me on a tour of the remodeled porches and the bedrooms. Each of them had been converted into dark, narrow closets. Storing stuff—rather than sleeping or relaxing—was about the only function those spaces were good for anymore. As the client kept saying when he first entered my office in Concord, the "work" was just crazy.

I spoke with the elderly parents, both in their early 80s and both visibly upset. They were still and quiet at first, staring downward as if penitent for committing some kind of crime or sin. They began to respond after I assured them repeatedly that nobody was going to jail and that they had done nothing wrong.

I drew very little information from them initially. My questions were a bit complicated and delivered at a pace that was inappropriately fast. That tendency of mine to get down to business, to get to the point, made clients defensive and had earned me poor marks during client counseling drills when I first came to work at LSSP. It was causing this elderly pair to clam up. I eased up on the verbal throttle and invited them to tell me the story of the contractor's visit.

The couple looked at one another and launched into a narrative. Whenever one of them hesitated or faltered, the other would jump in and continue. They recounted how the contractor drove up their long gravel driveway one morning as they were sitting on the front porch. After the dust settled and he emerged from his car, a big Buick, the contractor walked up to the base of their front steps. He said he was lost and asked for a glass of water. As he was waiting for one of the nieces to bring the water, he introduced himself. He asked the couple how their morning was going, complimented their beautiful property, and then asked how many people lived in the house and how many bedrooms it had. He quickly studied the outside of the home and announced that he could add some extra rooms to it for just a few hundred dollars.

Although they repeatedly told him they were on Social Security and their monthly checks amounted to just a few hundred dollars, he assured them they could make the monthly payments with little difficulty. "With four bedrooms instead of two, the nieces can both have their own rooms, plus the house will double in value! You're really going to thank me." Without giving them a chance to think it over, he went and sat in his car for several minutes. Then he returned with some documents and placed them on the small table in front of the couple. Before they knew it, he had gotten them both to sign, even though they told him they could not read. She signed her name with big block letters, and he employed a small "x." And with that, the contractor stuffed the papers in his pocket and declared, "These improvements will pay for themselves!"

A couple of days later, men arrived at the house with lumber, power saws and hammers. They walled in the porches and divided the tiny bedrooms. As quickly as they arrived, they were gone. Neither the contractor nor the workmen left a copy of the contract with the couple.

"I live 15 minutes away and I had no idea they done this to Momma and Daddy until after they left," said the son. "Nobody got my permission to mess with this house. Not my parents. Not the contractor. I called the deputies. They told me it wasn't a criminal matter."

I turned to the elderly couple. "Did the salesman ever ask if you were the legal owners?"

"No, sir. He just asked if this was our place. We live here, so we said yes. Then he asked if we had a mortgage. We said no. And right then is when he ran back down to his car and started filling out papers."

"It *is* their place … my wife inherited it and we let them live in it," added the son. "If he'd come to us like he should have, we would have told him to get off the property!"

It was pretty obvious what had gone down. The aluminum siding contractor had spotted this older couple living in an aging house and guessed they probably could not afford to pay for improvements to it. He would get them to enter into an installment contract with monthly payment terms that were difficult to meet, then assert liens and file suit when the couple missed payments. After the homeowners, clearly too poor to afford an attorney, failed to respond to the lawsuit within the 30-day deadline, the aluminum siding contractor would obtain a default judgment against them for thousands of dollars. He would then buy the property cheap when the sheriff auctioned it off on the courthouse steps in order to pay off the judgment. Then he could build a nice vacation home on the land. Or maybe three or four of them.

It was a classic property grab scenario, straight out of the Legal Services training manual.

There was just one problem with the aluminum siding contractor's plan. He had assumed that the older couple owned the place. As their son protested upon entering my office earlier that day, they could not legally bind him and his wife, the actual owners, to a contract for improvements to the property if they had no knowledge of the transaction. Likewise, the parents' signatures on the contract (assuming they were even competent to sign such a document) did not create enforceable liens against the property for the costs of labor and materials. At best, it simply created a contractual obligation on the parents' part to pay money for the work done.

But none of this stopped the contractor from trying to get the property. The civil lawsuit he and his attorney filed against the four family members alleged that the son and his wife both showed up and consented to the work when, in fact, they had not.

I consulted with the director of LSSP, Terry Roche, when I arrived at the main office in Charlotte the following morning. Terry wanted us to defend the case based on fraud. The builder never fulfilled his promise to build two more bedrooms for them. He had simply converted a two-bedroom house into a bizarre complex of closets. His promise that the work would increase the value of the home was false as well. It probably was worth less.

Terry also wanted our response to the lawsuit to include a counterclaim for money damages against the contractor for unfair and deceptive trade practices. After all, someone had to pay to undo the bogus work and that "someone" should be the contractor-plaintiff, not the homeowners.

By suggesting a strong countersuit, Terry was thinking "impact litigation," a philosophy of North Carolina legal services lawyers at that time. Under that theory, a case should benefit the individual clients in question yet also serve as a warning to others who engaged in similar misdeeds.

I filed the family's response to the lawsuit and quickly moved for dismissal of the contractor's claims. Attached to my motion for dismissal were sworn affidavits signed by the son and his wife explaining what they did and did not know about the transaction, plus a notice to the court that the elderly parents would be present to give verbal testimony, since neither of them could draft or proofread a written affidavit. Photos of the "work" were attached to the motion for good measure. They spoke volumes.

When the motion to dismiss came on for hearing a few weeks later, the judge opened the file and winced. "Counsel, I read this file over the weekend. If plaintiff is really, really lucky, all he will ever get out of this exercise is an uncollectable judgment against the two elderly parents. I will hold this motion hearing open until the end of the week so that you can try and resolve the case on your own." (Translation: Get the hell out of my courtroom, plaintiff, before I throw you out.)

And with that, the aluminum siding contractor's scheme to grab an elderly couple's home and land went up in smoke. He probably would have succeeded—and the couple would have been homeless—had they actually been the owners and no one had come to LSSP for help.

Early Case 2: "50 percent energy savings!"

Another such case was assigned to me just before I left LSSP in 1981. It involved an older homeowner whose house was in an African American neighborhood near downtown Charlotte known as Cherry. My staff attorney colleague at LSSP, Sharif Abdullah, had been working for over a year to organize the Cherry community, bring it better municipal services and, most important, preserve it from being totally wiped out by development the way other such neighborhoods near downtown Charlotte had been. Cherry was in an area of the city bordered by Mercy, Presbyterian and Charlotte Memorial hospitals, the posh Myers Park and Queens

Roads residential neighborhoods, a small shopping mall and busy commuter thoroughfares such as Independence Boulevard and Randolph Road. Cherry was most certainly in the developers' crosshairs, and there was no shortage of opportunists eager to buy up its tiny homes and lots before those developers struck.

The homeowner in question, let's call her Mrs. J, was brought to the LSSP office by Carrie Graves, the head of the LSSP Client Council. Ms. Graves reported that the client had just received a notice to pay almost $4,000 if she wanted to avoid losing her home in a foreclosure sale. Mrs. J, a retired hospital worker who had become blind with age, was shocked to her core when a neighbor read the foreclosure notice to her, as she had paid off her regular mortgage decades earlier.

It took a bit of discussion and a trip to the courthouse to pull certain documents, but we soon sorted out what was going on with this lady's home. The foreclosure procedure stemmed from a door-to-door sales transaction the previous fall in which Mrs. J purchased some electric baseboard heaters. Instead of just buying some heaters, she had bought into a web of deceit and confusing legal documents.

It all began when the baseboard heater salesman noticed smoke rising from her chimney. He also noticed a cord of freshly split firewood stacked neatly in her back yard near the base of her back porch. He knocked on the door, sized up Mrs. J's vision problem when she greeted him, then struck quickly.

"Ma'am, I notice you are heating your home here with wood. I have a heating system for you that will be easier to operate, is more energy efficient and will save you lots of money."

"Well, I've been heating this little house with my woodstove for decades. My nephew brings the wood from Lincoln County for free and it doesn't take much of it to keep the place good and warm."

The salesman had been waiting to spring his next comment: "At your age and with your vision problems, dear, you don't need to be going out to the woodpile in the dead of night to gather fuel for your woodstove. And you really shouldn't be hauling it up those steps when they are all covered with rain or snow or ice. What if you slipped or tripped and fell down those steps in the darkness and no one could see you or hear you?"

The salesman had a point. More than once Mrs. J had slipped while carrying firewood up to the house, landing on the cold ground with pieces of wood scattered all around her.

Before the hour was out, the salesman had convinced her to buy one electric baseboard heating unit for each of the four rooms in her little home. Although it would take a lot of expensive electricity for those heaters to warm up the uninsulated house the way the little wood stove in her living room could, he promised her "50 percent energy savings" and talked about how the evil OPEC oil cartel would be driving energy prices even higher. He then presented a contract for the purchase of the heaters, a financing agreement, a promissory note for the amount of the contract and a deed of trust (a mortgage instrument) securing her obligation to repay the note.

Before she signed these papers, Mrs. J asked him how much she was agreeing to pay. He told her it would be $100 per heater unit. What he failed to tell her was that he was actually charging her several hundred dollars per unit, plus installation fees, taxes and interest at 16 percent over five years. The total of payments for the heaters and the interest on the installment loan was more than $4,000, all secured by the mortgage on her home. If she missed a monthly payment, an "acceleration clause" in the finance agreement made all the remaining payments immediately due and payable.

And one other thing: he never told Mrs. J she was mortgaging her home to ensure payment of $4,000 for what he had told her would be $400 worth of heaters. How could she know the truth otherwise? She was sharp but she was blind.

The salesman returned the next day and screwed the four heaters to her baseboards, then plugged them into the nearest electrical outlets. "Just turn off the ones in the rooms that you are not using. It's called 'zoning.' It'll save you lots of money, dear." Then he left without ever giving her copies of the sales documents.

I asked Mrs. J if anyone else was present when she signed the documents, to which she replied, "No. Just him." One reason I asked this was because some of the documents were notarized and a notary public who was following the law would have asked her for identification before witnessing her signature and stamping the documents. Another reason I asked was that the notary's presence and the ritual of attesting to the signature on each document likely would have signaled that she was involving herself in a transaction far more complex than a straight-up purchase of four space heaters. Armed with that information, Mrs. J could have gotten a friend or neighbor to explain what she was signing.

Also interesting was the fact that, in addition to getting the notary to witness Mrs. J's signature sight unseen, the salesman registered the deed of trust at the county Register of Deeds office the day of the transaction. He had to have been anticipating a default in payments, a foreclosure on the home and the opportunity to buy her property for practically nothing once it was put up for auction on the courthouse steps.

I spoke with Terry Roche about the best legal strategy for saving Mrs. J's home. The plan we devised was similar to the one we had just employed to help the Stanly County family. We would file suit against the heater salesman for fraud in the inducement of a contract and for violating North Carolina's Unfair and Deceptive Trade Practices Act, then go straight to a judge for temporary restraining order stopping the foreclosure proceeding. The civil suit and supporting documents were drafted and filed the next day. Before we could schedule a hearing before a judge, a lawyer for the salesman contacted us and agreed to stop the foreclosure sale. "It's just a big misunderstanding, David." Within a couple of weeks, I had left LSSP, the transaction was cancelled voluntarily, the baseboard heaters were picked up and our elderly client's home was out of jeopardy. Mrs. J's nephew had a gas furnace installed in her home.

Early Case 3: John the Old Marine

From the time that I was 11 years old until the first few years I worked in the North Carolina Attorney General's Office, there was a wonderful couple in our church, the Kennedys. John Kennedy sold school textbooks for a living and Ann Kennedy helped oversee research grants at the University of North Carolina. Their children went to school with my sisters and me. John was a hail-fellow-well-met if ever there was one. Ann, too, was—and still is—quite a charmer.

In his later years, after he had retired, John became blind. That problem had little or no impact on his jocular personality. Like so many Irish-Americans of his generation, he never lost his gift for gab, and his sense of humor remained strong despite his newfound disability. He could also convey a gut-wrenching tale if he wanted to. At a church picnic one day, he told me a series of gripping stories from his experiences as a Marine fighting in the Pacific, stories that easily could have been transcribed and published as a bestselling book if only someone had recorded them.

One morning in the late '80s after Sunday services concluded, John said, "David, I need to talk to you about something that's troubling me. Can we go outside?" John seemed so cheerful all the time that I never pictured him being troubled by anything. He certainly was in this instance, though. You could see it all over his face.

"Sure, Mr. Kennedy. Let's go."

He unfolded his red and white cane and led me through the church kitchen, then out to a picnic table in the side yard.

"I've got this bill collector after me. It's all very embarrassing."

"What kind of bill is it?"

"Well, I don't really think it's a bill at all. It's … it's just plain fraud!"

"Hmm. Okay."

"Do you know what a 1-900 call is?"

"Sure. It's where you place a phone call to hear information on something, such as a stock analyst's report or a news story replay, and your phone bill is charged a fee for each minute you're on the line. It can get expensive really quickly." I felt too embarrassed to add, "And it is a way that guys can pay to have a woman talk dirty to them over the telephone." It seemed like he was too old to know about 1-900 sex-line calls.

"Well, this bill collector down in Miami claims I made repeated 1-900 sex-line calls and refused to pay for them. He says he's going to sue me to get the money for all my calls and that the lawsuit will be reported in the local paper. Claims I owe over $600!"

"And you didn't make the calls, I am guessing."

"Heavens no! I'm at home with Mrs. Kennedy almost 24 hours a day. How could I ever make such calls without her hearing me or seeing the charges on the phone bill? How would I even find out which number to call when I am blind? Still, I am about to pay the $600. It's all too stressful and could lead to lots of embarrassment."

"Did these 1-900 charges ever show up on your phone bill?"

"No. Never. Ann certainly would have asked about it!"

He gave me the bill collector's name and phone number, then described his demeanor over the phone.

"He's definitely ex-military—probably a former drill sergeant or something. You can tell by his voice and his attitude. He's very firm and commanding and only lets you talk if he asks a question. He tells you that you have one opportunity to make things right before he lets your entire community know that you are an old pervert and a cheat! Well, I'm neither a pervert nor a cheat." Then he smiled and said, "But I do plead guilty to being old."

"Let me look into this, Mr. Kennedy. I'll call the guy when I get to the office tomorrow. Bill collectors usually suspend their collection efforts against a supposed debtor if the Attorney General's Office gets involved."

"I'd be much obliged, David."

I called the bill collector first thing the following morning. I identified myself and my office and told him the reason for my call. His reaction was swift and sustained: "How can the government that I fought for and almost died for be harassing me for collecting on a legitimate debt?! You should be working to protect me from criminals like old Mr. Kennedy!" He went on and on, peppering me with questions about my integrity as a lawyer, my duty as a government official, and why he should not sue me.

Throughout my years of representing consumers, going way back to my early days as a Legal Services attorney, I knew that belligerent initial responses such as these were clear signs that the business knew it was engaged in something wrong. Legitimate businesses seldom responded in such a defensive and caustic manner. I told him I would be sending him an investigative subpoena for copies of all records supposedly supporting his claim that Mr. Kennedy dialed those numbers and to have his attorney contact me to discuss it.

"We have tapes of your client talking dirty to those girls. You will regret this!"

"Fine. Include the tapes with the other documents requested in the subpoena. While our office investigates this, refrain from further calls to Mr. Kennedy, okay?"

"I don't have to follow your instructions."

I asked Mr. Kennedy to contact me as soon as he received another communication from this bill collector. He never heard from the guy again. In the meantime, I scoured our consumer complaint index to see if we had similar complaints against the company. We did. I also skimmed recent monthly editions of the *Consumer Protection Bulletin*, which was compiled and mailed out by the National Association of Attorneys General, also known as "NAAG." Sure enough, it contained reports from various states about a Miami bill collector who tried to browbeat consumers into paying for disputed 1-900 sex-line calls. I contacted a couple of the assistant AGs from other states who had posted information about the collector and we agreed to form a multi-state group to address the problem. Using the newly popular tools of fax messages and conference calls, we soon mustered a posse of about a dozen of us from across the country.

When the assistant AGs from the 12 states began analyzing their consumer complaints against this collection agency and interviewing the complainants, it quickly became apparent that all of the recipients of the collector's calls were citizens in their 70s or older.

One AAG remarked, "This guy's whole shtick is to target old folks and humiliate them over the phone until they pay for calls they never made. What a racket!"

That was a new concept to us: phone scammers targeting older consumers exclusively. Within a year or two, all of us would be struggling with an epidemic of phone scams that targeted seniors.

The 12 states issued investigative subpoenas to the charmless, caustic bill collector, requiring production of all documents supporting his payment demands to their citizens for supposed 1-900 sex-line calls. We also invited him and his attorney to join us for a conference call on a particular date. He joined the call and told us he did not need an attorney. He defiantly argued all collection efforts were legitimate, we were defending fraud artists and he had documentation proving all the unpaid 1-900 charges were legitimate. One of the AAGs then asked why all of the supposed debtors in his collection portfolio appeared to be elderly.

"I don't know what you are talking about!"

A few days later, the collection agency was out of business. Its phone line was disconnected, and local officials found its small office abandoned. The only things left behind were lists, purchased from legitimate list brokerage companies, containing the names, addresses, phone numbers and ages of citizens over 75. We never learned who was behind the scam. The culprit or culprits had used aliases to set it up and run it. Ironically, this bill collector, who claimed he collected on unpaid 1-900 calls for phone companies, left an unpaid bill of over $30,000 for long distance debt collection calls that had been placed to seniors throughout the country.

John Kennedy was pleased when I saw him at church and told him he had helped take down a new scam that targeted American seniors exclusively.

We were still a few years away from using the phrases "senior scam" and "elder fraud."

The scammers who picked on the older consumers described in the first two cases above probably would scam—and did scam—persons of any age. It is doubtful that they were part of a specialized and sophisticated elder fraud industry, as described elsewhere in this book. Still, those salesmen knew how to spot age-related vulnerabilities and exploit them quickly. Those abilities coupled with audacity and a cold heart are at the core of elder fraud.

The Stanly County couple whose humble house was on the beautiful piece of land both were experiencing age-related declines in their cognitive abilities, particularly their abilities to process information as rapidly as it was coming at them. I spotted that problem shortly after initiating my conversation with them. By the time the fast-talking contractor was 18 sentences into his pitch, they probably were still processing the first sentence and totally bewildered. To use an old expression, he then "steamrolled" them into signing. The couple's inability to read was, in a way, an additional age-related vulnerability, as it was not that uncommon for lower income people born at the turn of the 20th century to be illiterate.

The age-related vulnerabilities of the client from Cherry did not include cognitive decline but did include failing eyesight and declining physical strength. The heater salesman seized upon those things quickly and effectively.

Owning one's house free and clear (or *appearing* to do so, in the case of the elderly Stanly County couple) was another age-related vulnerability that the scammers sought to exploit in the first two cases, above. Younger homeowners tend to have mortgages and little home equity. That makes it impractical to attempt such scams on younger persons in order to foreclose on their homes and buy them for a song.

In the third case, Mr. Kennedy had no particular age-related vulnerabilities that the scammer recognized and sought to exploit. He had purchased and was working off of an extensive list of individuals aged 75 years or older. The scammer seemed to recognize that people in that age group would be more susceptible to his abusive tactics and threats. As you will see later, this technique of purchasing commercially available lead lists of seniors who fit certain profiles, and then contacting them, would become standard tactics of the phone fraud industry.

An age-related vulnerability common to all three cases was the victims' presence at home during the middle of the day. Their working days were done, and they were easy to access. Younger adults tend to be at work during the day and much harder to approach with a deceptive pitch.

3

Generating Obsession:
The Fire Alarm Salesman
and Three Grandmothers

In the 1980s and 1990s there was something known as the "mechanical heat detector fire alarm scam." Investigator Jane Feather and I rolled into court several times to shut those scams down. The mechanical devices at the heart of the scams had been commonly employed as home fire alarms earlier in the 20th century, before relatively cheap and much more effective residential smoke detectors came on the market.

These mechanical heat detector fire alarms resembled the large metal alarm bells that hung on the walls of our classrooms when we Baby Boomers were kids. Round, heavy and almost a foot wide, the bells had a powerful metal spring coiled inside that was connected to a steel hammer. They also contained a soft metal fuse that kept the spring from unleashing the hammer. If the ambient temperature in the room rose to 124°F (116°F in later versions of the device), a temperature indicative of a fire that was well underway, the soft metal fuse would melt and unleash the spring and the hammer. The result would be a lengthy, ear-splitting peal from the alarm bell.

These devices wholesaled for less than $100, but a crafty salesman could peddle them to homeowners for as much as $1,000 apiece. Such a salesman could persuade a parent or grandparent to buy two, three or even four of them and place them in every room where a child slept. The parent or grandparent's love for the children was the main sales hook. The pitch usually began at a free "safety seminar" at a local steakhouse or cafeteria and continued with a visit at the customer's home that night or the next day. It always looped back to the protection of those children.

At the "safety seminar" the salesman would hold up a plastic smoke detector that had melted in a fire, then hold up a mechanical heat detector that had survived a fire.

"Look! This mechanical heat detector still works! Everyone, cover your ears now."

Br-r-r-iiiinng-g-g-g!!!

"And this amazing device can go back up on the wall in your grand-child's room as soon as you rebuild the house! There are no batteries to constantly replace and no electronics to malfunction. You can leave it on your wall undisturbed for 20 years and it will still go off if there is a fire. Now, which one of these devices would you trust your grandchild's life with, this melted little $10 smoke detector or this solid state, ear-splitting beauty?"

The main deception in the salesman's pitch was the suggestion that the melted smoke detector represented failure and a horrible, agonizing death for the child while the still-intact mechanical heat detector represented survival. Following the safety seminar, when he made his in-home visit, the salesman often punctuated this deception by pulling out pictures of fire-scorched children's rooms that appeared in a famous 1973 U.S. government fire safety report entitled "America Burning."[1] If a salesman really wanted to hook a parent or grandparent, he might pull out two particularly disturbing photos from pages 15 and 123 of that publication. One showed the charred body of a child crouched beside a dresser while the other showed a soot-covered child's bed with a sharp white silhouette in the middle of the blackened sheets where a child's body had been found after a fire. The pictures and the horrific events that they depicted were immediately and indelibly embedded in the mind of the customer.

"You wouldn't want this to happen to any of your grandbabies, would you, Mrs. Smith? Do you want this melted little smoke detector to be the only thing determining whether your grandbabies live or die? How many different rooms do your various grandchildren sleep in? Four? Great! I will install four heat detectors for you tonight and everyone can sleep safe and sound. I'll arrange financing too."

Most fire safety experts will confirm that smoke can incapacitate you when you are sleeping long before the flames of a fire reach you, that smoke typically precedes fire, and that by the time the bedroom temperature rises to 124° or even 116°, you probably could be so overcome by smoke and confusion that your chances of escape from the burning house (assuming you wake up) would be slim. Smoke detectors, on the other hand, are designed to go off early enough in the process that you can wake up, realize what is happening and exit safely. Who cares that the smoke detector will melt after it saves you while the big bell on the wall can withstand the fire and can be used again someday?

One day in the very early 1990s, Transylvania Sheriff's Detective Brian Kreigsman called Jane and me about a heat detector fire alarm salesman named Ronald Jordache. Jordache was targeting parents and grandparents in the mountains of western North Carolina, filling their hearts with fear and their homes with mechanical heat detectors at $1,000 a pop. Brian's DA told him he would not prosecute Jordache for criminal fraud because he was selling an actual product that did, technically, detect fires. Brian and local fire officials were hoping that the North Carolina attorney general could sue Jordache in civil court under the state's Unfair and Deceptive Trade Practices Act, get an order shutting his operations down in North Carolina and get customers their money back. Jane and I were happy to oblige and so was Attorney General Lacy Thornburg, whose hometown was just over the Blue Ridge Parkway from Brian's county. Jane and I filed the suit four days later.

Armed with sworn affidavits that Jane obtained from Jordache's customers describing his sales pitch and an affidavit from the state fire marshal explaining why that pitch was so deceptive, I persuaded a North Carolina Superior Court judge to issue a temporary restraining order shutting Jordache down. Jordache promptly left the state and never contested the case. As a result, we obtained a permanent injunction prohibiting him from resuming his sales tactics in North Carolina, an order that he pay the state $50,000 in civil penalties plus reimburse its attorney costs, and an order cancelling all the purchase contracts and finance agreements signed by North Carolina consumers. Brian and most of his citizens who purchased the heat detectors were quite pleased. But there were three notable exceptions.

"I've got three older victims, all grandmothers, who bought lots of these things from Jordache and put them up in their grandchildren's rooms," Brian told us. "They refuse to take them down and return them to the finance company, which means they can't get their refunds. They are obsessed with the images Jordache showed them and are convinced their grandbabies are gonna die if they take them down."

"I also think the grandmothers are embarrassed," he added. "Taking down the alarms and seeking a refund will be like admitting to their adult children that their attempts to protect the grandchildren were foolish. That makes them even more adamant that the devices need to stay up."

I almost volunteered to speak with these three older consumers but thought better of it. Brian was loved and trusted by the people of his county, and if he could not persuade these women there was no need to keep the devices, no government attorney in far-off Raleigh was going to do so. But he was describing three distinct behaviors that we eventually would encounter thousands of times in victims of the elder fraud industry. The first was a powerful, instinctive urge to protect precious younger loved ones that could trump common sense. The second was the fraud victims' inability to control or get past an obsession, regardless of whether the obsession was pre-existing or created and stoked by the scammers. This inability to control obsessions increases with age. The third behavior, refusing to admit to being scammed when the evidence is clear, stems from a fear that doing so would be an admission to being unable to make sound decisions anymore and perhaps needing someone to take over their financial affairs.

The next time Brian called us, it would reveal one of the most despicable and financially successful elder fraud groups ever to operate inside the United States. More on that later.

4

Sweepstakes and Lottery Scams: The Cases of Mrs. B and Mrs. D

By the early 1990s, state and federal consumer protection officials had recognized and begun to address the organized components of a large elder fraud industry. The most artful and successful members of this industry were fraudulent telemarketers who targeted older American consumers with phony sweepstakes and lottery pitches. They were based in the United States and operated out of hastily created call centers set up in struggling strip malls or older, half-vacant office buildings. Because they did not want to place expensive long-distance calls to targets who had no interest in what they were peddling, they purchased lead lists of older Americans who liked to participate in lotteries and sweepstakes.

It was easy to trace these phone calls or the victims' cancelled checks straight back to the scammers' lairs, then serve the scammers with court orders commanding them to stop calling our state and return all funds obtained from North Carolina victims. They usually did stop calling and sometimes returned the money—after perfunctory protests that our victims misunderstood their over-the-phone pitches.

These scammers tended to cluster in Sun Belt locations like central and south Florida, Arizona, southern California, suburban Atlanta and the reputed motherland of all North American telemarketing fraudsters, Las Vegas. Most of these locations comported with the lifestyle so many of them seemed to favor: bright sun, deep tans to punctuate lots of gold bling, hot babes, pool parties, endless summers.

This was also a time when fraudulent telemarketers arguably were marketing something. That something tended to be pure crap, such as wall calendars, overpriced magazine subscriptions or "Say No to Drugs!" bumper stickers that were sold in bulk. But the scammers were pushing merchandise, nonetheless.

> CALLER: Congratulations, Mr. Kirkman! This is Bob Jackson from Great Western Sweepstakes in Las Vegas. You have just won a million dollars in our latest contest!
>
> MR. KIRKMAN: But I don't remember entering your sweepstakes contest, Mr. Jackson.
>
> CALLER: You don't? Well, anyone who purchases $500 worth of our "Say No to Drugs!" bumper stickers automatically gets enrolled in our sweepstakes. And you won, sir. Says so right here!
>
> MR. KIRKMAN: But I never ordered any of your bumper stickers.
>
> CALLER: Uh-oh. That will disqualify you. Plus, we'll have to start the sweepstakes all over again, which will cost us a fortune. But we can fix that with your assistance. I'll send a federally licensed courier to your home in a moment. Give the courier a $500 check for purchasing the bumper stickers. Once the check is on its way, you'll be qualified to receive the million-dollar prize. Then we'll send you your bumper stickers and your million-dollar check. Problem solved, right?
>
> MR. KIRKMAN: That doesn't seem quite right, Mr. Jackson.
>
> CALLER: What could go wrong? By this time tomorrow, you'll have a million dollars and you can start your campaign to keep kids in your community off of drugs. It's a win-win situation, Mr. Kirkman! Just don't tell anybody about this until your million-dollar check is in your bank account. We don't want anyone to mug you and steal the check when you head to the bank!

The scammer would then contact Federal Express (or UPS or Airborne Express), direct them to dispatch a driver to Mr. Kirkman's house to pick up a check, and then have the company deliver the check to an address somewhere in the Sun Belt. The scammer would charge the courier's services to a credit card. Sometimes the card was legitimate and sometimes it was stolen. In any event, a few days after handing his check to the courier service's driver, Mr. Kirkman would receive a box of bumper stickers, together with a paid purchase invoice.

And no million-dollar check.

The fact that a courier showed up in the fraud target's driveway immediately following the phone call lent credence to the scammer's representations. The word "Federal" in one company's name and the military appearance of the vehicles and uniforms employed by one of the other companies also seemed to reassure the victims that the sweepstakes man's representations were legitimate and sanctioned by the government. Comforted by this, victims would not report the transaction to anyone until well after their big prize failed to arrive.

The scammers set their programs up this way for deniability purposes. They were certain that they could convince law enforcement that elderly Mr. Kirkman had entered into a straightforward contract to buy 500 bumper stickers and that he was simply confused about the operation of the sweepstakes promotion. "He simply *entered* our contest, detective. The drawing hasn't even taken place. It says so right there on his shipping receipt." Often this argument would work, and the overburdened law enforcement official would move on to other cases, but not always.

In North Carolina, the phrase "elder fraud" probably entered the Consumer Protection Division's vocabulary around this time. It was then that my colleagues in the Division regularly encountered older victims of sweepstakes and lottery scams who had lost $20,000 to $30,000 apiece. In 1992, we learned of a retired schoolteacher in Durham County who had been defrauded repeatedly by sweepstakes scammers. She had been conned out of $112,000 through the mail and over the telephone.

When we visited the victims, we found their homes packed with unwanted merchandise that they had ordered from various sweepstakes companies in hopes that such purchases would move their names to the top of each company's list of prize winners. The names of the companies ranged from long-established ones that advertised regularly on TV to obscure entities that investigators could never locate. It was clear from our conversations with these victims that they were quite captivated (one could say "obsessed") with prize contests. It also was apparent that their participation in the sweepstakes had gotten their names on "sucker lists" that were sold among sweepstakes scammers.

One such victim lived in Glen Lennox Apartments in Chapel Hill. She had lost over $30,000. I drove past her home twice each weekday as I commuted to and from work in Raleigh. Her daughter had been a few classes ahead of me at Chapel Hill High School. When my colleague Billie Rouse discovered this victim, I volunteered to visit her on my way home from work.

This woman, let's call her Mrs. B, had retired a few years earlier from a prominent position at the University of North Carolina. She was gracious and charming when she welcomed me into her small apartment. We had a long, pleasant conversation about life in Chapel Hill in the 1960s and 1970s when her daughter and I were growing up, and we learned that we had several family friends in common. On her dining room table sat piles of FedEx and UPS shipping invoices pertaining to checks she had sent to sweepstakes companies throughout the southern half of the United States. Her living room and her two bedrooms were stacked high with magazines, books and VCR tapes that she had ordered from the sweepstakes companies, most still wrapped in plastic, as well as tiny TV sets, cheap watches and jewelry, cheap plastic cameras and other worthless knick-knacks that represented her "prizes."

Mrs. B acknowledged that she had been tricked by these companies into purchasing unwanted merchandise. She had never won the multi-million-dollar cash prizes that had been dangled in front of her and, in some cases, absolutely guaranteed. This conversation caused me to think that she would not be scammed anymore, that she had learned her lesson.

But I was wrong. When I left that evening, I gave Mrs. B my home and office phone numbers and got her to promise to call and talk to me about a sweepstakes company's claims before sending money or ordering more merchandise. "Of course, David!"

She called me at the office the following afternoon. She announced she had just purchased $2,000 worth of additional merchandise because she found the sweepstakes official who called her the night before to be credible and sincere. This happened repeatedly over the next few weeks. Sometimes she would even say, "David, I think I made a mistake last night," but usually she just tried to convince me that the latest caller was legitimate.

We noticed this happening over and over again with other victims. They could acknowledge that they had been scammed by previous callers. Sometimes they could even explain in detail how the previous callers had tricked them and how they never should have sent money or bought something in hopes of receiving a valuable prize. But then they bought right into another scammer's lies as soon as the next call came in. It was as if all rationality and caution suddenly fled their minds whenever they received another exciting call or letter from a lying, phony sweepstakes official. It would be several years before medical professionals explained to us why this phenomenon occurred.

Another major sweepstakes fraud victim that our office encountered in the early '90s was a recently widowed former schoolteacher from Ohio who had moved to the North Carolina mountains near Asheville. Let's call her "Mrs. D." Two dozen telemarketer groups scammed her out of

$80,000 over the course of four months. Neighbors who reported her situation to us said that she had become very withdrawn, had turned her back on her new church congregation and her new North Carolina friends, and just seemed to want to stay at home—by the phone.

When we spoke with her, Mrs. D confided that, yes, she had been scammed out of more than $64,000. She gave us extensive notes detailing each call, each purchase, and each telemarketer's name, company and telephone number. She also provided us with copies of calendar entries, courier service invoices and cancelled checks. It was a complete roadmap to the scammers. She also reported that she just loved sweepstakes contests and always had.

Due to her apparent recognition of what was being done to her, we were confounded that she would stay by her phone and keep dealing with callers who promised her millions if she would just send money. She was a high-functioning, well-spoken individual whose internal BS-meter should have been the best in the world due to her decades in the classroom. She asked us to forgive her for being so foolish in those earlier transactions. Nevertheless, as soon as another sweepstakes scammer called, Mrs. D would be taken in quickly by his promises of riches being delivered to her front door, and she would start writing checks for large sums of money all over again.

My solution to Mrs. D's victimization was to do what any good consumer protection enforcement attorney might do: go to court, get the scammers to return her money and have them banned from calling into the state ever again. On behalf of then-attorney general Mike Easley, I filed a civil enforcement action against 18 different telemarketing outfits situated throughout the southern half of the United States, all of whom had gotten some of Mrs. D's money.[1] That same day, a Wake County Superior Court judge granted our request for a restraining order against the telemarketing companies, prohibiting them from making further calls into North Carolina.

Many of the defendants began returning Mrs. D's funds to us. Others simply vanished. In the end, we recovered $28,000 for her, a decent recovery percentage for a telemarketing fraud case. It was a pleasure to forward those funds to her as they came in, and each check provided an opportunity to counsel her against dealing with anyone else who might call and tell her she had won something. She was on the phone-fraud industry's notorious "sucker list" and they were not about to leave her alone.

Our press office publicized *Easley v. Eighteen Telemarketers* rather heavily. A New York–based investigator for a national television news program called and pressed us to arrange an interview with Mrs. D. At her request, we had not revealed Mrs. D's identity, not even in the court pleadings, and it was for good reason. Then, as now, older victims of fraud were mortified by the idea that their dealings with scammers might be revealed to their friends and neighbors. They did not want their adult children to know, either. And if those children did find out, they would be even more militant about not trotting Mom or Dad in front of reporters. Even when the reporters promised anonymity, disguised voices and obscured faces during on-camera interviews, the victims and their adult children were adamantly opposed to the idea. They did not want the humiliation. Objectively, I knew not to honor the reporter's request to interview Mrs. D.

Visions of appearing with Mrs. D on *Oprah* or on Dan Rather's evening newscast must have infiltrated my subconscious and overwhelmed my better judgment. I agreed to tell Mrs. D that a major news network wanted to interview her about her experiences and that they were promising not to reveal her identity. I convinced myself to make an exception to the "no interviews" policy described above because Mrs. D, as a former teacher, might embrace the chance to teach others in her age group about these scams.

When I called her number, Mrs. D did not answer. I left a message on her answering machine describing the opportunity to help others by sharing her experiences with the reporter anonymously.

The next morning, I arrived at work and heard the following voice-mail message: "Why are you trying to humiliate me, Mr. Kirkman? I told you I absolutely do not want to speak with any reporters about all this." Mrs. D went on to tell me what a breach of faith I had committed and how she was devastated by it. She ended with the words "You people just leave me alone."

Mrs. D's tearful message still haunts me more than two and a half decades later and probably always will. She went back to speaking with the scammers and sending her savings to them. Consistent with the phenomenon that Dr. Anthony Pratkanas of the University of California at Santa Cruz calls "psychological reactance,"[2] Mrs. D was rejecting those of us whose reactions made her feel as if she had done something wrong and foolhardy and needed to be restrained. Instead, she was embracing those who told her she was making the wise decision, she was doing the right thing, and she would prove her doubters wrong once she finally deposited all that sweepstakes money into her bank account. It was a response that we later witnessed hundreds of times when family members, friends, law enforcement officials or clergy members were less than gentle and reaffirming when they spoke to older victims about their losses. ("Mom! I can't believe you let yourself be defrauded like this!")

How much money Mrs. D lost after that we do not know. We referred her to local Adult Protective Services officials in hopes that they might obtain a financial guardianship order and preserve what little savings and retirement income she had left. The last word I received from them was that she had moved back to Ohio.

PART TWO

Will, Bill and the War Against the Home Repair Fraud Gang

5

"Something big and sinister"

In July of 1995, my efforts to fight elder fraud were sidetracked by a case assignment involving a new building product called Exterior Insulation and Finishing Systems, or EIFS. Essentially a plastic and fiberglass exterior wall coating that was applied to Styrofoam panels that had been glued to the wall of a structure, EIFS was developed in Europe to repair battle-scarred buildings during that continent's post–World War II reconstruction period. By the '90s, builders and architects across the United States and Canada were using EIFS to clad new wood-framed homes and apartment buildings. The product, also called "synthetic stucco," would give dwellings a solid and sunny Mediterranean villa look at half the price of traditional stucco. EIFS-clad homes looked especially striking when constructed in wide open, sun-drenched locations, such as coastal or desert areas or in golf course communities.

A hugely expensive problem with this new EIFS product soon showed itself in moisture prone areas of the country such as the Pacific Northwest and the Carolinas. In many recently constructed homes in North Carolina, the wooden exterior wall systems to which EIFS facades had been glued were rotting.

The EIFS manufacturers blamed this phenomenon on builders, saying they had applied their products to the homes incorrectly or had left gaps or other openings in the stucco around the windows and door frames, behind the exterior light fixture mounts or along the roof lines and other features of the structure. These tiny holes and gaps allowed rain water to seep in and become trapped against the wooden wall structure behind the Styrofoam and the plastic stucco. The result was wood rot.

The builders, on the other hand, claimed that EIFS was inherently flawed when it came to wood frame home construction, that moisture

36

inevitably would get behind any type of exterior house cladding system, be it brick, regular stucco or wooden siding, and that, unlike EIFS, those other exterior cladding systems all provided ways for the moisture to drain out or evaporate before causing damage.

North Carolina homeowners were stuck in the middle of this blame game. Making matters worse, they could not get their own homeowners' insurance companies to cover the staggering costs of repairing and recladding their rotting homes with something else. Collectively, those homeowners were facing about a billion dollars in losses. They were screaming bloody murder and demanding that the government of North Carolina break the impasse.

My division chief tasked me with making that happen.

So, as I sat in the middle of this circular firing squad featuring home builders, the EIFS manufacturers, homeowners and their respective engineers and lawyers, I was more than happy to take a call from my buddy Brian Kreigsman with the Transylvania County Sheriff's Department.

"Hey, Dave. You ever heard of a guy named Kenneth O.? He goes by the nickname 'Frog.'"

"Is he building houses with EIFS exteriors up there in the mountains?"

"Eeefs?"

"Never mind. Is he another one of your crazy heat detector fire alarm salesmen?"

Brian started to laugh.

"Naw, man! He rips off older folks by claiming there are major problems with their homes. Nothing needs repairing and nothing really gets repaired. He got a lady here in Brevard, Mrs. Barnes, for over $16,000."

Sixteen thousand dollars in losses seemed like a lot for a home repair scam back then. House painting and driveway paving scams were the most common forms of home repair fraud at the time. They were mostly strike-and-flee crimes where the perpetrators sprayed a useless dark substance on the gravel driveway or a powdery white substance on the sides of an older person's home. Then they collected a few hundred dollars for the supposedly "discount" job and fled the area. The next rain would wash their handiwork away.

Brian detailed how Frog got the $16,000 from Mrs. Barnes. First, he approached her and pointed out what he claimed was a minor problem with her roof. He offered to fix it for a few dollars. Upon completing the supposed repair, he told her of more ominous problems with her roof, problems that required expensive repairs right away.

After pretending to perform those additional repairs, Frog reportedly advised Mrs. Barnes of other problems with her home. Then others. And still others. With each report, he described the horrible consequences that might result if repairs were not performed quickly: a collapsing roof; water damaged walls and ceilings; toxic mold that would require her to move out of the house; floor systems weakening. Startled, Mrs. Barnes authorized every "repair" that Frog suggested. During a period of several months, she wrote him check after check for work in areas of the house that she could neither access nor see, such as the roof, the attic or the crawl space.

"Frog and his men didn't like it when I started dropping by her house in my patrol car," said Brian. "At first, they just jumped in the truck and headed away when I pulled up to the curb and rang her doorbell, but they'd be back the next day. Finally, they left her alone. Never performed any real repairs on her home so far as I can tell. Just hammered nails into rafters and floor joists, made lots of noise with the power saw and drill and installed unneeded two-by-four braces everywhere—basically made her think they were fixing all sorts of problems. Left a copy of *Hustler* magazine in her crawl space."

Brian was going to charge Frog with obtaining property by false pretenses but first he wanted to know whether our office had information showing that he had mistreated other North Carolina homeowners in the same manner. Brian was being smart. Proving to a jury that a defendant knowingly made a misrepresentation is always hard, but that's what the prosecution must show to win a fraud case. The defense often becomes "Well, I might have made a bad recommendation based upon a mistaken assessment of the situation, but it was not *intentionally* false and you cannot prove otherwise!" Proof of similar representations and transactions involving other victims, known as Rule 404(b) evidence,[1] can be introduced by the state to show that the representation in question was, in fact, knowingly false when the defendant made it. Such 404(b) evidence is especially compelling to juries.

I told Brian I would check for any 404(b) evidence in our consumer complaint files and walked down the hall to visit investigator Jane Feather. As I recounted what Brian had just told me, our antitrust investigator and office jokester, William C. Tucker, appeared in Jane's doorway. He had overheard my rendition of Brian's story from two offices away.

"Hey, tell Brian to mail us that *Hustler* so Jane and I can check it for fingerprints!"

Then Tucker shifted out of his jokester persona. He handed Jane a letter from an attorney.

"Seriously, guys, I just got this letter from a lawyer buddy in Wilson County. His elderly client experienced the exact same thing you're talking about. Started out with a simple offer to clean her gutters for $25. Then the scammers began reporting problem after problem with her roof and attic. Over time the scammers got permission to perform a long string of expensive repairs—all in parts of the house that she could not reach or see. Got her for over $100,000 in bogus repairs."

"Did this Wilson County scammer or anyone on his crew go by the names Kenneth or Frog?"

"I'll check. My buddy also says there is a building inspector in Rocky Mount named Frank Phelps who knows all about the guys who did it. We can ask Phelps if he's ever heard of Frog."

What really struck the three of us was the fact that Bill Tucker's Wilson County incident occurred at the same time as Brian's very similar case in Transylvania County. Transylvania and Wilson counties are on opposite ends of our very long state. Depending upon how badly one likes to damage the speed limit, the drive time separating the two counties is about six hours. The crimes could not have been perpetrated by the same scammer or the same crew.

The three of us looked at one another. Each of us had been working in Consumer Protection for several years and had developed highly accurate gut instincts when it came to fraud incidents.

Something big and sinister was lurking out there. All three of us felt it.

6

Road Trip to Rocky Mount

Bill Tucker spoke by phone with Frank Phelps, the building inspector in Rocky Mount who reportedly knew the guys who defrauded the elderly Wilson homeowner out of $100,000. Phelps told him about scammer after scammer and victim after victim. Apparently, the crooks were based in the Rocky Mount area and fanned out across the state and up into Virginia each Monday morning, then returned on Friday evening and divvied up their respective "takes." After his call to Phelps was over, Tucker appeared in my office doorway as I was talking with Jane about another case.

"The three of us need to take a short road trip to Rocky Mount and talk with that building inspector guy. He's got a ton of information about the guys who scammed that lady in Wilson County, and you need to hear it firsthand. Plus, he wants to introduce us to some other officials who are looking into them."

Sounded like a good idea. "Okay, but Jane and I don't want you smoking while we're in the car."

Tucker was pretty good about not smoking during the one-hour trip to Rocky Mount. When we arrived at the police department, Frank Phelps met us in the lobby and then took us upstairs to a small conference room where he introduced us to two officers with the Rocky Mount P.D. and Mark Rosenfield, a DEA undercover agent based just down the road in Wilson.

"Glad you guys developed an interest in these guys," said Rosenfield as he shook our hands. "But what took you so long?"

We were there for a couple of hours. Phelps was the talker in the group. The other three gentlemen remained rather quiet. Phelps claimed that the home repair scammers were led by Robert House, Sr., of Rocky

Mount and that Robert House, Jr., was one of his chief lieutenants. He said many of the other members of the gang were brothers, cousins and nephews of Bob Sr., while another member, David Viverette, had married into the family. Phelps rattled off additional members' names that did not have "House" in them, such as Ricky Repoza, Ricky Braswell, James "Dino" Wills, and "Colonel" Matthew Bales, who supposedly always carried a big knife.

"Bales," said Phelps. "He'd just as soon cut you open as look at you!" Phelps recited that comment each and every time he mentioned Bales. He always stated that Braswell was a "good guy" whenever he mentioned him. And he would mention both men hundreds of times during the ensuing months.

Bob House, Sr., had a grade school education, according to Phelps. Phelps also claimed that House had been running home repair scams on old people for years and had come upon the technique of victimizing a given homeowner repeatedly, sometimes for years, rather than defrauding him or her just once before moving down the road to another town and another victim.

Phelps named a local restaurant where everyone in House's organization reportedly met for breakfast early on Monday mornings before fanning out across Virginia and North Carolina to scam elderly homeowners. Sometimes the crews would decide during those breakfast meetings to switch victims and towns because certain victims they had been working on—or their bankers when it came time to cash the checks—were growing suspicious of them. The new crew would arrive at the victim's home, point out problems with the work the previous crew had done, and then scare the victim into believing that the local building inspector would spot the problems immediately, condemn the house and throw him or her out on the street. Terrified, the victim would consent to having the supposed repairs redone by the new crew at great expense.

"That lady in Wilson who lost $100,000? She's not that unusual. These guys talk about lots of victims like her—victims in towns like Warsaw, Fayetteville, Faison, Charlotte and Richmond, Virginia. They brag about an old man over in Raleigh called 'the Colonel,' who they've taken for over $100,000." His statement "These guys talk about victims like her" struck Jane, Tucker and me as a bit odd. Was Phelps in direct conversation with "these guys"? None of us asked him about it because we were so absorbed in all the other information he was conveying.

It did not take long to figure out that Phelps really hated these people. He claimed that a subgroup of them got his grandmother for $35,000 a few years earlier, that she was terribly loyal to them and didn't want them prosecuted, and that he had made it his mission in life to take them all down. One tactic that clearly galled him was how crew members would befriend the elderly victims, spending hours each day with them over the years discussing their family, life experiences, hobbies, religious and political beliefs, favorite pets and any and all dreams and aspirations the victims ever had.

The crew members would tell the homeowners about their own supposedly terrible upbringings, how they never had a wonderful and caring older person in their lives like the homeowner, and the homeowner had become like a second parent to them. Crew members would chauffer their victims to the store, the post office, the doctor and, of course, the bank when it was time to cash a check for another $9,000 in bogus repairs. They even brought birthday cards and birthday cakes to their victims, whereupon the entire crew would sing "Happy Birthday" in unison. The scammers were fraudulently obtaining loyalty and personal affection from each victim in addition to tons of cash.

This deceitfully obtained personal affection sometimes allowed these con men to run a form of sweetheart scam on their victims. After chatting with a homeowner over the course of several months, a guy on the crew might ask a female victim for gifts or loans of money for a new truck or for child support payments that would keep him out of jail. In some instances, female crew members would charm gifts and loans out of male homeowners.

Phelps related how "one of those guys told my grandmother, 'I ain't never had a grandmother or a mother. You're like a grandmother to me, ma'am!' And she fell for it and loaned him $10,000 which he never repaid." Phelps could never convince her that the guy had scammed her.

This loyalty toward one's victimizers, which sometimes became quite fierce, had proven problematic for prosecutors and law enforcement officers considering charges against members of House's organization. How does one prove fraud when the victim claims she or he was not defrauded at all, is happy with the job and does not want his or her money back? Another thing making it hard for a prosecutor to charge them with fraud was the fact that each "job" the gang members proposed and supposedly performed was memorialized in a written contract specifying parts, labor, taxes, etc. The contract might have been for work and materials that were totally unnecessary, plus the work might not have been completed in a professional manner, but the homeowner signed the document and paid when the work was finished.

When confronted with such a document, overworked prosecutors often declared, "It's just a contract dispute. Let the parties fight it out in small claims court if they want to. I've got a rape trial and two murder trials coming up." In those rare instances where one of the workers was charged criminally, someone from the House organization, or an attorney, would offer to repay the victim in exchange for dismissal of the charges. The overworked DA, unaware of how many other victims had been scammed and facing a lengthy docket of cases needing to be tried, often considered that a good solution.

Something else that this group liked to do, according to Phelps, was spot furniture, silverware sets or other items in the victims' homes that would fetch a good price in an antique store. Then they would accept those items as payment for an expensive job in lieu of a check.

Rosenfield also told us about transactions with local auto dealerships where House's group repeatedly bought and sold pickup trucks, half of them red and the other half white. "Don't know the reason for the color selection—red truck, white truck—but there could be money laundering going on there. You'll see small used car lots all over this area selling those red and white trucks."

Phelps also described how various members of the group were heavily into gambling, drugs and/or child support obligations, and money collected from a victim on a Friday probably would be gone by the following Monday. Even if some of the money was still around, it probably wasn't in banks. It was more likely buried in jars and metal cans somewhere on a gang member's property. The victims would never get anything back.

Phelps and Rosenfield mentioned an IRS criminal investigator in Greenville, North Carolina, Kevin Anderson, who was looking into the money laundering and tax related charges that might be brought against the gang. Rosenfield claimed he was in position to bring drug charges against a handful of Bob Sr.'s men at any time, but that probably would result in plea bargains through which they would receive little or no jail time in exchange for giving up the names of their drug suppliers. He wanted, instead, to bring down the entire home repair fraud enterprise. Phelps seconded the motion. Tucker, Jane and I were fine with that idea too.

We agreed to meet again in Raleigh in a couple of weeks. The AG's office would invite Curt Ellis, head of the State Bureau of Investigation's Financial Crimes Unit, the Wake County (Raleigh) DA and anyone else who might help. Rosenfield would get Kevin Anderson to come from Greenville, plus Tom Murphy, the assistant U.S. attorney in Raleigh with whom they both had been working. Phelps said he knew of an FBI agent in Virginia who was looking into these same scammers, and he would issue him an invitation. Same for his local DA, Howard Boney.

"Frank," I said, "I forgot to ask you something. Is a guy named Kenneth, aka 'Frog,' a member or this gang?"

"Frog! Yeah, Frog's big into it. Likes to run his scams in the western part of the state. Has a really nice log home just across the border in Tennessee…" Phelps seemed to know a lot about Frog and he was more than happy to share that knowledge with us. "Bad dude! But not quite as bad as 'Colonel' Matthew Bales, who'd just as soon cut you open as look at you."

Before heading back to Raleigh, we took a side trip to Gardner's for some eastern North Carolina pork barbeque and a chance to process what we had just heard. We realized that this consumer scam was not only the worst we had come across, but it was also the most perfect. Older homeowners were losing up to $200,000 apiece and there were a lot of them. They did not complain. Instead they were quite loyal to their victimizers. Overworked DAs were reluctant to charge fraud, and with good reason. To prove criminal fraud, a prosecutor must demonstrate beyond a reasonable doubt that the defendant knowingly misled the victim in order to obtain money or other things of value from them. Defense counsel's star witness in each case would be the victim, the satisfied customer, who would deny that the good young man ever misled him or her. The signed and written contracts would be the first defense exhibits introduced and published to the jury.

Without something else, these cases were going to be hell to prosecute. I did not know which case was going to drive me crazy first—this one or the EIFS wars.

7

Without Something Else, These Cases Were Going to Be Hell to Prosecute

When we gathered in Raleigh two weeks later to discuss the home repair fraud gang, Brian Kreigsman drove all the way from the mountains to join us. Kevin Anderson from IRS criminal enforcement was there representing the feds, along with Assistant U.S. Attorney Tom Murphy. Curt Ellis, Special Agent in Charge of the State Bureau of Investigation's Financial Crimes Unit, was there with his colleague, Special Agent Reggie Shaw. Prosecutor Shelley Desvouges from the Wake County DA's Office joined us. Frank Phelps, of course, was there with his law enforcement buddies from Rocky Mount as well as his local DA, Howard Boney. Phelps' FBI contact in Virginia did not join us that day.

Tucker, who was learning to create Excel spreadsheets, had compiled a database of victims, their losses and every crew member who worked on their homes. He handed out his first such spreadsheet at the beginning of the meeting and it was the catalyst for several discussions and lots of revived memories. Each attendee reported on the individuals and victims he or she knew to be involved in the scams. Tucker's list of known perpetrators quickly doubled to 20 and the number of known victims tripled to about 30.

Many of the additions to Tucker's spreadsheet that day involved incidents in Raleigh. House's group was said to hit neighborhoods in the city aggressively every week, often with as many as five crews. "Old Raleigh," a pie-shaped area of the city that begins near downtown and extends northwestward to the I-440 Beltline, was full of homes built in the 1940s, '50s and '60s. They were often owned and occupied by reasonably prosperous people in their 70s, 80s and 90s. Phelps explained why those particular homes and homeowners were the group's favorite targets. Homes of that vintage often were in need of real work, so the scammers' claims that a problem existed up on the roof or down in the crawl space were readily believed by the homeowners. In addition, homeowners in that age group were quite concerned with showing that they could maintain their homes, forestalling suggestions by their adult children that they needed to move into assisted living. Icing on the cake for the scammers was the fact that these Old Raleigh residents tended to be retired government officials, doctors, lawyers and North Carolina State University professors. They had healthy retirement savings and regular pension incomes.

We also learned that a group of home repair scam crews working the Raleigh territory was under the control of Andy Mazza. Mazza reportedly haled from the Danville, Virginia, area and so did many of his crew members. He now resided in Raleigh. No one knew what kind of understanding existed between Mazza and Bob House, Sr., in Rocky Mount regarding who could run scams in Raleigh and where, but it was clear that an accord was in place. And it was working well for them.

Our group discussed legal strategies and the challenges that prosecuting such cases would pose. The main challenge was the elderly fraud victims themselves. Having been scammed multiple times, they could not possibly remember all the deceptive representations the scammers had made to them. Many were dealing with short term memory issues, which made the problem even worse. If nobody could testify about a defendant's false representation to the victim, there could be no conviction for fraud.

Making matters worse was the previously mentioned tendency of our victims to hold strong and positive feelings for their victimizers. They would recoil at any suggestion that those guys had scammed them. In fact, many victims interpreted such suggestions as insinuations that they had mismanaged their personal affairs. That, in turn, made them even more adamant that they had not been scammed. (We would learn later that the crews often created these reflexive reactions in their victims. "Now your children are going to cite all this house deterioration we are fixing as an example of how you cannot maintain your own home anymore, and how you need to be put in an institution. It's best not to tell them anything about all this until the work is finally finished.")

We mulled over legal strategies and copious amounts of data at that second meeting, but our main take-away was that building criminal prosecutions upon the testimony of our victims could be a fool's errand. We were stumped.

Another challenge appeared during the meeting. Tom Murphy from the U.S. Attorney's Office really didn't seem to like the North Carolina State Bureau of Investigation. The few times he spoke were jabs at Curt Ellis and Reggie Shaw and their agency.

These stirrings of disharmony in the ranks notwithstanding, we did come up with a name for ourselves, the House-Mazza Home Repair Fraud Task Force. Calling ourselves the House Home Repair Fraud Task Force, as someone proposed initially, would have made it seem that we were from the Department of Redundancy Department, so we stuck "Mazza" in there. Another accomplishment was the decision on where we would go eat: Big Ed's Restaurant. For the next two years, the House-Mazza Home Repair Fraud Task Force would always adjourn to Big Ed's at lunchtime, whereupon we would feast on delicious, sometimes artery-clogging Southern cuisine and share even more information with one another than we would during the meeting itself.

8

Special Agent Will Garrett
Comes to Raleigh

The House-Mazza Home Repair Fraud Task Force held its third meeting at the federal building in Raleigh in October 1995. The multi-agency group had grown too large for the conference room in the North Carolina Attorney General's Office. Captain Mervin Roby, Captain William Leary and Lieutenant Frank Kotzian of the Elizabeth City Police Department in the coastal, northeastern corner of the state made the four-hour drive to Raleigh. Detective Brian Kriegsman again drove five hours from the other end of the state. Two dozen state, federal and local law enforcement officials and prosecutors from the mountains to the coast showed up as well. We also had our first attendees from out of state, U.S. postal inspectors, state police detectives and three FBI agents, all of them based in Richmond. One was Special Agent Wilbur E. ("Will") Garrett, Jr., the FBI guy Phelps spoke about during our first meeting.

I called the meeting to order, Tucker passed out his latest spreadsheet and then each law enforcement official gave a brief report. Returning attendees updated us on what they had learned since the last meeting while new attendees introduced themselves and spoke of their own investigations into members of the House-Mazza group. Energy and knowledge circulated throughout the room. Our lists of perpetrators and victims expanded by the minute. Members of the task force were becoming more familiar with one another and their comments often were punctuated by friendly jokes and facetious cracks at one another's expense. Things seemed to be going well.

Then all of that energy and good cheer got sucked out of the room. When it was their turn to report, the FBI-Raleigh announced that they did not believe they could build a federal criminal case against members of the House-Mazza organization and, therefore, would not participate further in the task force's efforts. They wished the group well, then excused themselves and returned to their offices upstairs.

An awkward silence gripped the room for several seconds. Then Will Garrett, the stocky, dark-haired FBI agent from Richmond, rose to speak.

"Hi, I'm Will Garrett with the FBI in Richmond. I cannot say this on behalf of the Bureau, but personally I find my Raleigh colleagues' position disappointing." With that, Garrett had our undivided attention. He made good use of the moment.

"There is a federal legal theory to nail these guys with. They use beepers and the interstate phone network to communicate with one another about the scams they are pulling. They will be in Virginia and they will call the big guy in Rocky Mount, North Carolina. Or they will receive a beeper message from Rocky Mount when they are in Virginia. And each time they use the interstate phone network in furtherance of one of their scams, they have committed the federal crime of wire fraud."

"As for the victims who can't remember certain conversations or don't want to go against the nice boys who have been working on their homes, that's no problem for me," he continued. "I have informants within the organization who can tell me exactly how one of my Virginia victims was defrauded and by whom. I can bring cases right now involving victims scattered from South Hill, Virginia, just north of the North Carolina line, all the way up I-95 to Dumfries, which you pass as you approach Washington, D.C."

"My only problem at the moment is finding a federal prosecutor in the Eastern District of Virginia who can clear the decks and indict some of these guys. Andy Mazza will be the first defendant listed on the pleadings, if I have any say in the matter," he concluded.

Will was an instant hit with everybody in the room. He was telling us things we were desperate to hear. His wire fraud legal theory might not be useful in intra-state North Carolina transactions, and we had not developed inside informants yet, but he had demonstrated that serious criminal fraud charges could be developed and laid on these guys. Unlike his Raleigh counterparts who had just spoken, Will had some age on him and was the sort of veteran law enforcement agent who possessed automatic credibility with the others in the room. On top of that, he seemed to care deeply for the older homeowners and was determined to put Mazza and company in prison.

Will held forth for the next hour. He told us how he had first noticed Andy Mazza's crews when he was out jogging one morning, that they learned their repeat victimization techniques from a guy named Robert Parlier from the Pennsylvania/Delaware region, and that Parlier and his home repair scams had been featured on the television show *America's Most Wanted* a few years earlier.

He explained how $100,000 worth of scams on a particular home-owner might begin with a guy knocking on the door and offering to clean leaves out of the gutters for $25. The gutter cleaner would come down off the roof after he was done, pull out some garden mulch that he had stashed in his pocket earlier that morning, then tell the elderly home-owner, "Sir, your roof is completely rotted! My leg just went all the way through it and I almost broke my hip. Here's some of the rotted wood. You'll need to repair the roof right away before the Henrico County build-ing inspector sees it and condemns your home. I know some guys who can repair it right away..."

And with that alarming statement, said Will, the first of a long series of expensive and unneeded "repairs" would be authorized by the victim.

As soon as the "guys" repaired the perfectly sound roof, usually by stapling an unnecessary new layer of cheap shingles over it, the crew chief (the scammers called him "the salesman") would come to the front door requesting payment, which would be somewhere just south of $10,000. As the homeowner made out the check, another member of the crew would position himself behind him or her and look to see just how much money was in the account when the homeowner recorded the check in the check-book register.

If a lot of money remained in the account following the issuance of the check, the salesman would get the high sign and move in for the "re-load," or next round of the scam: "Sir, with all the wood and new shingles we installed on your new roof, I sure would like to inspect your attic to see whether the rafters are able to carry that extra weight. Would that be okay?"

After spending a few minutes up in the homeowner's perfectly sound attic, the salesman would come down and announce, "Sir, I am afraid your rafters and attic beams are weakened from water intrusion and overloaded by all the material we just installed. We'll need to install rafter braces to ensure that the roof won't collapse in on itself. That would make all the work we just did worthless, and rebuilding the roof from the bottom up will be much more expensive."

Upon receiving permission to brace the attic, the crew members would simply nail vertical studs—made out of scrap two-by-fours—between the surface of the attic floor and the bottoms of the perfectly sound roof support beams. Then the salesman would collect several thousands of dollars more for that round of unnecessary work. The result in this instance, however, would be something that could actually harm the house instead of simply being useless and expensive. Roof support systems are designed to flex slightly as wind hits the roof or as snow piles on it. The scammers' vertical braces, also called "stiff knees," can defeat this flex feature and carry the impact of the wind or the weight of the heavy snow straight down to the ceilings of the rooms below, causing them to crack or break.

The third round of fraud usually involved a false claim that water intrusion (from the supposedly rotted roof) had caused serious problems in the walls and ceilings of the house, usually "toxic mold." The salesman might warn the homeowners to move into a hotel immediately for health and safety reasons if they could not pay to have the toxic mold treated. Upon securing permission to treat the mold in the walls, the scammers would go through the house spraying a pungent but useless concoction of water, kerosene and other agents, then collect several thousand dollars more from the victim.

The scams would continue as long as the victim had money to pay. While no part of the house was immune to a false claim that serious and expensive water damage had occurred, the scammers usually claimed that problems existed in portions of the house that the older homeowner could neither see nor visit, such as the roof, attic or crawl space. Will had come across some homeowners who had been reloaded three dozen times. One of his Virginia victims told crews she that thought her home was haunted. The crew reloaded her with thousands of dollars' worth of "ghost eradication" treatments and retreatments.

Then Will circulated a single-spaced, 43-page document. It was a summary of his interviews with an informant who was a longtime "salesman" for Andy Mazza in Virginia. It was a complete dossier on the House-Mazza organization and its activities in that state. The transcript detailed its structure, members, techniques, history and victims. It was both a how-to manual for home repair scammers and a roadmap to a successful prosecution of the House-Mazza group.

At page 28 of the summary, Will's inside source identified several older homeowners who were favorite targets of the House-Mazza group:

An individual identified by the nickname "the Colonel," of Raleigh, North Carolina, may have lost as much as $200,000 over the years;

Mr. [name redacted] of Boykins, Virginia, may have lost up to $150,000 over the years;

"The Three Sisters," [names redacted], who reside in Danville, Virginia, may have lost $30,000 to $40,000 over the years;

[Name redacted], of Lawrenceville, Virginia, off Route 58, may have lost $70,000 to $80,000 over the years;

An elderly retired prison guard, name unknown, of Brookneal, Virginia, may have lost $100,000-plus in the scams;

Mrs. [name redacted] in Yanceyville, North Carolina, may have lost $100,000-plus over the years;

Mrs. [name redacted] of Burlington, North Carolina, may have lost up to $200,000 over the years;

[Name redacted] and her sister, who reside in the Saluda/West Point area of Virginia, may have lost $100,000.

Nobody in the room wanted to give their report right after Will's, so we adjourned for lunch early and headed over to Big Ed's.

9

Tucker Seeks Out "the Colonel"

Throughout the early months of the House-Mazza home repair fraud investigation, stories abounded that crews visited and preyed upon a World War II veteran in Raleigh whenever they needed more cash. Rocky Mount building inspector Frank Phelps mentioned him at our first meeting. So did FBI Special Agent Will Garrett of Richmond. Nobody on our task force knew this victim's name, though. We only knew that the scammers referred to him as "the Colonel." Word also had it that he was a stickler for having his home in tip-top shape and that he would put the crews to work whenever they lied to him about another aspect of his home needing expensive repairs. They would approach him first thing in the morning when he was raising the American flag on a pole in his front yard.

Bill Tucker of our office was determined from the outset to locate this man. Tucker was a war vet himself. He had served in the Vietnam War and was aboard an aircraft carrier when it suffered massive and deadly explosions and fires following an accident during flight operations. "I never saw ground combat in Vietnam," he would tell us, "but I sure as hell would have preferred being in a fox hole with a rifle instead of pointing a fire hose as our ship was blowing up all around us!"

Beginning the day after our first meeting with Phelps and company over in Rocky Mount, Tucker started visiting the homes of North Carolina victims who had been struck by the House-Mazza crews. He loved the task for several reasons. First of all, his primary job responsibility was to investigate violations of antitrust and motor fuels marketing statutes. He seldom got to work on regular consumer fraud cases like Jane and me. Instead, he usually spent much of his time poring over financial documents, trying to divine from thousands of rows of numbers whether the companies involved were engaged in price fixing or some other illegal manipulation of the gasoline markets. Second, this elder fraud case tugged at his heartstrings, as it did with Jane and me. Third, Tucker loved working outside of the office because it freed him to chain smoke during business hours and listen to his favorite rock and roll station, WRDU, at high volume as he drove around in his car. And finally, he could take home 30 cents for every mile he put on his ancient Nissan. "If I speed enough when I'm out and about, I can take home almost double my monthly paycheck!"

Tucker cruised through the towns of central and eastern North Carolina and from neighborhood to neighborhood in Raleigh. He interviewed victims, copied their documents, and examined and photographed their homes. He showed them photos of some of the scammers in hopes that they could tell him which ones worked on their homes. He also photographed the victims' cancelled checks in order to record the payees' names and driver license numbers. Since the crew leaders did not want to expose themselves to law enforcement or tax authorities by having their names on a victim's checks, they routinely gave a lowly "hammer slinger" on the crew an extra cut for being the day's check casher. With photos of these checks in hand, Tucker was able to go to DMV and Department of Corrections databases and acquire valuable data for his growing spreadsheet of suspects and the victims they had conned.

Soon Tucker was able to spot homes that had been worked on by House-Mazza crews. All he had to do was drive through a neighborhood and look for houses that were a certain age, for outward signs that the place was occupied by an older adult (e.g., decals to alert first responders that a disabled or elderly person lived there, AstroTurf on the steps and porches to prevent slip and fall incidents, wheelchair ramps, aluminum awnings over windows to keep the home cool), and, most significantly, for horrible workmanship up on the roof and chimneys, such as shingles that had not been laid in straight lines.

He also looked for freshly installed basketball-shaped devices mounted on the roofs. These metal devices would spin with the wind, ventilating the attics below. They could be purchased for $40 at Lowe's or Home Depot and were easy to install, but crews would charge an elderly homeowner thousands of dollars for installing one of them after advising that a state-of-the-art automatic ventilation system was needed on the roof to alleviate mold and other moisture problems supposedly discovered in the attic.

One very obvious sign that these guys had struck someone was their absolutely awful workmanship in replacing the fascia boards just below the lower edge of the roof. Tucker could spot this feature instantly while driving down a street. For some reason, these guys couldn't nail the long boards on straight and were often too lazy to even paint and caulk them adequately.

Yet another victim identification tool that Tucker learned was something called a reverse phone directory. This was a special phone-book—made obsolete by today's online reverse lookup websites—where telephone service customers and their phone numbers were listed not by the customers' last names but by the street names and street numbers. These directories also listed the number of years that a subscriber had held a particular phone number at that address, which made it even easier for crews to confirm their suspicions that an older individual lived in a particular house. If the directory showed 35 or 45 years of phone service at a particular address, they knew to go knock on the door and offer to clean the gutters. Phelps and Garrett both reported that House-Mazza crews carried such directories in their trucks. Tucker purchased his own reverse directories so he could confirm suspicions that he should visit a home bearing some of the House-Mazza fraud indicators.

One day Jane received a call about a House-Mazza scam in progress in northwest Raleigh, not far from Andy Mazza's house. Such incident-in-progress reports were rare, and Tucker was not in the office, so Jane and I jumped in Jane's car and headed out to the victim's address. Even the two of us could spot the appalling fascia board work, the wind turbine attic vent and the poorly aligned shingles as we pulled up to the curb in front of the house. We recognized Carl Allen Smith, one of Will Garrett's suspects, standing in the carport and went to talk to him. He had the same vacant, snake-eyed look that appeared on his mug shot hanging on Tucker's wall back in the office.

As Smith calmly denied that his crew was doing anything wrong and questioned why we were bothering him, Tucker pulled up. He had been patrolling neighborhoods in the area, saw the red and white trucks, and spotted the horrible work.

"Hey, Jane. Hey, Dave. How did you guys beat me to this one?" Tucker was smiling as he made this inquiry but he seemed genuinely perplexed.

"Tucker, meet Carl Allen Smith." Instead of acknowledging my introduction attempt, Smith turned his snake eyes toward the far end of the street, one eyebrow raised higher than the other.

Suddenly we heard the horn of a white pickup truck that was parked at the end of the street. The driver held his hand out the window, pointed to the sky and made a twirling motion. Smith and the rest of the crew immediately piled into their own trucks and roared out of the neighborhood.

"Bill," Jane said, "you're getting so good at this you are spotting scams in progress!"

"Yeah, but how did you two beat me here?"

"'Cause Jane's good," I replied. He remained perplexed. After Jane and I picked on him for a few minutes, we explained the phone call Jane had received.

Despite his keen eye for the crews' handiwork, Tucker spent weeks searching in vain for a particular Raleigh home with a flagpole in the front yard and the telltale signs that House-Mazza crews had run their scams there. He even resorted to scouring the Raleigh phone book for names preceded by the appellation "Col.," but he struck out on that time-consuming approach too. He appeared in my office door regularly to update me on his fruitless quest.

"Still can't find the Colonel, Dave. Spent four hours yesterday driving around town. I did find a couple over on Glen Eden who lost $80K. Retired bankers."

"Great work. Let's grab some beers at The Players' Retreat this afternoon and talk about it."

"Sure! Wanna meet there at 3:00?"

"Gotta work. How 'bout I come by at 5:30?"

"Oh, I'll still be there at 5:30! Should be on beer number eight."

Tucker probably wasn't exaggerating too much about the eight beers. He could consume that beverage with great efficiency. Same for cigarettes.

PART THREE

Victim Mindsets and Vulnerabilities

10

Mrs. S and the Twins

One of the first victims of the House-Mazza home repair fraud group that Tucker, Jane and I met was Mrs. S, a woman in her 80s from Wake Forest, North Carolina, who had been scammed out of $107,000. Her situation was reported to us by her adult daughter who lived at the North Carolina coast. Mrs. S had been ripped off by a home repair contractor earlier in the 1990s and local police and the Wake County DA had prosecuted that contractor successfully.

The defendant in that earlier case had obtained $5,000 from Mrs. S. His sentence included prison time and a requirement that he repay her. The case was reported in the papers and the House-Mazza group took notice. Members of that group soon showed up at her home promising to fix the problems that the convicted scammer had caused in her home. They spent the next year and a half defrauding her over and over again.

Mrs. S's deceased husband had been a skilled professional who had worked at Wake Forest University prior to its move to Winston-Salem, North Carolina, in the 1950s. Their longtime home, which she still occupied, sat on a large lot not far from the old Wake Forest campus. It bore the hallmarks of most of the House-Mazza victims' homes: at least 50 years old and still in sound condition.

We were welcomed into the home by Mrs. S's daughter. She introduced Mrs. S to us, then took us through the home, pointing out things the scammers supposedly had repaired. At each location, her mother argued that the repairs were necessary and that the scammers had done right by her. The daughter was correct in her conclusion that her mother had been scammed. The original, 50-year-old wooden roof decking, which supposedly had been replaced, was still there. The attic rafters had useless stiff knees scabbed onto them. There were unneeded rotary vents mounted on the roof. The walls of the basement were adorned with fresh, sloppily applied white paint ("water proofing"). Useless eight-foot-tall red screw jacks were wedged between the basement floor and the floor joists above. Some were only inches from the basement's concrete walls and begged the question: How can a few metal screw jacks hold up the floor system of a 100-ton home if the concrete foundation wall just two inches away cannot?

We also noticed a new wooden screen door adorning the outside entrance to the basement. At that time, a standard-size screen door like that could be purchased for $35 at Lowe's or Home Depot. "Momma paid $1,000 for that door," said her daughter. Mrs. S., having overheard the comment, rushed over from the other side of the basement and chastised her: "They did a beautiful job with that door! They had to special order it because of the doorway's unique size—plus they had to paint it! Why do you keep criticizing those boys? They are all good to me."

As you can surmise, Mrs. S held her victimizers in high regard. Twice she told us they were like sons to her. As for the screen door, however, it was definitely a standard size.

We soon learned that the home repair fraudsters had taken Mrs. S to the store or out to lunch regularly, had presented her with cakes on her birthday, and regularly took her downtown for ice cream on hot afternoons. Individual crew members sat in the living room and conversed with her for hours at a time, diverting her from the fact that actual repairs were not being performed on her home by other crew members. They learned everything they could about her life, her family, even the dogs that she owned when she was a girl. They told her about their own lives and how they wished they had had a mother like her. After all of this personal attention, it would have been surprising had she not become fond of them—even though they were deliberately draining her savings.

The flare-ups between Mrs. S and her daughter were the first time we witnessed the non-financial losses that that elder fraud criminals inflict upon families. We never learned whether the scammers had suggested it to her or she had developed such an attitude on her own, but clearly Mrs. S felt that her daughter was questioning her competence and trying to take over her financial affairs by claiming she had been defrauded repeatedly. This angered Mrs. S and she was having none of it.

Mrs. S claimed her daughter was jealous of the young men who had showed her such kindness and perhaps feeling guilty over the fact that they demonstrated it each day while her daughter enjoyed life at the coast.

Mrs. S was adamant that she still knew how to care for her home and that she was still in charge.

The daughter clearly was distressed by Mrs. S's attitudes. "We can live without the $107,000," she told me. "The wedge that these guys have driven between Mom and me is far more costly and painful." She felt that her mom would come around once the scammers were charged with fraud. For the next several months, she contacted us to complain that such charges had not been filed.

Another pair of victims we dealt with early during the House-Mazza investigation were twins in their 90s who lived in the heart of Old Raleigh, not far from downtown Raleigh. Like so many inhabitants of that area, the twins had been politically connected during the primes of their lives. In fact, they still were and could drop names with the best of them ("We had lunch with Governor Jim Hunt and UNC president Bill Friday last week...").

The House-Mazza group had been performing work on the twins' home for 10 years. They had run every type of home repair scam on them at least once, and a few of them had been run two or three times. For example, we could find rusted screw jacks or faded stiff knees mounted alongside brand-new ones. The twins told us the roof had been "completely reconstructed two times" during that 10-year period, the second reconstruction "necessitated by the incompetence of the crew that did the first reconstruction job." We could tell via a quick visit to the attic that such was not the case. As usual, the original roof decking and roof trusses were still in service.

The twins, just like Mrs. S., would not stand for any criticism of the work we had examined. They, too, spoke of being taken to the store by the scammers, long conversations with members of the crew, lunch outings, birthday gifts and comments about their being like kind-hearted mothers the crew members never had. They were quite enamored of their victimizers.

It made us sick.

11

As Little as $1400
Can Be Devastating

Many of the cases discussed in this book feature victims like Mrs. S and the twins who were upper middle class or wealthy. In terms of dollars and cents, their losses sometimes were breathtaking. As reflected in my two 1981 LSSP cases featured earlier, however, having a limited income does not immunize one from these devastating scams. My low-income clients in those two cases easily could have ended up homeless or worse—and they were scammed only one time.

Another such example was a one-off fraud incident that almost cost a lower income couple their lives.

Erwin, North Carolina, is a small town an hour south of Raleigh, down in tobacco country. The town itself used to be known as the "Denim Capital of the World" due to the textile product once manufactured there. Late one cold January in the year 2000, we received a call from the county Adult Protective Services office there. They had just started working with an elderly couple who had been defrauded by someone claiming to be with "the California Lottery."

The phony lottery company representative called the couple out of the blue and congratulated them for winning a $100,000 prize in one of the company's contests. He told them the money would be delivered the day after they paid $10,000 to cover California state income taxes on the prize. They replied that they did not have that kind of money and that they barely brought in $1,400 each month through Social Security.

"Have your January checks arrived yet?" (This was when Social Security payments came in the mail.)

"No. They should come tomorrow."

"Fine. Just cash them and then wire me that amount of money immediately. I'll release the prize to you. You can settle up with me for the rest of the taxes after it arrives. But you have to act now before my boss discovers that I'm letting you pay the balance of the taxes later. He might nix the whole arrangement!"

Excited about this wonderful news, the husband and wife did as they were told and wired the entire proceeds of their January Social Security payments to California. They were already in a situation where their Social Security payments often failed to get them to the end of the month. Whenever they found themselves in that predicament they skimped on food, stopped purchasing needed medications, and delayed payment of utility bills until the next monthly check arrived. Their November and December power bills were already overdue. This arrangement with the sweepstakes man would put them even further into the hole, even though it was just the first week of the month. But at least the $100,000 would be arriving in a few days, and soon they would never again have to worry about stretching their Social Security payments to the end of the month.

The $100,000 never arrived and no one picked up the phone when the husband and wife called the lottery man's number.

Around the 29th of January, a neighbor called Adult Protective Services and reported that the couple was sick, freezing and starving in their small house and that the wife was in dire need of her Parkinson's medications. The power had been cut off and the cupboard was bare. The outside temperature at night had been in the mid-teens and was expected to go down into the teens again that night. APS immediately took them to the hospital. Both had the flu. The doctor observed that the wife probably would not have survived another night in the house.

The scammer who almost killed this poor couple was never found.

12

"I found the Colonel!"

One Monday morning in the early fall of 1995, just as I was about to head to the county courthouse for the weekly calendar call, Tucker burst into my office with a huge grin. He was always an upbeat guy and usually arrived at work on Monday mornings full of energy and eager to regale us with tales of his weekend misadventures. The rest of us just wanted to drink another cup of coffee before we tackled a new week. On this particular morning Tucker was as ebullient as I had ever seen him. I could tell that he was ready to unleash some particularly interesting stories.

"I found the Colonel!"

"Fantastic! I've got two motions on the calendar this morning and need to head to the courthouse. Can you walk with me and tell me about it?"

"Sure thing. It'll give me a chance to smoke another cigarette." We headed out the door and down the sidewalk to the Wake County courthouse. Tucker could hardly contain his excitement.

"The Colonel is about 90 and almost blind, although you'd never know it. He lives right off of Wade Avenue." Wade Avenue is a tree-lined, undulating thoroughfare in west Raleigh that extends from the state fairgrounds to the edge of the downtown area. Many victims of the House-Mazza crews lived in neighborhoods on either side of that boulevard.

"He lives on a tiny street just off Canterbury Road. I didn't even know that street existed. He is still very military and very much in charge. Saw him Saturday morning hoisting his flag. I got out of my car and asked him, 'Are you the Colonel, sir?' He replied, 'They call me that. What can I do for you, son?'"

Tucker had spent most of his Saturday talking with the Colonel and inspecting his house and his cancelled checks. The crews had taken him for just under $240,000 during the preceding 12 months. Sure enough, the scams started out with a knock on his door and a humble looking fellow offering to clean out his gutters for $45. Once the gutters were clean, the man told him the roof was rotted. "It is so rotted, sir, that my leg plunged into it all the way up to my hip. Almost broke the bone!" The Colonel then got the usual warning about the Raleigh building inspector being in the neighborhood and that he would condemn the Colonel's house on the spot if he saw the hole up there. "You'll have to move into a hotel and your neighbors will have to stare at a big sign in your yard that reads 'Condemned,'" the scammer told him.

Then the scammer mentioned some friends doing roof work in the neighborhood who could fix the problem ASAP. He asked if he could use the Colonel's phone to call them.

The Colonel agreed. Minutes later, several trucks pulled up in front of the house. The crew chief requested permission to go up on the roof and inspect, received permission to do so, and then spent 20 minutes atop the house. He eventually came down the ladder and told the Colonel that the roof was in much worse shape than the gutter cleaner had described. The whole wooden roof decking system from one end of the house to the other was rotten and in need of replacement. It would cost several thousand dollars to strip off the shingles, replace wooden roof decking, and lay new roofing felt and shingles. He would need a deposit of $3,575 to purchase the materials, and the rest when the job was done. The crew chief also mentioned the building inspector in the neighborhood and the likelihood that he would see the problem and condemn the house on the spot.

The Colonel directed the crew chief to take care of the problem immediately, then wrote out a check for $3,575. Ladders promptly went up all around his house and he could hear what he thought were workers tearing off shingles, cutting into the roof, yanking boards loose, and flinging them to the ground. A few days later, the crew chief announced that the work was finished, the roof was as good as new and the final payment due was $8,800.

Little did the Colonel know, according to Tucker, but the crews had replaced almost nothing on the roof, the shingles already on the roof were fairly new and most were never pulled off, and the scammers had simply laid another layer of cheap shingles over them. While a complete roof replacement might cost $9,000, such a simple "shingle overlay" job usually went for $2,000 to $3,000 then.

As the Colonel was writing the $8,800 check for the supposedly rebuilt roof, the crew chief asked if he could go up into the attic to examine how the rafters and beams were handling all the new material up on the new roof. He also told the Colonel he wanted to ensure there was no damage in the attic from the water intrusion that had rotted the roof decking. The Colonel directed him to go up and check it. Sure enough, when the crew chief descended the attic steps, he reported that the rafters were weakened from the water intrusion and about to buckle under all the weight of the new roof. They needed bracing if the roof was to be saved.

That evening, the crew had hammered two-by-four studs vertically between the rafters and the attic floor (the stiff knee scam).

"I counted 17 of those stiff knees, multiplied that by $100, since that's what Will and Frank told us they charged, and asked if he had a cancelled check for $1,700. Sure enough, there was a check for $1,750. I guess they charged him an extra $50 for the nails. It was the check he wrote right after the two for replacing the roof."

The crew also convinced the Colonel that his house had toxic mold that needed to be treated, plus water damage to the inner walls, all resulting from the "totally rotted" roof. He paid thousands for those bogus mold treatments. After performing that round of phony repairs, a crew member asked for permission to use his toilet, received that permission, and a few minutes later emerged from the bathroom reporting that there was water on the floor surrounding the toilet base and the toilet needed to be pulled up so they could inspect for possible damage to the floor system below. This was the "toilet bowl scam" where a worker pours a cup of tap water around the base of the toilet, then reports a serious toilet leak to the owner.

As one might expect, the Colonel directed them to pull out the toilet plus go into the basement and inspect for any floor system damage below the bathroom. Sure enough, the crew chief returned and reported that there was extensive damage to the subflooring and that it was going to be expensive to repair. The Colonel replied, "Do it."

"That was $6,500," said Tucker. "I checked in the basement below the toilet. Nothing had been replaced. Apparently, they just went down there and partied. They wacked the floor joists with their hammers every now and then to make the Colonel believe they were actually working. You can see all the hammer marks in the wood."

The crew also hit the Colonel with the failing floor scam. This is when a heavy-set member of the crew walks across the floor with a deliberately ponderous gait trying to rattle the furniture and the contents of shelves and cabinets. The crew chief asked the Colonel if he noticed what was happening with the furniture and all the items in the cabinets when his worker walked by. "They shake badly when my man simply walks across the floor, sir. All the water that poured in through your rotted roof must have damaged the floor system! We need to go underneath the dining room here and inspect."

A half an hour later, the crew chief convinced the Colonel that the floor system was indeed failing, that the entire house could be impacted if it did fail, and that an expensive system of hydraulic jacks was needed to re-lift the floor and keep it stable. The cost would be $16,000.

What the crew did next was purchase metal screw jacks from Lowe's or Home Depot and install them throughout the basement and crawl space. Tucker knew from Phelps and Garrett's briefings that crews typically charged $500 for each "hydraulic jack" they installed. When he counted all the screw jacks installed, there were 16 of them. Sure enough, the Colonel had issued two checks totaling $8,000 and bearing the notation "hydraulic jacks."

"They also ran the basement waterproofing scam on him, the rusted chimney flashing scam, the frozen pipes scam and the inspector scam," Tucker told me. The phony inspector said that most of the earlier jobs were done incorrectly and had to be redone, then summoned a different crew to the Colonel's house to redo all the work. The Colonel paid for all that too. Just the other day, he lent one crew member $3,500 so he could make the down payment on a new car. It goes on and on."

"The good thing is, the Colonel realizes he was defrauded and he wants to help us. He remembers each transaction, each fraudulent statement and each check he wrote. He is as sharp as a tack. He's going to be a fantastic witness!" Tucker concluded.

Tucker had every right to be so happy that Monday morning.

13

Twelve Key Victim Vulnerabilities and One Myth

What makes seniors prime targets for fraud? One key reason can be found in Willie Sutton's supposed response when asked why he robbed banks: "Because that's where the money is."

Historian and economist Neil Howe, writing in *Forbes* in 2018, cited statistics that explain why many in the world of crime now prefer robbing American seniors to knocking off banks. While a large but declining number of them struggle with poverty, Howe noted that seniors have become the wealthiest age group in the United States. The average American retiree's net worth is $264,750. He observed further that the average net worth of members of the 75-plus generation, sometimes called "the Silent Generation," is 1.3 times that of the Baby Boom generation, two times that of those in Generation X and 23 times that of the Millennials.[1]

Their generation's place atop the generational wealth chart is not the only factor that makes seniors the targets of fraud artists. Over the years, and based in large part on information shared by victims, their family members and the scammers themselves, Dr. Virginia H. Templeton and I compiled the following list of 12 common senior fraud victim vulnerabilities[2]:

1. Good credit, easy access to savings, 100 percent equity in one's home.
2. Fixed, limited income and worries about making ends meet.
3. Depression.
4. A strong desire to be a decision-maker again.
5. Difficulty controlling obsessions.
6. Physical or emotional isolation.

7. Loneliness stemming from the death of a spouse or close friends.

8. Fear of losing one's independence, especially the abilities to manage one's own finances or live in one's own home.

9. Impairments in mobility, sight or hearing.

10. The effects of medications during the course of the day ("sundowner effect").

11. Accessibility—seniors who are retired are easier to catch at home or on the phone than younger adults who are working.

12. Age-related cognitive decline.

In later chapters of this book, we will discuss other vulnerabilities that were unique to particular victims, but the list above contains the most common ones. Some are closely related to one another and often seen together, e.g., No. 2 (financial insecurity), No. 3 (depression), No. 4 (desire to be a decision-maker again), No. 6 (physical isolation) and No. 7 (loneliness), while others are not. Most of our victims had a combination of at least two or three of these vulnerabilities. Some had as many as 10.

Oftentimes a victim's unique combination of vulnerabilities changes after several re-victimizations. For instance, as the scams continue, No. 1 (good credit and readily accessible assets) might turn into vulnerability No. 2 (worries over a shrinking nest egg) and No. 4 (desire to be a decision-maker again) might change to No. 8 (fear of being declared incompetent and losing one's independence).

Members of the elder fraud industry map and re-map a target's unique pattern of vulnerabilities and tailor the nature and timing of their pitches to take maximum advantage. Criminals who defraud over the telephone spend a lot of time conversing with their targets and searching for these vulnerabilities. Home repair scammers, as we have already seen, typically accomplish this by having one member of the crew sit with the victim and engage in lengthy conversations while the rest of the crew pretends to repair the house. Internet scammers, especially romance scammers, will do the same from their computer terminals in Nigeria, Spain, Russia or wherever they are located. Put another way, all of them are profiling their victims.

Some of these vulnerabilities are rather obvious. For instance, home repair scammers, when they notice that their fraud target suffers from impaired vision or mobility, will pretend to repair areas of the home that the victim can no longer see or access. Other vulnerabilities had to be pointed out to us. Take No. 4, for instance, "a strong desire to be a decision-maker again." Many of our victims who lost enormous sums of money once held important, high pressure jobs where others relied upon them to provide guidance and make important decisions. They missed those heady days when they were go-to persons in their organizations. Scammers exploit that vulnerability by using a tactic they call "putting them back in the captain's chair." They adjust their pitches and their false narratives in order to make every issue a question of huge importance that only the victim can resolve.

In the late '90s, Professor Lisa Gwyther, director of Duke University's Alzheimer's Family Support Center, gave a presentation to the North Carolina Senior Consumer Fraud Task Force on age-related vulnerabilities to fraud. Many of the vulnerabilities we were well aware of. One key vulnerability was new to us: difficulty in controlling obsessions. Lisa explained how many older individuals developed this problem as they aged. An enjoyment of sweepstakes, for instance, might become an obsession later in life. Yep, we frequently witnessed that in sweepstakes scam victims. So had the scammers! Similarly, a desire to keep one's home tidy and in good repair might become a fixation later in life. You have just read about one such victim—the Colonel. There were many, many more like him.

Professor Gwyther also spoke of the prevalence of age-related depression among older individuals. Sometimes the cause was metabolic and sometimes it resulted from sad developments later in the person's life, such as the passing of a spouse, siblings or friends, or from declines in health and mobility. Scammers know how to tap into their victims' depression, especially those dark moods when the victims are feeling resentful, impatient or hostile toward those who love and care for them. The scammers will seize upon such feelings to drive a wedge between the victim and his or her personal support network. "If they get wind of these transactions before they are complete, they will just use them as excuses for their plans to take away your checkbook and put you in a nursing home, so don't talk to them. Okay?"

You will notice two different kinds of isolation listed in vulnerability No. 6. People living alone in rural areas often are physically isolated from the network of friends and family that might help them see through scam attempts or debunk the scammers' tales. Oftentimes, however, victims may have plenty of friends and family members nearby who physically interact with them often, but they feel ignored or patronized by their family and friends and detached from their day-to-day activities. For example, adult children and grandchildren might regularly include a grandparent in their activities, but they tend to converse with one another or be totally focused on the children's activities, seldom engaging in any meaningful conversations with the grandparent. These older adults are not physically isolated, but they might as well be. Scammers take advantage by developing very close (but fake) friendships with such victims. They engage in the types of meaningful conversations that the adult children and grandchildren no longer include them in and make them feel valued.

The twelfth and final category, age-related cognitive decline, definitely overlaps with some of these other vulnerabilities. Vulnerability No. 7, difficulty controlling obsessions, probably falls completely within its scope. Age-related cognitive decline includes what experts refer to as normal cognitive aging, problems that develop slowly with age and are subtle in their onset, such as short-term memory issues or difficulty processing information as quickly as before. It can include impaired judgment in exciting or alarming situations. I definitely witnessed the latter in one of my parents as they got older. Individuals experiencing such problems can still enjoy normal, productive lives and even learn new things just as before, but they might need a little more time to carry out such tasks. It is like an older computer that is slowing down but can still perform most of its original functions—if you are a little patient with it. Senior scammers, as the cases so far illustrate, tax these declining cognitive abilities by doing exactly the opposite.

Also included in this final, rather broad vulnerability category are conditions that cause more rapid declines in cognitive abilities: Alzheimer's disease, Parkinson's disease, vascular dementia, Lewy Body Dementia. Scammers appear to have an evil gift for finding and financially exploiting people in the early stages of these medical conditions. As is discussed in Chapter 35 ("What Do the Scientists Have to Say About All This?"), research has shown that financial competency, which is the ability to handle one's financial affairs in one's best interests (including the avoidance of fraud), disappears early in the Alzheimer's progression.

The following is purely anecdotal but it is something my colleagues and I experienced frequently. Often while working with repeat victims of senior fraud, we would recommend that the family arrange for their mother or father to undergo a cognitive assessment during the next doctor's visit. Most of the time, the result of the assessment was that the parent's cognitive functioning was normal for his or her advancing age. A few years later, however, many of those families would contact us to report that their parent had just been diagnosed with Alzheimer's disease. The fraud artists, it seems, had spotted the early stages of that condition long before anyone else had. It was almost as if they had been studying the aforementioned research.

Interestingly, on April 16, 2019, the *Annals of Internal Medicine* published the results of a long-term research project about older adults and heightened vulnerability to fraud. They showed that "[d]ecreased scam awareness may be an early indicator of Alzheimer dementia and its precursor, mild cognitive impairment..."[3]

One vulnerability that people often ascribe to older adults is a myth: "They just grew up during a kinder, more trusting time." I worked for two attorneys general who repeatedly said that. Never during the two decades that I worked for those AGs did I encounter a repeat victim who fit that profile. Most had made their livings in professions where skepticism and a willingness to challenge or contradict others were vital skills. As children during the Great Depression, they grew up in a time when bankers were distrusted, millions joined labor unions because they distrusted employers and corporations, and others fervently believed that labor unions were linked to Bolshevism. They had to fight World War II because governments and businesses around the world had messed things up so terribly. Theirs was a tough, skeptical generation, and you can experience those traits rather quickly when you try and persuade one of them that they are being defrauded.

Something else that debunks the "kinder, more trusting time" fallacy is the fact that these so-called Children of the Depression, aka the Greatest Generation and the World War II generation, are passing into history. The Korean War (or "Silent") generation and the Baby Boomers are now taking its place. The leading edge of the Boomers, a generation notorious in the 1960s for its skepticism, its irreverence and its willingness to challenge norms, is now being hit hard by the elder fraud industry.

And that is why "they grew up in a kinder, more trusting time" is not listed above as the thirteenth common vulnerability.

14

Our House-Mazza Posse
Gets Mired in the Mud

As 1995 drew to a close, attendance at the meetings of the House-Mazza Home Repair Fraud Task Force grew so fast that Jane Feather and I kept having to find larger and larger meeting rooms to host the gatherings. We switched from the meeting room at the U.S. Attorney's Office to the North Carolina State Bar's huge hearing room, then later to the North Carolina Highway Commission's palatial hearing room across from the capitol building. Law enforcement officials kept joining us from various North Carolina towns, cities and counties. So did Virginia officials and officials from the U.S. Department of Justice in Washington, D.C.

Kurt Ellis of SBI Financial Crimes brought in analysts Evelyn Poole and Glenn Fanelly Covington from the intelligence unit at bureau headquarters. Their participation proved extremely helpful because of the computer firepower at their disposal. Tucker's spreadsheets contained a wealth of information and had become eagerly anticipated handouts when each meeting began, but Evelyn and Glenn's data sheets soon made them obsolete.

Certain individuals had become the stars of the group. Will Garrett probably took top billing, followed by Tucker. Their senses of humor and wealth of knowledge about the scammers were the reasons everyone looked forward to their comments during the meetings and wanted to dine at their tables when we adjourned for lunch at Big Ed's. Jane grabbed the spotlight quite often with her charm and sense of humor. Glenn grabbed it too. She did not say much, but that did not matter to some. She was tall, young and smart, and she had at her fingertips a wealth of intelligence on the scammers. (She went on to become an investigator with the Federal Trade Commission and, later, a U.S. postal inspector who busts child pornographers.)

Frank Phelps still felt that he was a big player in the group, but there were already whispers that he might be way too close to the scammers, one scammer in particular, Ricky Braswell. His protests that "Ricky is a good guy" started to wear on the rest of the group. Because Frank was not with a criminal law enforcement agency, some in the task force did not want him to attend any further meetings at all.

Despite the expansion of both our ranks and our knowledge of the scammers, challenges grew. Will Garrett was still having trouble getting an assistant U.S. attorney to bring charges in his cases. It was not that he was being told "no." The prosecutors he worked with simply had a backlog of pressing cases that had already been indicted and needed to go to trial. In the late spring of 1996, Will announced that he might not be able to work with us for quite some time. Two hikers had just been murdered near the Appalachian Trail in Virginia's Shenandoah Valley and he was being pulled off his cases to go investigate. A lot of that investigating would involve hiking up and down the trail and interviewing through-hikers who might have encountered the victims or possible suspects days or weeks earlier.

I was pulled away by the synthetic stucco wars. Assistant Attorney General Beth Smoot and I were trying to put together a half-billion-dollar claims settlement program funded by the builders, the manufacturers and their insurance companies. At the same time, we were working behind the scenes to make North Carolina the first state to ban the use of non-drainable EIFS synthetic stucco in wood-framed homes.

What really reduced the task force's momentum to a slow, ponderous slog during this time period was the inability of North Carolina members to cultivate informants inside the House-Mazza group like the ones Will Garrett had developed in Virginia. It was not that the scammers refused to speak to any of us when they were arrested for something, such as drug violations, assault, drunken driving or driving with a revoked driver's license. They would talk, but they seldom told us anything that would build our cases. It was worse than just blowing smoke. They wasted our time by fishing for whatever information we had on their operations.

By way of example, one day Jane, Tucker and I drove to Louisburg, the seat of Franklin County, just north of Raleigh. The local sheriff told us there was a member of the House family who wanted to speak with us about the House organization. When we interviewed him, he claimed that he was "legit" and had never scammed elderly homeowners like many others in the House clan. He named Bob House, Sr., and Bob Jr. as major players, something we already had been told. He could not seem to remember who else might be involved and asked us to name a few, just to jog his memory a bit. He also invited us to name certain victims there in Franklin County, which also might jog his memory. His ploy was "Show me your cards, but I won't show you any of mine."

We declined. Repeatedly. Then we drove back to Raleigh empty handed. Jane spent much of the return trip carrying on about how creepy our unhelpful source had been. "Every time that damn man referred to me as 'Honey' or 'Shug,' I just wanted to vomit! Can you imagine any woman wanting to be with him?" (To this day, one can make Jane cringe and protest simply by slipping the word "shug" into a sentence.)

Other North Carolina law enforcement agents encountered the same show-me-yours-but-I-won't-show-you-mine ploy. All of us were being played by these lowlife con men. It got to a point where many of us were reconsidering our strategy of building cases through inside informants. The original strategy of building fraud cases via the testimony and recollections of our elderly victims crept back to the forefront. The Colonel should be able to help prove a criminal case against several of the scammers. Surely, we would find other victims who would make great witnesses.

15

Call the Doctor!

The North Carolina contingent of the House-Mazza Home Repair Fraud Task Force was facing an existential crisis by the spring of 1996. We could not develop inside informants, nor could we find more victims who could help us prove our fraud cases through their own testimony and recollections of events. Most of them simply could not remember what was said to them by whom about each supposed problem in their home. The scammers had been in their homes almost every day for months or years, making non-stop representations and promises. Even the Colonel experienced these issues sometimes. The more we tried to tease the details of those conversations out of them during interviews, the more these victims froze up or grew agitated. From a prosecution standpoint, we were stuck on the starting line. How could a prosecutor make the required showing that (1) a false representation was made, (2) it was made by the named defendant and (3) the victim reasonably relied upon it and paid money?

The most vexing of our victims, and there were a lot of them, were not the ones whose memories were cloudy. They were the ones who maintained, often with raised voices or wagging fingers, that they had *not* been scammed, we were picking on "good boys" or "dear friends" and we needed to leave their house.

We were stuck.

If we could not get some criminal prosecutions going, we probably needed to shut down the task force and direct our time and resources to other crimes. After all, we had been at this for months. Everyone had plenty of other cases to address.

At one of our meetings in mid–1996, there was an animated discussion about cult members who just could not accept that they had been manipulated and scammed. Many of us had investigated or brought enforcement actions against charismatic individuals who ran pyramid schemes, Ponzi schemes or other investment scams. Those criminal schemes were similar to cults. Victims of those schemes fiercely defended the schemes' leaders once our investigations were revealed, and they often packed courtrooms, got in our faces when court was recessed or adjourned and harangued our coworkers back at the office while our trials against their victimizers were in progress. Sometimes they even harangued the judge—which was rather counterproductive.

Only when the pyramid or Ponzi scheme's leader was perp-walked off to jail and it dawned on them that they would never recover their life savings did any of the cultish victims change their position. Even then their view of us tended to be adversarial ("Why didn't you protect me before I gave my life savings to that crook? What good are you?"). Until that awkward moment of enlightenment was reached, however, those victims remained prisoners of the hypnotic spells that the leaders of the pyramid or Ponzi schemes had cast, and they would have drunk the poisoned Kool-Aid willingly had those leaders directed them to do so.

The House-Mazza crews seemed to have placed our elderly victims under identical spells. Even when we persuaded a few of them never to do business with the crews again, that they had been defrauded, such victims often re-engaged with the crews when the convoy of red and white trucks pulled up in front of their homes a day or two later.

Many on the House-Mazza Task Force had heard of psychiatrists and other professionals who could "deprogram" cult members and speculated that perhaps some of our older victims could be deprogrammed as well. With specialized counseling, perhaps they might recognize their repairmen as victimizers rather than as dear friends or newfound sons or grandsons. While we were at it, perhaps there might also be some sort of additional counseling or drug therapies that would help our victims retrieve memories of important conversations with the scammers. After all, there were techniques that enabled trauma victims to remember important details of their horrible experiences. Such deprogramming and memory retrieval might be the House-Mazza gang's undoing.

We were grasping at straws. It was an interesting discussion nevertheless.

As the discussion wrapped up, I mentioned that I knew a geriatrician and that I would run these points by her. Afterward, I called Dr. Margaret

Noel at Thoms Rehabilitation Hospital in Asheville, North Carolina. Had I known any other geriatricians, I still would have called Dr. Noel. She was a biology major when we both attended Davidson College back in the mid–'70s. She subsequently completed medical school, an internal medicine residency and a geriatrics fellowship. During her college days, her combination of smarts, charm and working girl sensibilities enabled the future Dr. Noel to soak up complicated facts and scientific principles, then explain them to individuals with fewer intellectual gifts—pre-law students like my buddies and me, for instance—in a clear, non-patronizing manner. Now, as a practicing physician, she was employing those gifts on a daily basis as she explained to concerned family members the mysteries behind their older loved ones' troublesome behaviors and declining cognitive abilities.

Sure enough, busy Dr. Noel listened to all my descriptions of our elderly victims, suppressed any urge she might have had to laugh at our theories, and kindly offered some thoughts on what was going on. She started out with an explanation of age-related cognitive changes and how our intellectual capacities peak in our late 20s. While these changes are identifiable on detailed testing in most individuals by their 40s, alterations in reasoning and spatial recognition skills, speed of processing, working memory or attention, and ability to "multi-task" are not noticeable until the person is into their 50s or 60s. These changes are generally annoying but not disabling, she said. She spoke of how this progression eventually can affect judgment during excited situations or one's ability to keep up with directions or conversations. Such problems stemmed, in part, from a reduction in the brain's ability to process information as quickly as before. Other faculties like patience, self-control or recognition of risk might be impacted by age-related stressors. Which of these various mental skills and faculties would be impacted, and when, could vary greatly from one person to the next.

Normal cognitive aging, she said, would not mean that persons experiencing such issues were incapable of handling their own affairs or learning new things or processing new information like before. Often, those persons just needed a little more time to do the processing and learning. They could maintain their independence and enjoyment of life with certain lifestyle modifications.

Some of our fraud victims, she said, might be experiencing mild cognitive impairment, a subtle condition often "clinically dismissed as normal aging" that can be marked by executive dysfunction (judgment and decision-making impairments) and/or mild short-term memory and mood changes. The scammers were likely recognizing and exploiting those issues. In many persons, she said, mild cognitive impairment is heralding the earliest stage of Alzheimer's or another dementia process. Dr. Noel stated that over half of persons with dementia were likely undiagnosed.

Dr. Noel also made it quite clear that no magical medical or psychological fixes would reverse our victims' strong and positive feelings for their victimizers or restore their poor recollections of the conversations that they had had with them. She concluded her comments by saying patients often were brought to her after a critical financial mishap by families who felt helpless to intervene. She expressed hope and gratitude for our efforts to educate the public and put safeguards in place against those who prey on the vulnerable. These efforts, she said, would make a tremendous difference for the patients and families she served.

At the next monthly meeting of the House-Mazza task force, I shared Dr. Noel's comments. I feared that it would unleash a round of pessimism and that North Carolina task force members might start to bail out of the whole project.

The first reaction came from Mark Rosenfield, the DEA agent.

"Well, we've still got some federal drug charges that can be brought against some of these guys. Maybe now is the time." He rattled off the names of eight or nine suspects and the possible charges against each. They were key players.

Then Kevin Anderson of the IRS chimed in. "There are some tax and 'structuring' charges that can be filed against many of those same guys, plus some of their buddies. They aren't declaring all of this income on their tax returns."

"Structuring" is a federal crime designed to fight money laundering. It is committed whenever one splits a cash transaction into separate, smaller components in order to avoid the cash transaction report (CTR) that must be filed when certain financial transactions exceed $10,000. The CTR requirements probably were why House-Mazza crews studiously avoided collecting checks for $10,000 or more from their victims. Instead they would ask a victim to write two or three checks in smaller amounts, often on the same day and sometimes on successive days. The crews "structured" so much that each member probably could be charged with multiple counts of that crime. Such charges would not be as sexy as bank fraud, wire fraud, money laundering or drug possession, but at least the gang members could be sent away to federal prison for up to five years on each charge.

After Rosenfield and Anderson spoke, some of the criminal prosecutors chimed in. If some of Rosenfield and Anderson's defendants "flipped" and helped with the investigation and prosecution of the hundreds of home repair fraud incidents we now knew about, the entire North Carolina contingent of the House-Mazza organization could be taken down. Then, as trial lawyers love to do, they narrated how they would present their cases in court. Cooperating crew members would testify first about how each homeowner was intentionally defrauded and by whom. A local building inspector like Frank Phelps would then confirm that the repairs were unnecessary and really didn't fix anything. The prosecutors would put the homeowners on the stand as their final witnesses, not to prove the fraud itself but to prove the amounts lost to the crimes. They would have each homeowner go through a stack of checks that they had written to the scammers, read off the dates, payees and dollar figures, verify their signature, and testify that each check was for a supposed home repair. With each check presented and acknowledged by the victim, the defendants would be guilty of another felony charge.

One prosecutor in the room observed, "At this point in the trial, I'd love for defense counsel to ask an elderly homeowner about how wonderful these boys were to her, how their work was just fantastic, and how she loves them all. The jury would see how the victim remains under the scammers' spell and they would demand the death penalty!"

Another prosecutor predicted that few defense lawyers would let their clients face a jury trial if any of their fellow scammers and the elderly homeowners were on the prosecution's witness list.

The federal charges that Rosenfield and Anderson were discussing could, collectively, bring lengthy federal prison sentences. Would such charges scare these members of the House-Mazza organization into cooperating with our home repair fraud investigations? Would the filing of those charges make other members who had not been charged nervous enough to come forward and help us? Would they finally break ranks?

Or would the leaders of the organization keep their 50 guys under control?

In a few months we would know the answer.

PART FOUR

Payoff

16

The AG Calls Channel 11 Troubleshooter Jennifer Julian

As the task force struggled to build cases against the House-Mazza group, a related problem developed. The House-Mazza crews were still ripping off elderly victims all across North Carolina. Multiple crews were operating in some of the larger communities, like Charlotte, Raleigh and Fayetteville. We needed to warn the public that this was happening. Several months had gone by since Detective Brian Kreigsman's call to report Frog's $16,000 scam in Brevard.

Most of the prosecutors and law enforcement officials on the House-Mazza Home Repair Fraud Task Force operated under agency policies that strongly discouraged talking to the press about investigations that had not yet resulted in criminal charges. Jane, Tucker and I, however, worked for an elected official whose consumer protection mission included warning the public about new frauds and scams. We told the others on the task force we would try and get the word out via the press, but we would not name our suspects or the agencies that were looking into them.

When we ran our public warning idea past the higher-ups in the AG's office, they discussed and quickly quashed any notion of the AG calling a press conference to describe the scams and warn consumers. Because we could not name the suspects or the agencies looking into them, and because almost none of our victims thought they had been scammed, the higher-ups worried that members of the press would ignore the story or, even worse, tear into Attorney General Easley for not giving them any specifics to work with. They would want victims to interview, bad guys to chase with their cameras and microphones, and examples of useless repairs to show to viewers and readers.

The strategy for warning the public soon shifted to sharing the story with a specific reporter and then letting him or her run with it.

There were several reporters we thought would be suitable, including consumer reporter Monica Laliberte with WRAL-TV in Raleigh, C.J. Underwood with WBTV in Charlotte and business writer Ames Alexander with the *Charlotte Observer*. Each had worked on consumer protection pieces with us over the years.

Jane and I suggested consumer reporter Jennifer Julian with WTVD Channel 11 in Durham. People who resided in central North Carolina in the 1990s and early 2000s remember her as "The Troubleshooter" for Channel 11 News. Jane and I had made several trips to Durham when Jennifer would host "Ask Consumer Protection" phone-in events during that TV station's evening news hour. Throughout those newscasts, anchors Larry Stogner and Miriam Thomas would cut away to Jennifer, who stood in front of us on the far side of the studio and narrated as we and other Consumer Protection Division colleagues manned the phones and answered callers' questions about everything from child car seat recalls to credit card scams. Those call-in events were great ratings boosters for the station, and Jennifer Julian, because she had such a nose for compelling consumer protection stories, already was one of the station's star reporters.

During the course of several of these call-in events, many in the Consumer Protection Division got to know Jennifer well. Over time, we tipped her off to several newly developing consumer protection issues and she did compelling stories on them. Jane and I thought that she could do a good story on the House-Mazza group without demanding to know the names of victims and perpetrators. Deputy Press Secretary Amy Laurel Friedman gave the green light to contact Jennifer.

As it turned out, there was a victim willing to go on camera, Brian Kreigsman's original victim up in Brevard, Mrs. Barnes. Brian was more than willing to go on camera, too, and demonstrate all the useless "repairs" to her home. When we called Jennifer and pitched the story, she jumped on it. Within a couple of days, she had interviewed Attorney General Easley in his office and had gotten her counterpart at WTVD's ABC sister station in Asheville, WLOS, to film interviews with Brian and Mrs. Barnes.

Jennifer's story soon aired on the two stations and it was spectacular. Brian demonstrated all the phony repairs to Mrs. Barnes's roof, attic and crawl space, including beams into which the scammers had hammered dozens of nails for no reason whatsoever. "They just hammered nails into it to make her think they were doing real work under the house." Mrs. Barnes, a sweet older woman if ever there was one, spoke of all the problems and repair recommendations the scammers kept presenting to her, and how she found it so overwhelming and confusing.

Jennifer described how the scammers had taken millions of dollars from older homeowners across the state, how they were based mainly in the Rocky Mount area and how dozens of law enforcement agencies were investigating them.

The attorney general's interview at the end of the story featured comments about how polite and courteous the crew members might appear to be, but that many of them had serious criminal records. In preparation for the attorney general's interview, Tucker and Jane had printed out one crew member's lengthy rap sheet using an old daisy-wheel printer that printed text on one long scroll of 8½-inch wide paper. In the "killer moment" of the interview, Attorney General Easley picked up the top end of the four-foot-long document and then unfurled it over the front of his desk and onto the floor, as if he was unfurling a sail or a fishing net. "And here's the criminal record of just one of them!" He never stated the scammer's name or itemized his crimes, and the camera could not pick up the individual entries on the list. Nevertheless, that five-second "visual" really tied the whole piece together with the closing message: "These are truly bad people! And we are onto them."

Jennifer's story reaped rewards on several fronts. It warned the public about the pervasiveness and high cost of the House-Mazza repair frauds and helped older homeowners to recognize the scams and avoid them. Family members recognized their own loved ones as victims of the frauds and reported their situations to us. Other law enforcement agencies wanted to join the task force. Most important, the story made members of the House-Mazza group very nervous. Some of them called us and wanted to talk.

Maybe now we would secure our own inside sources to build the North Carolina fraud cases.

Perhaps the most beneficial result of Jennifer's story was Attorney General Easley's reaction to it. He was already attuned to the elder fraud industry's telemarketing fraud component and how it stole millions of dollars from North Carolina seniors. In fact, he had recently created a public-private partnership to fund and produce a series of catchy and compelling TV commercials warning seniors about the dangers of tele-marketing fraud. Those commercials had just hit the airwaves. Some of them featured recreations of telemarketing fraud incidents that Jane, Linda Matthews and I had worked on. After doing Jennifer Julian's piece, General Easley seemed personally invested in stopping the House-Mazza group, just like he had become invested in the telemarketing fraud issue.

Attorney General Easley had another reason to be so interested in stopping the House-Mazza group. Like the House clan, he was from Rocky Mount. He did not appreciate their bringing Rocky Mount's good name into disrepute. Soon after the interview, General Easley began communi-cating directly with Jane, Tucker and me about House-Mazza, calling us out of the blue, asking for the latest and wanting to know how he could help. This meant that we would no longer need to communicate with him through multiple layers of middle managers.

Like Brian Kreigsman's initial call to our office a year earlier, Mr. Easley's personal investment in the case following Jennifer Julian's story would prove pivotal.

17

"We need to go check on the Colonel!"

On the day that Tucker proudly announced he had located and interviewed the Colonel, he drove Jane and me out to meet him. The Colonel lived in a modest home in an Old Raleigh neighborhood where many of the city's elite resided. The structure had been built in the 1940s. It possessed a picture-perfect yard with well-trimmed shrubs, lots of dogwoods and Japanese red maples and a plush carpet of blue fescue grass. And just as the FBI source in Richmond had stated to Will Garrett, in the middle of the lawn stood a flagpole. The American flag was billowing in the breeze. The roof of the home bore all the telltale signs that House-Mazza crews had scammed the Colonel repeatedly.

The Colonel fit the mental image that I had developed during Tucker's long quest to find him: straight and upright, chin held high as he looked you squarely in the eye, confidence in his voice and firmness in his handshake. He was efficient in his conversations, decisive and no-nonsense. His personality was so commanding that it was hard to think of him as being in his early 90s. He reminded me of my late grandfather, who also had been a colonel during World War II and who went by his military title until the day he died.

While Tucker and Jane explored and photographed the house, I chatted with the Colonel in his study. He told me his eyesight had been failing in recent years but that he still had passable peripheral vision and could go about his life just fine. He showed me the magnifier he used to read short items, plus the ruler-like device that enabled him to fill out and sign documents and checks.

I did not ask him about his dealings with the House-Mazza crews at first, preferring instead to hear his stories about serving with General

Douglas MacArthur in the Philippines before the Japanese invaded, followed by his military service after America declared war. We also discussed his service during the Korean War. Then he listened with interest to stories of my grandfather's days in World War I serving as an army engineer in France, his days in World War II building and rebuilding American airfields in England, and his three decades commanding the Florida Highway Patrol. The Colonel seemed to have a good impression of combat engineers and opined that they never received due credit for the success of important military operations, and he gave me several examples from the battles in the South Pacific.

It was clear that the Colonel's long-term memory was quite sound.

When our discussion turned to the crews that had worked on his house, it was evident that, outwardly, at least, they had accorded him all the deference and respect that he had received as a senior military officer. He said he liked how they punctuated every sentence, question or request with the word "sir" ("Sir! Request permission to enter the basement"). When he gave a directive, they responded with a collective "Yes, sir!" They arrived each morning in time to join him in the yard for the raising of the flag, and they mustered up to "police the yard" (pick up litter) each evening before they left.

The Colonel spoke of how crew leaders might summon the entire crew to the front yard and publicly rebuke one of them for tossing a cigarette butt in the grass or damaging shrubbery with a ladder. "You're not going to disrespect the Colonel by throwing your cigarette on his lawn. Apologize to him now and then get out of here!"

"Colonel, sir, I am sorry for littering your yard. I have enjoyed working for you, sir. Goodbye."

One thing that stood out was the Colonel's pride in the condition of his home and yard and the scammers' desire to exploit those feelings. He told me more than once that keeping a camp, a barracks or an entire base in tip-top shape was important, that it reflected on the person in charge, and that he felt the same way about his home. He did not want his children to inherit a less than perfect house. The scammers, he said, constantly sounded that theme as they recommended expensive and totally unnecessary repairs. "Sir, it will be a shame if your children inherit this house only to find that there is water intrusion going on down in the basement." Upon reflection, he realized that they were exploiting this characteristic of his and that he might have paid them more than the cost of tearing down his house and rebuilding it from scratch. (This was true. The replacement cost of the house, according to his insurance policy, was $40,000 less than what he had paid the scammers to date.)

Yes. The Colonel was going to be a compelling witness. During the months that followed, he would give Tucker and Reggie Shaw of the SBI Financial Crimes Unit lengthy descriptions of each transaction he had with the scammers, pairing each transaction with invoices and cancelled checks. He was an evidentiary gold mine.

Ten months after we started working with the Colonel, a powerful and deadly hurricane named Fran made landfall near Wilmington, North Carolina, and wreaked havoc all the way up Interstate 40 to Raleigh, Chapel Hill and points further west. The hurricane's eye passed directly over Raleigh, leaving the city a tangle of fallen trees, downed power lines, smashed automobiles and badly damaged homes. Making the hurricane particularly devastating during its march through North Carolina were the days upon days of heavy rain that preceded it. By the time Fran plowed over us, the streams were swollen and the ground everywhere was saturated. Tall hardwood trees, especially fully matured oaks with their enormous leaf canopies and their shallow, sprawling root systems, captured the powerful winds like large sails and soon toppled over, their root systems pulled out of the soggy ground. Pine trees, with their flexible trunks and deep tap roots, as well as smaller hardwood trees, fared far better, but many of them also were pulled down by the large oaks, hickories and maples. During the middle of the night when the edge of the hurricane eye passed over us, we could hear through the howling winds the sounds of trees and tree limbs crashing down all around us and debris striking our homes and cars. The warm, wet air, if we stepped outside, smelled of freshly cut lumber and salt water from the ocean 150 miles away.

Considering that Raleigh's official nickname is "the City of Oaks," it is easy to imagine why Hurricane Fran inflicted so much destruction there.

Governor James B. Hunt, Jr., ordered all non-essential state employees in the hurricane-stricken areas not to report for work during the week following the storm. Inasmuch as many of us could not even exit our driveways or drive down our streets, we probably were not going to make it to work anyway. The governor's directive notwithstanding, Attorney General Mike Easley ordered employees in his Consumer Protection Division to report for work first thing Monday morning unless doing so proved dangerous or impossible. He wanted us to address citizen complaints about post-hurricane price gouging and home repair scams— common occurrences following any big storm.

That Monday morning, Tucker and I and a few other Consumer Protection colleagues made it to the office. None of the receptionists showed up that day, so we all took turns manning the switchboard and taking complaints. Our switchboard was functioning just fine but calls were barely trickling in. Most of the phone lines outside of downtown Raleigh were down, and besides, people throughout the state probably thought we were closed along with all the other government offices. So we just hung out in the reception area sharing stories and jokes, feasting on fast food from the Wendy's next door and answering an occasional call.

I don't know what triggered it, but as Tucker was in mid-joke he stopped, looked straight at me, then declared, "We need to go check on the Colonel!" I didn't need any convincing. I, too, suddenly felt something might be happening with the old fellow.

We wound our way out of downtown Raleigh in Tucker's old Nissan, then inched our way up Wade Avenue toward the Colonel's. The avenue looked like a war zone, with debris and fallen trees everywhere, all of it entwined in downed power lines, roofing materials and campaign signs touting Bill Clinton, Bob Dole or Jesse Helms. Crews had managed to clear one lane in each direction, so it only took a few minutes to make it to the Colonel's neighborhood. Stately Canterbury Road, which leads up to the Colonel's neighborhood, was a complete mess and several homes on both sides were badly damaged by fallen trees. When we arrived at the Colonel's place, however, the house seemed to be intact and there was only modest damage to the yard. None of the signature red or white pickups of the House-Mazza home repair scammers were parked nearby. We felt good about the old guy's situation as we exited Tucker's car and walked up to his door.

The Colonel's grandson came out and greeted us. He told us that one of the House-Mazza crews had shown up at his grandfather's house on Saturday, just hours after the hurricane passed over, then took him for another $28,000. (That brought his total of payments to the scammers to $267,000.) Most of that $28,000 was payment for the removal of a supposedly enormous pine tree before it could slice through the house and destroy it. The grandson managed to contact the bank in time to get the check cancelled before the scammers cashed it first thing Monday morning, but the repercussions of Saturday's incident were still reverberating throughout the household.

When we talked to the Colonel, he was distressed by what he feared was massive damage to his home. He was also disturbed because family members thought he had let himself be scammed again. Outside of his presence, one of them confided to us that they were going to move him into a retirement community with assisted living facilities, since his eyesight and judgment were so impaired.

"What kind of impairments in judgment are you talking about?" I asked.

"He won't stop dealing with these con men. He's going to impoverish himself."

The Colonel stood alone in his study. Gone were his air of confidence and control, his direct stare and his crisp, authoritative sentences. His head, neck and shoulders tilted forward. His hands were fidgety. Invoking the period in his life that made him most proud, I asked him to compare this hurricane with typhoons he had experienced in the South Pacific before and during the war. He replied that this one had been the worst, mainly because of all the huge oaks crashing down in the neighborhood.

I asked him about the tree that needed to be removed from the house. He said it sounded like a bomb going off when it hit the roof, then took me to the door of a back porch to show me the damage. There were still pine branches and a tangled gutter dangling along the edge of the porch roof and interfering with the operation of the screen door. In the yard beyond, I could see the stump of a small pine tree. It was five or six inches in diameter and leaning towards the door at a 45° angle.

"How big did they say the pine tree was?"

"They said it was the huge pine tree out there in the back yard and that they needed to bring in a crane to take it apart. Said the cost of renting the crane was sky high due to all the other houses that had trees on them. Took them several hours to get the tree off this house, and that's why they had to charge me so much to do it. But it saved my house! They would not let me go near this part of the house to check it out because the tree could have sliced through the roof at any second. And look, there are still branches from it blocking the door."

He seemed quite desperate to hear us say that it was wise to pay $28,000 to have the tree removed.

Neither Tucker nor I could tell him this, but all the large trees behind his house were still standing straight and tall. It probably took the crews only a few minutes to cut the little tree off of his house. Then they must have sat on the roof for another couple of hours, smoking and making occasional noises with sledge hammers or the chain saw in order to convince him they were still removing a monster tree.

Tucker and I then spoke with the grandson while the Colonel disappeared into his study. After a few minutes, we could hear him down the hallway, speaking into the phone in a tone that he probably thought was loud enough for the party on the other end to understand but not loud enough for us to hear. (I still cannot figure out how his phone might have been working that day.) We could hear him nevertheless. "I can't talk right now! They are all here. My family, the SBI, the attorney general—all of them."

It was clear to all of us that the Colonel, as sharp as he still was and as willing as he had been to help prosecute the scammers, was still vulnerable to terrible lapses of judgment during excited situations, a phenomenon Dr. Noel had described. The first people he had reached out to for help after the storm were the House-Mazza fraud artists. They knew exactly how to tax that momentarily impaired judgment and make another $28,000 off of it. Here he was days later, his house full of concerned family members and government officials, none of whom would praise his response to the storm and the damage it had inflicted. Once again, he was reaching out to the scammers, this time over the phone. We didn't know whether he was trying to warn them not to come to the house while we were there or obtain their reassurance that what he did immediately following the storm was correct. I suspect it was the latter but it could have been both.

The family moved the Colonel to assisted living just as they had vowed. He passed away two months after Hurricane Fran struck his neighborhood and is buried in Arlington National Cemetery. His grandson told me that his health followed a steady, downward trajectory after the post-hurricane scam.

18

"Boom-Boom!!!"

"**B**oom-Boom!!!" That's the sound that an object makes as it breaks through the sound barrier. Or a boxer as he delivers a devastating one-two punch. Or a hit man after walking up to his mark and raising a gun to his head. Two loud thunderclaps within a fraction of a second. "Boom-Boom!!!"

In the early fall of 1996, the House-Mazza gang experienced their own shocking "Boom-Boom!!!" moment. On October 15, a federal grand jury in Raleigh, North Carolina, indicted Robert Marshall House, Sr., Robert Marshall House, Jr., David Joseph Viverette, Richard Van Johnson, Edward Dawson, Steven Nelson Churchill, Steven Earl Shaw and Paul David House for conspiracy to distribute cocaine in violation of Title 21, Section 841 (a)(1) of the United States Code.[1] These were the drug charges that DEA agent Mark Rosenfield had mentioned at the task force meeting earlier in the summer. They were being prosecuted by fellow task force member Assistant U.S. Attorney Tom Murphy.

Two weeks later, a federal grand jury in Richmond, Virginia, returned a 76-count indictment naming Anthony F. Mazza, Jr., Christopher Donald Burke, Christopher S. Williamson, Carl Allen Smith, Marvin Anthony House, Allen Dwayne Stallings and Ted Michael Stallings. The charges were wire fraud and conspiracy to commit wire fraud in violation of Title 18, Sections 371 and 1343 of the United States Code.[2] These were the wire fraud charges that now-retired FBI agent and current Virginia State Police investigator Will Garrett had spent several years developing.

When the Richmond indictments were announced, federal authorities referred to it by the same name Will Garrett had typed onto his folder full of notes before an official case was opened—"Operation Spray Jug."

Not every count in the Richmond indictments named all seven

defendants, but each man was named in enough counts to make him worry about ever getting out of prison if convicted on each of them. The prosecutor for these cases was Assistant U.S. Attorney David Schiller of Richmond, an avid fan of Will Garrett and his work. He said to me when the case was filed, "It's an honor to prosecute Will's final FBI case, especially this case. He did a fantastic job building it. These are some awful crimes."

The Richmond indictments repeatedly mentioned an unindicted conspirator, Gary Anderson Barker. Barker was one of Will Garrett's inside sources. "Bah-kah," as Will pronounced his last name, would be charged later and enter a guilty plea.

After the double concussion rocked the House-Mazza network, things began to change. Network members who had not yet been charged started contacting law enforcement officials throughout North Carolina and Virginia. They weren't trying to tease out of us important facts about our investigations either. They wanted to come in and spill the beans on their fellow fraudsters so that they might receive lighter sentences once they, too, were charged. And they all thought they were going to be charged. It was sweet.

One member of the extended House family who had jerked us around during an interview months earlier called Tucker and Jane in tears, begging to know when he could come to the AG's office and talk with us. The SBI would not schedule an interview with him, even though his buddies were already speaking to them.

I, too, received such calls. One was placed by a group member's angry wife. She was pretty caustic toward me and claimed that we in law enforcement were treating her man like dirt by refusing to meet with him. I asked her if he was anywhere near the phone.

"He's standing right here."

"Can I speak with him?"

"Why do you think I'm calling you, mister?"

When her man came on the line, he was blubbering and crying. His new and desperate demeanor was in striking contrast to the badass dude that one pictured while looking at his rap sheet and seeing all the convictions for assault and communicating threats. But there he was, pleading and promising. And whimpering.

"Mr. Kirkman, I know I am going to be charged next if nobody in law enforcement is willing to talk to me. But I can give you dozens of guys on a platter, plus their victims and how they scammed them. I can also give you the guys who supplied all the drugs mentioned in those indictments too. I can be in Raleigh in 45 minutes!"

"I appreciate that, but we'll need to put you in contact with a field investigator for the feds, the SBI or one of the local law enforcement agencies working on this."

"But Mr. Kirkman, all them guys keep blowing me off! The AG's office is my only chance. Can't you help? I can sure help you."

"Just give me your phone number and I'll see what we can do. Can't make any guarantees. As you said, they are talking with lots and lots of folks in the organization now."

This last comment did not go over too well. He began to howl and curse. Then he screamed, "Baby, he won't talk to me either!"

"Baby" then snatched the phone from him.

"Attorney Kirkman, you are one shyster piece of shit!"

PART FIVE

The Losses Are Seldom Just Financial

19

You Can't Assign
a Dollar Figure to It

If you are the type of reader who absorbs every detail of a story, you will note that the Colonel passed away just after many of his victimizers were indicted by federal grand juries in Richmond and Raleigh. We do not know whether he ever learned about the indictments or, if so, whether his reaction was positive or negative. I cannot see how it would have been positive.

To have a victim like the Colonel pass away shortly after a major fraud event was nothing new. We witnessed the phenomenon repeatedly during the quarter-century that I worked on elder fraud issues. Sometimes it was difficult to tell whether the family's reactions to the fraud incidents triggered the victim's swift decline and demise versus the victim's own realization—deep down inside, perhaps—that he or she had been conned and could no longer protect himself or herself from fraud.

During my final years with the North Carolina Attorney General's Office, I shared an office suite with three other enforcement attorneys. One of them was a particularly brilliant attorney who regularly handled complex cases against major corporations. In most of those battles, she was badly outgunned by the huge corporations' top-drawer law firms, yet she prevailed far more often than one would ever expect. Her father, a successful businessman from whom she inherited much of her brilliance, was a vibrant fellow in his late 80s who lived independently in nearby Durham, North Carolina. One day in 2015, he received a phone call. Here is my office suitemate's description of what followed:

> The person who called posed as a tech person from IBM who provided tech support for Time Warner. Dad had cable and Internet through Time Warner,

so nothing seemed amiss about the call. The scammer spent a lot of time talking to Dad to help with his computer before Dad gave him credit information. (I remember spending a long time on the phone with a tech person setting up my router, and suspect it seemed like that sort of thing to Dad.) Right after the call ended, Dad realized that he'd given out sensitive personal and financial information and took action to protect himself and his financial accounts. With help from my brother and me, he had his accounts blocked and we reversed a couple of transactions that already had been made in his name. Then his health declined rapidly.

Another elderly friend of mine was caught in the same scam. She is also a very intelligent, highly educated, successful retired professional who still functions just fine. I helped her by suggesting steps to take: contacting her bank; putting on a credit report block; taking her computer to a reliable store in Carrboro to have it cleaned; etc. She didn't want me to tell her daughter, so I didn't, and she is still chugging away, happily independent. My experiences made me realize the importance of reassuring the person. Not all elderly are scammed because of declining capability. They are bombarded with scams and embarrassed when taken in. Our responses (as their children) can make it worse. It is important to try to figure out the circumstances of the individual, not assume how things happened.

While she probably would have done so anyway due to her nature, my colleague knew from working in our office that she had to remain calm and assure her dad that such an experience was common, that lots of sharp people fall victim to such scams, and that it did not warrant feelings of embarrassment, self-doubt or shame. Nevertheless, he experienced those intense and depleting feelings.

"Even though I don't think that what happened indicated a decline in Dad's ability to watch out for himself, he was inconsolable about his mistake," she added.

During the weeks that followed, her father's physical health deteriorated so rapidly that he had to be moved to a nursing facility. Shortly after that he passed away.

When I do presentations on elder fraud, the audience's attention seems riveted to the eye-popping dollar figures that I display on the screen showing average individual victim losses and total victim losses across the state. Unfortunately, I cannot come up with a slide reflecting the non-financial losses that the elder fraud industry inflicts. How can one put a dollar figure on the despair and physical decline experienced by victims like my colleague's father? How can one quantify the toll inflicted upon family members as they witness Mom or Dad going through tormenting defensiveness or self-doubt at the end of his or her life, or as they ponder the additional years of normal life that Mom or Dad might have enjoyed but for the crimes perpetrated against them?

Worse still is the way elder fraud criminals often destroy loving relationships between seniors and their adult children and grandchildren during the parents' final years. The embarrassment and defensiveness felt by many of these victims are pronounced to begin with, but those feelings quickly morph into resentment and bitterness—often on both sides—especially if the younger family members' reactions and follow-up conversations with their older loved ones are not restrained and compassionate.

As has been mentioned several times already, often the scammers deliberately alienate their victims from their own families before the victimization is ever discovered. One way they do this is by filling their victims' heads with the notion that any criticism or questioning of their sweepstakes, home repair, or sweetheart scam transactions by their adult children simply proves that those children are just itching to declare them incompetent and take control of their hard-earned life savings. When the scammers employ that tactic successfully, they become their prey's victimizers and support network at the same time. ("Let's show them that their accusations against you are just wrong, Mr. Kirkman! Go wire the final $20,000 to the bank in Nigeria so that we can get this $24 million transferred into your checking account once and for all. That will change their tune!")

As Mom or Dad re-embrace and do more deals with these scummy victimizers, the younger family members' frustrations grow stronger and, quite often, more noticeable. Mom or Dad usually picks up on the frustrations and becomes all the more adamant, defensive and determined to prove the children wrong. In turn, the family's vicious, downward emotional cycle picks up speed and momentum. The longer the cycle persists, the more difficult it is to break.

In the North Carolina Attorney General's Elder Fraud Unit, we encountered several families who endured this tortuous cycle for years before the victimized parent passed away or went into a nursing facility. During those agonizing years, if the courts would not step in and appoint a financial guardian for the repeat-victim parents, many adult children simply threw up their hands and let Mom or Dad keep sending their money overseas until it was all gone. Silently watching their parents impoverish themselves was a form of agony that was preferable to the agony of struggling in vain to get them to stop.

The daughter of a $100,000-plus lottery scam victim in Asheville once told me, "I can't keep pissing him off by trying to stop him. Perhaps when his final penny has been wired away and the scammers stop calling it will dawn on him that I was trying to protect him all along. I don't want him to go to his grave holding so much animosity towards me."

The daughter of this Asheville victim tried to remain close to her father for the next several years, hoping in vain for that moment of awareness and forgiveness. Her approach was employed by others across the state. The added strain of watching what was going on caused the "caregiver fatigue" of many of these adult children to kick in years before their parents actually became incapable of living independently. That is the point when older adults need the help and energy of family caregivers the most.

Unfortunately, many of our repeat victims and their families completely abandoned one other. The emotionally draining battles over the suspect transactions took too much of a toll. Both sides had had it with one another.

Also quite distressing are those situations where families successfully petition the court to declare Mom or Dad incapable of handling their financial affairs and to appoint a family member to take control of their finances and real estate before the scammers drain those assets to nothing. When families are forced to take this draconian step (sometimes with our encouragement and assistance), the bitterness felt by the fraud victim parents can go off the charts. But at least the guardianship will ensure that there will be enough money to sustain Mom or Dad in their final years.

So yes, while the reported losses inflicted by the elder fraud industry against North Carolinians might be $10 million in a given year, and while the 1 percent report rate for those frauds multiplies that figure to $1 billion a year, the true extent of the losses inflicted by the elder fraud industry is incalculably more than that.

Just ask the family of the Colonel, or the daughter of the lottery scam victim in Asheville, or my office colleague whose father's life was cut short by the tech support scam.

20

"Reloading" and
the Cycle of Fraud

Richard M. Titus, who studies fraud victims, once made the seemingly circular observation, "It appears that one of the surest ways to become a personal fraud victim is to have been a victim."[1] Titus's point, however, makes perfect sense to those familiar with the tactics of the elder fraud industry. With elder fraud, once a scammer defrauds someone, he will strike that person again. And again. And yet again.

Whenever I give presentations on elder fraud, I liken this phenomenon to a fisherman always returning to a successful fishing spot. When the fisherman pulls the first fish of the day into the boat, he never says to himself, "One fish from this spot is enough. I should be sporting and move on." No, he will keep fishing that same spot until he reaches his legal limit or it no longer yields fish. And as long as a victim of senior fraud continues to possess money or credit and has identifiable vulnerabilities to fraud, a scammer is going to keep working those vulnerabilities and reeling in the cash. After all, it took time to locate that victim, develop a rapport with him or her, learn his or her vulnerabilities, create a narrative to exploit those vulnerabilities and then execute the scam. Why go through that multi-step process all over again with a total stranger when the first victim can still hand over fistfuls of money?

As was mentioned earlier, scams targeting younger victims tend to be one-off events. Younger victims are hard to scam a second or third time because they possess less savings, are in debt or lack easy access to credit. Additionally, they have much less equity in their homes and they possess few of the age-related fraud vulnerabilities discussed throughout this book.

Reload. Then Reload Again

A gripping narrative enables a skillful elder fraud criminal to scam the victim repeatedly. Home repair fraudsters weave a convincing tale about water intruding into the structure of the house over a long period of time, rotting the wooden roof decking, weakening the attic rafters, causing toxic mold in the walls and ceilings, damaging the floors, rotting the floor beams, deteriorating the home's foundation, etc. As soon as the bogus repairs to one of these nonexistent problems are paid for, the crew chief will claim that another expensive, moisture-related problem exists which must be remedied right away. Fraud artists call this segue into another iteration of the scam a "reload."

Overseas sweepstakes and lottery scammers typically embed a reload opportunity in every iteration of their scams. They often start off by congratulating their victims for winning *second* place in their contest, then direct them to wire money overseas to cover taxes or other expenses related to the prize. Once the victim sends the money, the phony sweepstakes official will reload by calling again and announcing that the first-place winner failed to send money as required, that the victim has moved up and become the first-place award winner, and that more money needs to be sent overseas to cover taxes or fees on the much larger prize. If the victim sends those additional funds, he or she will be reloaded again and told that he or she is now the grand prize winner, that the prize amount has tripled, and that more money must be sent.

After the initial round of reloads has borne fruit, the scammers tell their victim that the prize is being released and will be arriving shortly. Within hours, the victim starts receiving a series of communications, such as the following:

- A supposed U.S. Customs official states that a large prize has arrived at a port of entry and that thousands of dollars must be wired to a particular address to cover customs duties on that prize.
- A phony representative of "Lloyds of London" or some other insurance company calls and warns that thousands of dollars must be paid to cover the policy insuring the prize while it is in transit, otherwise it will have to be returned to the contest company.

- A fake IRS agent calls from Washington and announces that, although overseas taxes on the prize have been paid, the victim must wire thousands of dollars to cover U.S. income taxes, otherwise the prize will be returned.
- A scammer claiming to be with the Department of Homeland Security calls and announces that his agency is concerned that the large prize might have ties to overseas companies or banks that support terrorism and that the victim must wire thousands of dollars to cover the costs of a "terrorism audit," otherwise the prize must be returned.
- A phony attorney or barrister from the country where the contest company is based calls and reports that he sued the company and got the court to freeze its assets because it was engaged in fraud and that he will help the victim to recover the huge prize upon receipt of several thousand dollars for a retainer fee.
- That same phony attorney will call repeatedly, claiming that the customs duties, taxes, insurance premiums, and terrorism audit fees mentioned above must be paid again, otherwise the prize cannot be delivered. He will claim, also, that the earlier paid fees, duties and taxes will eventually be repaid once the court case against the fraudulent company has been resolved.

With grandparent scams, the caller might reload his victim with the following shocking announcements in order to collect $60,000 over the course of three or four days:

- Grandchild has been in an accident while driving a car in Mexico or Europe and needs money for his or her hospital expenses,
- Grandchild has now been charged with reckless driving by the police and needs more money for bail and an attorney.
- Crooked jailer won't release grandchild despite bond being posted because he wants a bribe.
- Grandchild now needs to pay for the hospital expenses of the occupants of the other vehicle, otherwise he or she will be re-arrested.
- One of the occupants of the other car has died. Grandchild now has been charged with homicide. Thousands of additional

dollars are needed to hire an attorney, cover an increased bail bond and pay for the deceased passenger's funeral.
- The rental car company needs to be paid for its destroyed car, otherwise the grandchild must go back to jail.
- The owner of the other car must receive compensation for his destroyed vehicle, otherwise the grandchild goes back to jail.
- More charges have been lodged because a second passenger in the other car has now died. The grandchild is back in jail. Thousands of dollars more are needed for attorney's fees, increased bond, funeral expenses, etc.

Fraudulent "money transfer" pitches coming from Nigeria and other countries long ago earned the nickname "Nigerian 419" scams; 419 is the section in that country's criminal fraud code that is being breached whenever the scams are committed. For decades, Nigerian 419 scammers have posed as the spouses or children of corrupt former dictators whose names appeared regularly in the American news. They ask for help in moving millions of dollars to the United States and promise their elderly target 25 percent or even 33 percent commissions. They have also posed as American soldiers who discovered a secret fortune that once belonged to former Iraqi dictator Saddam Hussein, former Libyan dictator Muammar el-Qaddafi or some other corrupt foreign leader. In each one of these scenarios, the Nigerian 419 scammers claim they need to move millions of dollars out of their countries and into the United States, and they promise their targets that they can keep 25 to 33 percent of the funds if they simply allow their U.S. bank accounts to receive the money.

Sometimes a Nigerian 419 scammer pretends to be an attorney in another country who represents the multi-million-dollar estate of a supposedly distant relative of the scam target. The attorney claims that the target is the only known heir of the deceased and that the multi-million-dollar estate will be seized by his very corrupt government if it is not disbursed to the rightful heir soon.

Whichever iteration of the Nigerian 419 money transfer scam is being run, the perpetrators launch endless requests for money to cover an assortment of supposed expenses, transfer fees and taxes so that the fortune can be sent to the United States. As these reloads continue, each requested payment is represented to be the final hurdle. As soon as the victim pays this supposedly final expense, however, another problem crops up:

- A crooked banker or probate court clerk wants a bribe before releasing the funds.
- More assets of the decedent have been located, requiring payment of more probate fees, legal fees and taxes.
- The estate tax in the country where the distant relative died has just doubled and the higher amount must be paid.
- Just before the transfer of funds was to begin, someone else came forward claiming to be an heir. Their claims must be defeated in court, which will require additional attorney's fees.
- The millions of dollars were just transferred out of the country, but a crooked customs officer in London's Heathrow Airport has intercepted them before they could reach the United States and is holding them hostage until he receives $30,000.

In each of the fraudulent schemes outlined above, be they home repair, grandparent, sweepstakes or Nigerian 419 scams, the criminals will reload the victim with requests for more money as many times as they can. In doing so, they continuously stoke the false narrative about a home that is about to receive its final necessary repair (or be condemned if it is not repaired immediately) or a large sum of money that will arrive soon. After a couple of reloads, overseas scammers might even wire a few thousand dollars into their victims' bank accounts and tell them, "We needed to make this small transfer to ensure that the $24 million transfer will go into the correct account later this week." Such payments back to the victims leave them even more convinced that the narrative, now firmly embedded in their minds, is real and that anyone saying otherwise is wrong. At this point, they are ripe for a final series of reloads.

A Troublesome Risk-Reward Calculation

Many victims are aware that it is risky to pay money in order to collect a larger sum of money later. Despite this knowledge, many of our repeat victims told us of a mathematical calculation that kept going through their minds as they fell deeper and deeper into the scammers' narratives: "What's another $10,000 if it guarantees that I will receive my $24 million tomorrow, or if my grandchild is freed from jail in a foreign prison? This additional payment is a risk worth taking."

Sometimes, as many victims have told us, they focus on what they have paid out already: "I've already invested $65,000 in this thing. I don't want to lose all that I have paid in by refusing to fork out this final $10,000."

Another risk that seems to go through many victims' minds, according to the scammers, is the notion that refusing to pay any more money is an admission they were duped when they made all those previous payments and perhaps an acknowledgment they should not be trusted to manage their own finances anymore. The scammers might not be too subtle in driving this point home either. "Mr. Kirkman, you've already spent $65,000 on this. If you lose $65,000 just because of one last $5,000 payment, your family will think you are incompetent and seize control of your finances. You must take this last step and show them!" Many repeat victims choose the "show them" route.

Stop the Reloads and Break the Cycle of Fraud

By employing your finest conversational skills and many of the lessons and tips scattered throughout this book, and by avoiding words, voice tones or facial expressions that make the victim feel foolish, demeaned or patronized (e.g., "Momma! I can't believe you got scammed like that!"), you can interrupt the reloads and break the cycle of repeat victimization.

Regardless of your relationship with the victim, try to begin with the comment that con artists skillfully run transactions just like these on very bright people every hour of every day and that they can make those transactions seem very real. Invite them to explore with you the signs that the offer or request is legitimate and the signs that it is a ruse. At some point, discuss the types of payment requests listed above and ask whether the victim has encountered any of them. Ask about any payments or "refunds" the scammers might have made to the victim and explore why such a payment might have been designed to keep them on the hook. Discuss the types of payment requests the scammers might make next and extract a promise that the victim will talk to you about each request before making another payment. It is amazing the impact you can have on the victim if you successfully anticipate the next reload and predict what the scammer will say next.

Scammers often move on if they detect their carefully crafted narrative and their cycle of "reloads" have been interrupted or debunked.

With home repair frauds, the reload cycle can be broken when a local law enforcement officer, building inspector or family member shows up at the house repeatedly and asks questions about the repair work or if a bank employee balks at cashing a check for the crew member without first contacting local officials about the soundness and necessity of the repair work. With any of the overseas-based scams just mentioned, the reload cycle can be interrupted when bank personnel or representatives of independent money transfer companies like MoneyGram or Western Union block wire transfers from the victim. (The latter two will place such "blocks" at the request of the victim's state attorney general or on their own initiative.)

The best way to break the victimization cycle—the reloading—is for you or someone else the victim knows or loves to convince him or her that it is in their best interests to stop paying, that what has been lost already will never be recovered, and that any further payment is throwing good money after bad. Such conversations require patience, calmness, and words and a tone of voice that do not cause the victim to feel chastened, scolded or foolish. Several conversations might be required. Be fully aware that you may encounter defensiveness and resistance, especially at first. Not all victims can be convinced to stop, especially on the first try. Sometimes you might be the third or fourth person to have the same conversation with them, and they will respond positively to you (or to the person right after you). The three main things to bear in mind when you try to help a repeat fraud victim are the following:

1. The criminals will reload and strike this person again.
2. Be patient and avoid emotional reactions, facial expressions or words that make the victim feel embarrassed, attacked or under scrutiny.
3. Avoid doing nothing.

21

Lewis the Elder Orphan

Except for pyramid and Ponzi schemes, I never handled investment scams during my career in the Attorney General's Office. Other state agencies, mainly the secretary of state's Securities Division, prosecuted securities fraud and most other investment scams. Elderly victims of investment scammers came to my attention quite often, however. One was an unforgettable fellow whom I will call Lewis.

Lewis was in his mid–80s and lived in the Triad area of North Carolina, a region in the central part of the state anchored by the cities of Greensboro, High Point and Winston-Salem. The Triad was home to three key industries that powered so much of North Carolina's economic growth during the 20th century: tobacco, textiles and furniture. All three have been in decline in recent decades, but when they were in full swing, Lewis was a prosperous local businessman whose success and philanthropy made him a Triad hero.

When I first heard about him, Lewis was widowed and had no children. He had no living siblings, but he did have a few nieces and nephews living in California and Texas. His relationships with them were all but non-existent. His "family" throughout his adult life had been his wife, his business partners and his employees. For decades, he devoted almost every hour of every day to that family, and he had few friends outside of that realm. When his wife died and he accepted a Fortune 500 corporation's offer to buy his business, his bank account became quite full but the members of his fictive family soon drifted out of his life.

Lewis was what we called "an elder orphan," someone with no real family, few friends, and hardly any personal support network. The elder fraud industry loves elder orphans.

I first heard of Lewis when his CPA called me.

"I've got this client who's turned over $2 million to a really sketchy individual. That guy cleaned out his investment accounts. After getting my client to execute a full Power of Attorney, he also transferred his CDs and other bank accounts to who knows where. He also got my guy to take out a mortgage on his home and obtained all the proceeds from that too! When I sought details on these transactions so I could do his taxes, my guy really couldn't tell me a thing, and he had almost no records."

"Who is the sketchy individual?"

"Some guy he met at an estate planning seminar at a steak house over in Archdale. His name is Angelo…"

The CPA gave me as many details of Angelo's scheme as he could. He also noted that Lewis had lost thousands to phony sweepstakes officials calling from overseas. I thanked him and said I would try to drop by Lewis' place after doing an elder fraud training program in Winston-Salem later in the week. My pretext for the visit would be the sweepstakes scams, but my main purpose would be to learn about Angelo's activities. For some reason, there was no information on the Internet about Angelo.

Lewis' street address gave me confidence that we could get him some meaningful help. He appeared to live in a county where the district attorney and county Adult Protective Services professionals were quite attuned to the plague of elder fraud and willing to address it forcefully.

Another factor that gave me confidence was that Angelo still lived in the community. Chances were good that Angelo and the assets he stole from Lewis could be located and seized. Such is almost never the case when the criminal is running a sweepstakes, lottery or Nigerian money transfer scam from overseas and the victim's life savings have been wired across the ocean.

As it turns out, the CPA only knew part of the story. When I visited Lewis a couple of days later and eventually started discussing Angelo, he told me of credit card accounts being maxed out, personal loans being taken out and rental properties being deeded away. The proceeds were now held by Angelo. The two of them had some sort of business partnership, the exact nature of which Lewis could not describe.

From what I learned that afternoon, a lot of the questionable transactions were executed by Angelo via the Power of Attorney form he had pulled off of the North Carolina General Assembly's website and had gotten Lewis to sign. The document was so thorough in its conveyance of authority over Lewis' personal and financial affairs that Angelo was even empowered to make unlimited gifts to himself from Lewis' holdings. And Angelo was not shy about using that power either, gracing himself repeatedly with large gifts of cash and real estate. He even acquired the title to Lewis' two rather expensive cars.

I had seen or heard of POA abuses like this hundreds of times already, and I knew that the POA form in question gave local DAs and Adult Protective Services officials fits. After all, how does one convince a judge or jury to convict a defendant of a financial crime when the supposed victim knowingly authorized the transactions in question by signing and then initialing every paragraph of the POA form in front of a notary public? Such a task is even more hopeless when the victim of POA abuse seems outwardly competent and asserts that he or she signed the document without coercion.

Lewis was just such a person. During my visit he offered profound insights on the news of the day, analyzed the UNC basketball team's victory the night before with great skill, and scoffed at the woeful course I had set for my meager retirement portfolio. His words were slow yet precise. His house, attire and personal grooming were neat, clean and stylish. He seemed mentally sharp. If a medical professional with zero knowledge of his risky financial dealings were to make a quick assessment of Lewis' ability to handle his financial affairs in a manner consistent with his own best interests, that professional would conclude that Lewis was financially competent.

Some states in the early 2000s had clear prohibitions against self-dealing by people holding powers of attorney. Angelo would have needed a good criminal attorney had his repeated abuses of the self-gifting powers in Lewis' POA form occurred in one of those states. Other states imposed strict fiduciary standards that made any POA transactions inconsistent with the client's best interests legally voidable. When I met Lewis, however, North Carolina law offered few such protections. That changed in 2018.

Trying not to set Lewis off by implying that he had been scammed, I asked him what kind of return he and Angelo expected to achieve through their new business venture.

"Angelo projects a 100 percent return in just two years. People are going to love this new business!"

"How much have you put into this venture?"

"Something north of $4 million."

"That's a nice chunk of change."

"Multi-million-dollar transactions were common chores for me when I was running my company. This venture is just a little hobby business for me. I enjoy being back in the game."

"So you're fine with all this, I'm guessing."

"Of course. I know what I am doing."

It was obvious that Angelo had recognized and exploited a longing on Lewis' part to be a major player in the world of commerce once again.

Back in the 1960s, when I was about nine years old, I acquired an invaluable insight while watching an episode of the popular Sunday night TV western *Bonanza*. That lesson served me well in the elder fraud wars. Part of the episode's subplot involved an older man who was determined to beat up a young man who had disrespected him in full view of other men of the town. The older fellow could not be persuaded that a brawl with the younger man would surely cause him substantial regret and pain, if not death. Hoss Cartwright, great observer of human nature that he was, offered something like the following to another onlooker: "Just about every feller thinks he can still fight like he could when he was 22 years old. Hard to convince him otherwise." Hoss and company had to diffuse the conflict through other means. I think Hoss ended up whupping the younger guy himself but can't recall for sure. I just remember the "like he could when he was 22 years old" comment.

Lewis' self-view was not too different from that of the older gentleman Hoss spoke of. Hundreds of elder fraud victims whom I have met—male and female—exhibited that same characteristic. Lewis was convinced that he could still evaluate, plan and successfully execute complex financial transactions, just like when he was running his business back in his younger years. It excited him to be doing it once again, to be the go-to guy, to be the captain. He resisted any suggestion that he no longer could handle such transactions. Nevertheless, he was completely blind to the signs that Angelo was fleecing him. He had not checked Angelo out or learned that he had never run his own company. No longer could Lewis bring a healthy degree of skepticism and financial street smarts to his dealings with Angelo, qualities that had enabled him to avoid bad deals back in the day.

Lewis clearly could not follow fast-moving conversations anymore, and I repeatedly found myself slowing down and reframing my comments and questions so that he could keep up with them. Angelo must have had a field day with Lewis' slowness in processing things. He probably talked to him a mile a minute.

The more I posed questions about Angelo's business plan that he could not answer, the more defensive Lewis became. Finally, he just exploded.

"I don't have to waste my valuable time explaining simple business concepts to a government official! Why are you even here? Do you want to tax me before I even make money on this venture? Do you want to squash it because you don't understand free enterprise?"

I had just wandered into a psychological trap that scammers set for their elderly victims, traps designed to keep them from talking to government officials. They convince the Lewises of the world that the sneaky government might come around making inquiries because it wants to tax the transaction or, worse, have him declared incompetent so that Social Services (an arm of the government) can take over his finances. I could almost picture Angelo saying, "It's none of the government's damn business, Lewis! Don't talk to 'em!" The tactic clearly was having its intended effect here. Lewis was going silent on me.

I backpedaled, then tried to use the same technique on him that Angelo had employed.

"We definitely want business expansion and more people making money in North Carolina, Lewis, and you've done a lot of that during your long career. We just want to make sure that your business expertise is being utilized wisely. Angelo is our concern, not you. He does not have much of a business record, especially not one as extensive as yours."

Lewis' agitation subsided.

None of the remainder of our conversation that afternoon pertained to Angelo or money. We spoke of how our respective families had settled in the Triad in the 1700s and about my days growing up in Chapel Hill during the '60s and early '70s as well as his days in pre-flight training there before the navy sent him off to fight in World War II, his experiences as a naval officer in that war, and life in the Triad before it was interlaced with interstate highways. He showed me photos and other mementoes of those times. It was a pleasant conversation.

My plan during that final hour at his home was to build up more personal rapport with Lewis and perhaps counteract some of the false friendship that Angelo had developed with him. There was no way I could be 100 percent successful in that endeavor. Angelo lived there in town somewhere and could visit Lewis anytime. I could not. He also had the ability to call Lewis on the phone repeatedly throughout the day while I could not. He could fill Lewis' head with visions of earthshaking profits while I could only be the advocate of caution. Angelo inspired dreams and excitement while I was a dream crusher, a scold, a downer. Angelo definitely had a huge advantage over me. But I hoped that building a friendly relationship with Lewis might generate a few more tidbits of information that would be Angelo's undoing.

As I left, I assured Lewis that I would call him in a day or two.

During the drive home to Chapel Hill, I considered strategies and colleagues who could help put a stop to Angelo. Kevin Anderson with IRS Criminal Investigations might have Angelo on his radar screen, or he might know a DEA or FBI agent who was looking at him for drug activities or money laundering. Donna White at the Division of Aging and Adult Services in Raleigh might have trained a Victims Assistance Program volunteer in the Triad who could hit it off with Lewis and slowly help him realize what was going on. I would call John Maron at the secretary of state's Securities Division in Raleigh to see if they were already looking at Angelo for investment fraud. I would contact the county DA and my police detective contacts in Lewis' community and game plan this thing with them as well.

It seemed like a good plan. If we were lucky, perhaps we could claw back a substantial chunk of Lewis' life savings before Angelo pissed it all away.

22

Will We Save the Elder Orphan?

When I arrived at my office the next morning, I contacted the officials on the list that I compiled in my head during the drive home. While none of them had heard of Angelo, Kevin Anderson, John Maron and the DA all said they would check to see if others in their agencies had anything going on him. Donna White promised she would try to find a Victims Assistance Program ("VAP") volunteer in the Triad who could work with Lewis on a day-to-day basis to recognize what Angelo was pulling and, hopefully, gain Lewis' assistance in the investigation and prosecution of Angelo.

The DA got back with me first. "The P.D. really wanted to look into this one. Unfortunately, Lewis doesn't live in town or even in my county. He lives just over the county line. We can't help."

My heart clutched when I heard this. As I mentioned, Lewis' address and zip code gave the appearance that he lived in a municipality and county where it was very likely officials would address Angelo's misdeeds aggressively. Unfortunately, as is often the case in North Carolina, the town and zip code in Lewis' mailing address did not reflect that he lived outside the city limits and the county where the town was actually located. He lived one county over, and that small county's DA, sheriff and Adult Protective Services personnel were far less skillful and aggressive in addressing elder fraud incidents like this one. Before calling my DA buddy, I should have checked MapQuest to determine exactly where Lewis resided.

Kevin Anderson indicated that the IRS had nothing going on Angelo, but he welcomed any information we might develop on him, given the millions of dollars he allegedly had obtained from Lewis. He said he would check with the other federal agencies that might have an interest in Angelo or his business practices as well as Suspicious Activity

Reports (SARs) filed by banks or other entities in hopes of spotting Angelo's name.

John Maron gave a similar response. State securities officials did not have anything going on Angelo. Additionally, simple two-person business partnerships often did not fall within the coverage of securities laws which his agency enforced. Nevertheless, John's colleagues would be interested in anything we developed.

Donna White had a VAP volunteer in the Triad who was trained and hopefully ready to go. He was a former business professional from the area just like Lewis. They probably knew one another. VAP volunteers had proven extremely effective in negating the false friendships that scammers had developed with other victims around the state and in getting those victims to accept that they had been scammed. Their success rate in breaking the re-victimization cycle was almost 100 percent.

Before we could introduce a VAP volunteer to a victim, however, there needed to be some sort of awareness on the part of the victim that he or she had been scammed. Without that, the victim would never consent to the placement. Lewis was nowhere near that point yet. If we could somehow get him there, it might result in Angelo going to jail. The timeframe might be longer and the amount of funds left to recover might be greatly diminished, but something good could still happen.

Then something really bad happened.

I spoke with Lewis a few times during the next two weeks. While his faith in Angelo remained strong and Angelo was in his home almost daily working on "partnership matters," Lewis seemed to enjoy speaking with me. At some point, hopefully soon, some doubt about Angelo might creep into Lewis' mind and we could place the VAP volunteer with him.

During the third week, Lewis never responded to my calls. It was the same the week after that. Had Angelo convinced him to stop talking with me? Had Lewis died? I Googled his name together with the word "obituary" but found nothing indicating that he had passed away. I called Lewis's accountant. He did not know anything either, but he noted, "I have copies of his health care power of attorney and his living will in the file. I'll call the fellow listed on those documents to see if Lewis is in a hospital or nursing home or something."

Sure enough, Lewis was in intensive care at the hospital. He had suffered a massive stroke and his condition was deteriorating. He was about to be taken off the ventilator and have his feeding tube removed per the instructions in his living will. Two days later he passed away.

Lewis bequeathed all of his property to a pair of local charitable organizations. Had Angelo not obtained almost every last dime of his personal wealth, those charities would have received millions to fund good works in Lewis' name for years and years to come. Even still, the executor of the estate and the two charities perhaps could have pursued Angelo in court and, if they were lucky, proven the fraud and recovered the assets. Without any statements or records from Lewis that would show exactly how Angelo had defrauded him, such a suit would be next to impossible to win, plus very expensive. Moreover, Angelo had left the area suddenly and nobody knew where he was. Nobody was sure he had even used his real name while scamming Lewis. The executor (an old friend of Lewis') and the two charities elected not to pour time and resources into the matter.

Angelo got away with it.

23

George Love,
Elder Fraud Fighter

George Love was married to a Chapel Hill, North Carolina, woman who had been my ninth-grade civics teacher, a fellow law school student years after that, then my state legislator, and eventually my county's chief district court judge. Her name is Patricia Stanford Love. In the late '90s, George contacted me at Judge Love's suggestion because he had been conned into sending $100 to phony sweepstakes officials who told him that he had won their contest. The supposed prize was rather large and the requested fee seemed tiny in comparison so, like many first-time victims, George made a quick risk-to-earnings calculation and elected to take a chance. The prize never arrived. What did arrive over the next eight years was a torrent of letters and phone calls telling him he had won other sweepstakes and lottery contests.

George learned his lesson from that first incident and refused the scammers' never-ending entreaties to send money. Until his death in 2008, George regularly shared with us the latest pitches he was receiving. In so doing, he kept my colleagues and me apprised of some of the newest lures and enticements being waved at older U.S. citizens by overseas-based sweepstakes and lottery scammers.

Over the years, the mailings George forwarded grew more and more sophisticated. While the early mailings seemed amateurish and the products of cheap 1990s desktop printers, in later years the graphic design and printing work behind the mailings made them appear as legitimate as they were eye-catching. The mailings' countries of origin grew more numerous as well. Initially the mailings George received all came from Canada, but soon they were arriving from points all over the globe—the UK, Spain, Costa Rica, Hong Kong, Malta, Jamaica, Australia. It became a running joke between George and me that he had just won another round of the Spanish National Lottery, known as "El Gordo." George must have been informed a dozen times over the years that he was El Gordo's grand prize winner and needed to wire thousands of dollars to Madrid or Malaga or Barcelona before millions of Euros could be delivered to his doorstep.

Somewhere around 2003, the prize notification mailings that George was receiving contained some fairly convincing looking checks, most of them in amounts ranging between $1,000 and $3,000. Each check bore the name and checking account number of an actual U.S. company. The cover letters informed George that the checks were to cover foreign taxes and fees that he would be charged in the process of collecting his big prize and that they were issued by U.S. companies that were promotional partners in the overseas sweepstakes or lottery contests. The cover letters directed him to deposit the checks into his bank account immediately and then call a special toll-free number for further instructions.

Had George done this, he would have been instructed to visit a particular grocery store or Walmart near his home and wire cash in the same amount as the check he had just deposited. The scammers would then promise him that as soon as his cash was received in Toronto or London or wherever the sweepstakes or lottery company supposedly was located, his prize would be released. George knew better than to do any of this. The gigantic prize would never be delivered to his doorstep and the large check he had deposited would be returned, marked "counterfeit" once the company on whose account it was drawn realized that they had never issued such a check to begin with. George's bank then would have required him to compensate it for the amount of the counterfeit check, and it would have been within its legal rights to do so.

Variations on this theme would have been employed on George repeatedly if he had deposited the check and made the initial wire transfer as directed. He might receive a follow-up phone call minutes later informing him that another fee or tax needed to be covered and that he should go back to the store to wire more money. He might be told that other prize winners had failed to wire money to cover their taxes or fees, so he would be receiving their shares of the prize if he simply wired even more money to cover those taxes and fees. He might even receive a call informing him that one or more of his wire transfers had not been received, that the sweepstakes company would work with him and Western Union or MoneyGram to get those funds back, and that he needed to wire the funds again ASAP if he did not want the whole transaction to collapse. George might lose tens of thousands of dollars this way before the original check came back marked "counterfeit."

But, again, George knew better. Unfortunately, thousands of North Carolinians did not, nor did hundreds of thousands of seniors living in other states.

George appeared in anti-fraud public service announcements produced by then-attorney general Roy Cooper that warned about the techniques and persistence of the elder fraud industry. George also allowed us to feature the mailings and counterfeit checks he had received in our other senior fraud awareness events. He wanted to protect his fellow seniors.

There was one thing in particular that George wanted all seniors to know. From the day he mistakenly paid them in 1998 until the end of his life, the scammers kept peppering him with their calls and letters and phony checks. George's decision to chance a hundred dollars on a caller's promise to send him a huge prize had landed him on a "sucker list" that was sold and exchanged among fraudsters around the world. Once on the list, there was no getting off.

PART SIX

Judgment Day

24

"What were you trying to run on my grandmother yesterday?"

L et us return to the House-Mazza home repair fraud group. Once federal charges were brought against key members of that group in the fall of 1996, the spotlight shifted to the state of North Carolina and the charges that it and local officials would bring. Without those charges, the remaining members of the group—and there were dozens of them—would simply recruit new crew members and continue the lucrative scams unabated.

Repeatedly ripping off the same elderly homeowners was the only employment skill that most of those guys had. Plus, it paid well. Well enough that a man with only a ninth-grade education and his family could live very comfortably. And he could also drive around in a $40,000 pickup truck. And he would have plenty of money on top of that to fund, say, a hot girlfriend, a drug habit, a gambling addiction, the services of prostitutes, or whatever other recreational interests he might have. These unindicted fraudsters were never going to stop their crimes voluntarily, even after watching their buddies on TV being perp-walked to federal prison. The state needed take them down and send them off to its own penitentiaries.

Only they weren't being taken down.

During the months after the federal indictments were announced, remaining members of the House-Mazza group seemed to sense that nothing was going to happen to them. Reports of heavy losses by elderly homeowners across the state started to creep upward again. Whenever we or local law enforcement officials received new scam reports, they were sent to Reggie Shaw at SBI Financial Crimes for further investigation and workup. Financial Crimes then coordinated with local law enforcement and local DAs to investigate and bring state charges, but none had been brought yet.

"Financial Crimes is swamped," Jane complained. "They need reinforcements."

Tucker chimed in. "Reggie's got enough on his plate to choke a pig!"

They were right. By now, hundreds of victims and scores of scammers had been identified. Some victims had been scammed up to two dozen times at the hands of different members of the gang. And with all of the "structuring" the scammers did, the number of checks and check payees was even higher. Reggie and company had to sort through all of that in order to determine which suspect scammed a particular victim on a particular day, then find cooperating suspects who could confirm it. On top of that, House-Mazza was not their only investigation by any means. SBI Financial Crimes had a lot of other white-collar crimes to solve.

One official with the power to get Financial Crimes some much needed reinforcements was our boss, Attorney General Mike Easley. As the elected official whose department included the State Bureau of Investigation, he could get more SBI agents on the case. He had been front and center in the press on the House-Mazza matter, first with the Jennifer Julian interview and then more recently with the major newspapers and TV news channels when the federal charges were announced. In each interview, the AG vowed that state charges were being planned for members of the group, and members of the press were sure to ask him about those vows eventually. Some of the adult children of our victims, such as the daughter of Mrs. S in Wake Forest, were already threatening to go to the press over the fact that no state charges had been brought and the guys who had scammed their parents were still out on the street.

Tucker, Jane and I hatched a plan to get more local SBI offices involved in the House-Mazza cases. That plan included reminders to the AG via our friends inside the executive suite that newspaper and TV reporters soon might ask for updates on his promises of state charges.

Our plan proved unnecessary. One morning a team of SBI agents showed up in our office. They were from various SBI districts and they wanted copies of all of our consumer files involving the House-Mazza group. Mr. Easley had ordered them into the fray. The document request was huge and it would see Jane and Tucker and their administrative assistants hunched over copy machines for the rest of the day, but they were quite happy to oblige.

Soon after that, swarms of SBI agents were interviewing victims and suspects all over the state and clearing out the investigative backlog. One agent in particular, Karen Nenstiel, traveled to the Rocky Mount area constantly to interview House-Mazza crew members who hoped to earn special consideration from judges and prosecutors by cooperating with the investigation.

Karen Nenstiel's activities became so worrisome to certain members of the House-Mazza group that she had to change hotels frequently because of threats made against her. At one point, it was widely rumored that a key House-Mazza crew chief who had not yet been indicted had put out a "contract" on her.

From what many of them told me, these SBI reinforcements did not resent being pulled into the House-Mazza investigation. After all, their elderly neighbors, parents and grandparents were just like the victims. One of those agents learned that his grandmother in Goldsboro, North Carolina, had just been approached by a House-Mazza crew member. She did not bite on his offer to clean her gutters for $25, but that did not stop the SBI agent from having some fun with him. That afternoon, he drove from his office in southeastern North Carolina to the Rocky Mount area, met with Special Agent Nenstiel, then went to the crew member's home and to have a heart-to-heart conversation with him.

"What were you trying to run on my grandmother yesterday?"

The scammer was flabbergasted. How in the world did this SBI agent know who he was, where he lived and what he had done the previous day?

"If somebody—anybody—runs one of those home repair scams on my grandmother, I'm holding you personally responsible. Y'all work together and we know that. I also know where you live and can get here pretty fast!"

Although the agent never threatened any particular action against him, the scammer was quite concerned. Attempting to defraud an SBI agent's grandmother probably was not the best way to move to the top of that agency's list of cooperating subjects who were entitled to special consideration on charges and sentencing.

The SBI agent's grandmother was never approached again by members of the group. Nobody attempted to whack SBI Special Agent Karen Nenstiel either.

25

House-Mazza: "Soon, every day will be Saturday!"

The spring of 1997 was a heady time in the Consumer Protection Division of the North Carolina Attorney General's Office. We were about to move out of our cramped, moldy, windowless office suite in the old Raney Building and into a spacious, newly renovated 1930s art deco structure across the street from the capitol. Attorney Phil Lehman was successfully bringing cases that would make North Carolina forbidden territory for payday lenders and the astronomical interest rates they charged lower income consumers, while attorney Kristine Lanning and investigator Linda Matthews were doing likewise with an infestation of pyramid schemes that had swept in. Attorney Beth Smoot and I helped launch an enormous claims resolution program for the state's homeowners who had suffered expensive water damage from non-drainable synthetic stucco, or EIFS. We had also helped to get non-drainable EIFS banned from wood-framed residential construction projects in the state. The state criminal charges against the House-Mazza gang were shaping up nicely and expected to take down the remainder of the gang.

In Richmond, defendants in Will Garrett's federal case entered into plea agreements with the government and were sentenced as follows by Judge Robert R. Merhige, Jr., in case number 3:96-cr-00124 (E.D. Va)[1]:

1. Anthony F. Mazza—60 months active sentence, three years supervised release.
2. Christopher Shane Williamson—33 months active sentence, three years supervised release.
3. Ted Michael Stallings, 24 months active sentence, three years supervised release.

    4. Christopher Donald Burke—27 months active sentence, three years supervised release.

    5. Allen Dwayne Stallings—24 months active sentence, three years supervised release.

    6. Ted Michael Stallings—24 months active sentence, three years supervised release.

    7. Carl Alan Smith—46 months active sentence, three years supervised release.

    8. Marvin Anthony House—51 months active sentence, three years supervised release.

In a related case, number 3:96-cr-00141, Judge Merhige gave Gary Anderson Barker, one of Will Garrett's inside informants, a 27-month active sentence plus three years of supervised release.[2]

In a non-legal matter of utmost importance to the Consumer Protection Division of the North Carolina AG's office during the spring of 1997, the University of North Carolina and Duke University basketball teams were expected to compete for the NCAA championship. North Carolina had just defeated Duke for the Atlantic Coast Conference Tournament Championship, giving Coach Dean Smith his eighth victory over Mike Krzyzewski's Duke Blue Devils during the last 10 encounters. Smack-talk between UNC and Duke fans in the office was intense. Bill Tucker, just as he had done every spring before that, was busy administering the office's NCAA Basketball Tournament pool and collecting bracket sheets and "donations" from most of the staff.

Tucker's retirement from the state of North Carolina was only 18 months away. He equated being that close to retirement to being a month or two away from graduating from high school or college. "You can see the light at the end of the tunnel, even though there is still some crap to put up with. But busting your ass from here on out won't boost your salary or improve your retirement benefits, so you might as well just come to work, enjoy what you do, and think to yourself, 'Soon, every day will be Saturday!'"

Tucker repeatedly told Jane and me how much he loved working the House-Mazza cases. It was going to be his last big legal project and it meant a lot to him. The victims were all good people and he had interviewed scores of them across the state. The victimizers were low-life scum. Nobody had ever taken up a home repair fraud case as enormous as this. If it succeeded, it would represent the largest take-down of a home repair fraud operation in the United States—a nice exclamation point at the end of a long career.

Other things were making Tucker happy that spring. He loved being married to his new bride, Terry. The two of them had a new home on a golf course just east of Raleigh. He was slimming down and he needed to do it. Being a heavy smoker and a partaker of large quantities of beer each day—especially when he played golf—had taken its toll on him. By getting away from all that, Tucker hoped to enjoy decades of happy retirement life with Terry.

He was also really happy with a new weight loss drug he was taking, something called "Finfan."

On the first morning following the three-day Easter weekend, receptionist Jessica Gill buzzed me and said that Bill Tucker's brother-in-law was on the line. I had never met or heard of his brother-in-law. Jessie put him through.

"Bill died yesterday. Something to do with his heart. He was enjoying Easter at the beach with Terry and the family when he started feeling poorly. She drove him to the emergency room at the little hospital near Shallotte. He got tired of waiting to be seen, said he felt better, and asked to be driven back to the cottage. They were barely a block from the hospital when he went into cardiac arrest. Terry drove straight back to the ER but they could not revive him. The funeral will be Thursday in Raleigh."

Tucker was only 50 years old. The entire Consumer Protection Division was stunned and grief-stricken by the news. So, too, were the members of the House-Mazza law enforcement task force. Tucker and Will Garrett up in Richmond had bound that task force together for two years with their jocular personalities and dedication to putting the scammers in jail.

A couple of months after Tucker died, an event occurred that would have made him proud. Most of the defendants who had been charged the previous fall by the U.S. attorney for the Eastern District of North Carolina had entered into plea agreements and were set to be sentenced by federal judge W. Earl Britt in Wilmington. Among the defendants who would be sentenced were Bob House, Sr., and Bob House, Jr. Jane Feather and I decided we could not miss that.

After making the 120-mile drive to Wilmington without inflicting irreparable damage upon the speed limit, we parked along the waterfront just across from the battleship USS *North Carolina* and headed into the fortress-like federal courthouse. Judge Britt seemed to be in a rather poor mood that morning, chastising prosecutors and defense attorneys alike as he heard sentencing evidence in other cases and then announcing how long each defendant would reside in the federal penitentiary. As for Jane and me, our spirits were high. They were buoyed further by the presence of DEA Agent Mark Rosenfield, IRS Special Agent Kevin Anderson and Will Garrett, who drove all the way from Richmond even though these were not his cases. Frank Phelps was in the audience too. It was a terrible shame that Tucker could not join us.

Judge Britt finally called the cases that we had come to see. One by one, the members came forward with their attorneys. By the end of the morning, Judge Britt had entered the following sentences against them in case numbers 5:96-CR-11-BR and 5:96-CR-174-BR (EDNC)[3]:

Robert House, Sr.—186 months
Robert House, Jr.—135 months
David Viverette—15 months
Edward Dawson—65 months
Richard Van Johnson—98 months

Each defendant was also sentenced to three to five years of supervised release following their prison terms. (Co-defendants Paul David House and Ricky James Braswell were sentenced to 60 months of supervised release and no prison time a month and a half earlier.)[4]

Afterward, all of us except Phelps gathered in the parking lot to debrief. Members of the defendants' families were filing out of the courthouse and heading to the same lot, so we tried not to appear happy—even though we were. We quickly decided to have lunch together in celebration of the day's events and to raise a toast to our departed colleague, Tucker.

There were plenty of good places to dine along the riverfront in downtown Wilmington, but we decided to honor Tucker by finding a beachfront eatery. Tucker loved a good beach as much as anything. Kevin Anderson suggested the Oceanic Pier in nearby Wrightsville Beach. It had a restaurant with an outdoor dining area out on the pier that looked straight down onto the beach and the waves. We immediately jumped into our cars and convoyed up Oleander Drive to Wrightsville.

It was a perfect time to be on that pier. The lunch crowd at the Oceanic was filtering out so we secured a table next to the pier railing. The weather was sunny with a light, cool breeze. Surfers, beach walkers, sunbathers and shore birds were doing their things below us. For the first and only time in my career, I violated my never-drink-at-lunch rule and ordered a beer. It was a brand that I never would have ordered in a restaurant, but this time I did because it was Tucker's favorite: Natural Light.

We all raised our glasses and toasted our departed colleague. Then we toasted the bad fortune that rightfully befell Bob House and company about an hour earlier, thanks in large part to Rosenfield and Anderson. The two of them, of course, demurred and protested that it been a group effort. It was the two of them, however, who came up with the new prosecution strategy once Dr. Noel let it be known that our elderly fraud victims' failing memories of the home repair transactions could not be rehabilitated or their frustrating loyalty to their victimizers somehow "deprogrammed."

Later that summer, Will Garrett returned to Raleigh. He was gathering information for state prosecutions of members of the House-Mazza gang in Virginia. Before heading back to Richmond, he visited Jane and me in our snazzy new offices across from the capitol. He gave us both FBI baseball caps and some other souvenirs of his federal case against Mazza and company and talked about how much he enjoyed working with us, especially Bill Tucker. He discussed how much longer he might work as an investigator for the Virginia State Police, confiding that he wanted to ease out of his career rather than leave law enforcement work cold turkey the way Tucker had planned to do.

"I don't know if I want every day to be a Saturday. Saturday is when I have to do chores!"

Will told us that he, like Tucker, needed to get his physical health in better order while he still had good health insurance. The comment seemed odd because we knew how Will had stayed in shape during his last few years with the FBI. But he was not talking about getting more running in, dieting or lifting more weights. He needed to undergo a procedure to remedy some blood flow issues. He told us we should expect to see and hear less of him in the coming days as he got that procedure behind him.

A week after that, we received a call from David Schiller, Will's federal prosecutor buddy in Richmond. "I don't know if there's any way you and Jane can make it on such short notice, but Will Garrett's funeral is today. We just learned that his colleagues there in North Carolina had not been invited."

"What? We did not know that Will had died!"

"It happened a few days ago. There were complications during his medical procedure. Stuff broke off and cut off blood flow to his brain, if I understand it correctly. It was all very unexpected."

David Schiller was right; we could not make it to Richmond on such short notice. We were grateful that he had called us, though. He later reported that the turnout for Will's funeral was huge, with heavy attendance by members of the judiciary, the legal profession and the federal and state law enforcement communities.

Schiller said that Will's law enforcement career had been filled with celebrated cases. Just as Tucker had told Jane and me a few months earlier, Will had told him that the home repair fraud investigations and prosecutions were his favorite cases and that he was glad he could end his FBI career with them.

Will was in his mid–50s when he died. It had been three and a half years since he had spotted the House-Mazza crew members on his morning run and something deep down inside told him, "This isn't right."

26

"Frog" and the Habitual Felons

In the fall of 1997, Wake County District Attorney C. Colon Willoughby announced that his office had secured 127 felony indictments against members of the House-Mazza home repair fraud group for violating the state's false pretenses (criminal fraud) statute, North Carolina General Statute § 14-100. With that, the first of the long-promised state of North Carolina prosecutions had begun. The Wake County cases were being prosecuted by a team led by Assistant District Attorney Shelley Desvouges, a longtime participant in our task force. The defendants included crew members who had defrauded Mrs. S in Wake Forest and the Colonel in Raleigh.

Soon after these Wake County cases were announced, felony charges were brought by DAs in several other counties. Defendants ranged from crew chiefs all the way down to "hammer slinger" workmen who cashed the victims' checks. According to information compiled by SBI Special Agent Karen Nenstiel, over 250 state felony charges ultimately were brought, and just about all of them resulted in guilty pleas. As Shelley Desvouges and other prosecutors predicted in one of our task force meetings almost two years earlier, no right-thinking criminal defense attorney seemed willing to let his or her client face a jury in one of those cases. It was certain that a jury would take a very dim view of their clients' actions.

One of the strategies in this state prosecution initiative was to secure multiple felony convictions, if possible, against each defendant and take advantage of North Carolina's habitual felon statute in order to secure lengthier prison sentences. A first-time violation of the "false pretenses" act, North Carolina General Statute § 14-100, was only a Class H felony and carried relatively light punishment compared to the federal charges that had been brought against others in the group. In a state fraud case, if a convicted defendant's record was not that awful, he or she could get off with probation or just a few months in jail for each offense. Defendants who had been convicted of multiple felonies, however, automatically received lengthy prison sentences under the habitual felon statute. That is what happened with many of those guys.

In Virginia, similar cases were initiated by state prosecutors.

By the time the new millennium arrived, these state cases had worked their way through the local court systems and most of the remaining House-Mazza crew members were sent to prison. Some of the members who had been convicted in federal court were also convicted in these state proceedings and had to serve time in state prison after doing federal time.

There were still a few members running scams, however, with the most notable being Frog, the guy whose alleged victimization of Detective Brian Kreigsman's elderly constituent in Brevard kick-started the formation of the House-Mazza home repair fraud task force five years earlier. The situation involving Frog eventually was remedied.

In 2004, the U.S. attorney for the Western District of North Carolina charged Frog and four others with various offenses relating to alleged home repair frauds in the college town of Davidson, North Carolina. By the spring of 2005, Frog's four co-defendants had pleaded guilty and some had agreed to testify against him. In late 2005, Frog pleaded guilty to seven counts of wire fraud and one count of conspiracy to defraud the United States and received a 102-month prison sentence from U.S. District Court Judge Lacy Thornburg.[1]

Thus ended the largest, most successful law enforcement take-down of a home repair fraud ring in the United States.

PART SEVEN

Going International

27

Whack-a-Mole Leads to the "Means and Instrumentalities" Approach

When the telemarketing fraud component of the elder fraud industry was operating mainly from bases in the United States, its members preferred to set up shop using assumed names, reel in the cash, then quickly shut down. The shelf-life of a phone fraud operation rarely exceeded one month. Then the scammers would change names again, secure another short-term lease in a vacant office building or strip mall storefront, move all of their tables, chairs, phones and employees there, and start the fraudulent pitches all over again. Such constant movement was a key reason why recouping any amount of money from those guys via court proceedings was extremely tough and why our recovery of $28,000 of the $64,000 lost by Ms. D was such a rarity. It was a frustrating game of Whack-a-Mole. Making matters worse, the moles had rigged the game against us.

When the state AGs and their federal counterparts recognized and started addressing the elder fraud scourge in the early '90s, they quickly surmised that there were three ways to attack the problem. Elder fraud was equated to fire, with its three necessary components: fuel, oxygen and heat. Remove any one of those elements and a fire will either die or never ignite to begin with. Elder fraud's three necessary components are a criminal, a victim and the victim's money. Take any one of those components out of the mix and the elder fraud attempt, just like fire, dies.

Elsewhere in this book there is a great deal of information on how we took the criminals out of the equation through court action. There are also chapters on educating seniors or working with specific repeat victims in order to take them out of the equation. When overseas criminals ramped up their elder fraud activities and learned to target seniors who were immune to public awareness campaigns, the option of cutting them off from their victims' funds became the only one available. This chapter summarizes 25 years' worth of efforts to block the criminals' easy access to these funds.

A Multi-Day Window of Opportunity to Foil the Scammers

During the early to mid–'90s, quick, coordinated action with banks and other key businesses proved highly effective in stopping victim losses. Personal checks that fraud victims sent to the scammers usually took a day or two to arrive via overnight courier, so the victim had that much time to direct the courier to return the check rather than deliver it. If the check had already been delivered, another day or two might elapse before it was presented to the victim's bank for payment. During that additional two-day window, a stop-payment order could be placed on the check, thereby preventing any financial loss.

Whenever scammers collected payment by securing victims' credit card numbers over the phone, there was a much larger time frame in which to contest the charge. We counseled many victims to contact their credit card company immediately and contest the fraudulent charges that they had agreed to over the phone. At the same time, we would send letters to the victims' credit card banks, on AG letterhead, advising that we had determined the credit card transactions to have been the result of telemarketing fraud. The credit card banks usually removed the charges from the victims' accounts and debited them back to the credit card bank used by the scammers.

The Window Starts to Close: Remotely Created Checks and Electronic Debits

"Remotely created checks" were used widely by businesses in the latter half of the 1990s and the early 2000s to collect payment from customers who ordered merchandise or services over the phone. When a sales transaction approached conclusion, the business would ask for the customer's bank account number, then print out a bank draft that looked almost identical to a personal check made out by the customer. The only difference was that the remotely created check never contained the customer's signature in the lower right corner, just the notation "Payment Authorized by Customer."

The remotely created check could be deposited into the scammers' bank account immediately and the funds would be available to them the next business day. The phone fraud industry loved this. Meanwhile, the check itself would make its way back to the customer's bank for payment via the banking industry's check clearinghouse network, just like a regular check. The result was a debit to the consumer's bank account one or two days after the fraudulent transaction, thereby cutting in half the timeframe in which the victim could place a stop payment order.

Automated Clearing House, or ACH, debits are initiated in similar fashion, except that no paper check is created. Instead, the entire payment transaction is done electronically via the banking industry's automated clearinghouse network. The debit to the consumer's checking account usually occurs that evening or the next business day. If you pay bills out of your checking account online, you are utilizing the ACH system. Scammers in the United States and Canada discovered the benefits of this system in the late '90s, too, and by the early 2000s they were using it with gusto.

Wire Transfers Close Window of Opportunity to a Few Minutes

Since the late '90s, those who scam seniors over the phone or via the Internet have relied heavily upon wire transfers to reap the fruits of their crimes. This is especially true when criminals are calling or emailing from overseas. Western Union and MoneyGram terminals have long existed in grocery stores, pharmacies and other businesses just about everywhere in the United States. Most fraud victims can drive to one of them in just a few minutes. In addition, and for quite some time, Western Union and MoneyGram both have had networks of thousands upon thousands of wire transfer outlets throughout the world. As a result of these extensive networks, the scammers have been able to receive their U.S. victims' cash in almost any neighborhood anywhere in the world without fear of detection or apprehension. In addition, their receipt of those funds can occur just minutes after their victims hand cash to the Western Union or Money-Gram terminal operator in their favorite store.

Wire transfers pretty much shut the window of opportunity discussed above.

The "Means and Instrumentalities" Approach

When the state attorneys general first approached the business community for help with telemarketing fraud in the early '90s, their goal was to block the scammers' access to these various payment systems. Cutting off the money flow would be like cutting off the oxygen supply to a fire—it would be snuffed out. By resorting to this tactic, we were making a tacit admission that the phone fraud industry could not be defeated through vigorous consumer education campaigns or prosecutions alone.

The National Association of Attorneys General Means and Instrumentalities Subgroup came up with this strategy of reaching out to the business community in 1993. The subgroup was comprised of assistant attorneys general around the country like me who struggled daily to stop telemarketing fraud. The first company we contacted was FedEx. Led by Assistant Attorney General Steve St. Clair of the Iowa Attorney General's Office, a group of seven of us traveled to Memphis to meet with FedEx officials and discuss ways to keep the company's services from being misused.

FedEx Impresses

We arrived in Memphis with data and case histories showing how phone fraud artists often wiped out older consumers' life savings by repeatedly sending FedEx couriers to the consumers' homes to pick up checks. Steve presented a chart itemizing how an Iowa farmer lost almost $100,000 to sweepstakes scammers during the course of a few of months, thanks to repeated visits by FedEx drivers. We pressed them to train their drivers to recognize and report the telltale signs that an older consumer was being exploited, and we urged the company to utilize special computer programs, like the credit card industry employed, to spot and act upon transaction patterns among senders and receivers that suggested fraud.

FedEx's lawyers responded, "We are doing all those things and more." Then they introduced us to Gail Grauer, whose unit worked with FedEx drivers and customers to spot and interrupt such transactions. Gail took us to the building where this work was performed.

When we got there, we found several FedEx employees seated in front of giant double computer screens and wearing telephone headsets. Gail paired each of us with a member of her staff and we listened as they took calls from drivers who were concerned about the checks they had just been dispatched to pick up. The staffer would either ask the driver to put the customer on the phone or call the customer's phone number directly. As the staffer did this, he or she would bring up on the left computer screen the customer's shipment history. On the right screen would be the shipment history of the intended recipient of the envelope containing the check.

We often saw on the left-hand screen that FedEx had been dispatched to the customer's house several times recently to pick up checks for various parties. It was also apparent from the data on the right-hand screen that the intended recipient had been receiving checks from numerous other parties all around the country. The patterns on the two screens left almost no doubt that the customer, who usually sounded elderly, was being scammed. The FedEx staffer would inquire whether the check was being sent to collect a prize of some sort, and if the customer said yes, counseling would ensue on how legitimate contests were prohibited by law from collecting any sort of payment prior to releasing the prize. Most of these conversations ended with offers by FedEx to cancel the deliveries, followed by the customer's request to do just that.

Following our session with Gail Grauer's staff, we asked company attorneys whether FedEx could report such customer data and experiences to the appropriate state AGs as the suspected fraud incidents occurred. They steadfastly refused. There were follow-up conversations about our offices styling subpoenas to the company so that we could obtain what would almost be real-time data on transactions like the ones we had witnessed. Immediate access to the types of information we saw on those computer screens would enable us to jump on the scammers right away—before they could close up shop and reopen somewhere else. Those conversations never bore fruit. FedEx believed it could not share customers' transaction information with the government in real time without their expressed permission.

Still, we were impressed with FedEx's in-house fraud interdiction program and decided to pitch it to the other two major overnight courier services, Airborne Express (now DHL) and UPS. Scammers had dispatched couriers from those two companies to pick up seniors' checks as well. Airborne quickly agreed to implement something similar. UPS was less responsive.

The ACH Processors

Members of the means and instrumentalities subgroup also launched investigations against, secured settlement agreements with, and filed enforcement actions against companies that allegedly processed ACH debits and remotely created checks on behalf of fraudulent telemarketers. These companies appeared to do this despite alarmingly high rates of ACH chargebacks by the consumers' banks and despite written warnings from agencies like ours that they were collecting money for criminals.

One company which allegedly did this was an ACH demand draft processor Your Money Access, also known as YMA. In the mid–2000s, several state attorneys general and the Federal Trade Commission sued YMA in federal court in Philadelphia.[1] The assistant state AGs who prosecuted that enforcement case were all long-time veterans of the telemarketing fraud wars and the NAAG Means and Instrumentalities Subgroup: Philip Heimlich and Elizabeth Blackston of Illinois, Steve St. Clair of Iowa, John McGlamery of Nevada, Elin Alm of North Dakota, Erin Leahy of Ohio, Elliot Burg of Vermont, and me representing North Carolina. Our longtime colleagues from the Federal Trade Commission, Michelle Chua and Gary Ivins, worked that case as well. The defendants eventually settled without taking the case to trial.

The bank through which YMA processed fraud-induced ACH debits totaling millions of dollars was Charlotte-based First Union Bank. Evidence and testimony developed in the YMA case suggested that First Union employees were well aware of the extremely high chargeback rates for YMA's telemarketer clients but failed to act. Wachovia Bank, which subsequently bought First Union, was forced by federal authorities to pay $125 million to phone fraud victims, most of them seniors, whose accounts were debited through YMA and other payment processors.[2]

The YMA case and the closely related Wachovia case apparently caught the attention of the banking and ACH processor industries. So did our group's discussions with the National Automated Clearing House Association, or NACHA, pressing them to tighten the financial industry's rules prohibiting ACH debits for outbound telemarketing transactions. ACH debits and remotely created checks quickly faded as means of collecting money from fraud victims.

Western Union and MoneyGram

From 2002 until 2017, the state AG group's efforts focused heavily on the wire service industry. Canadian, Jamaican and Costa Rican phone fraud groups loved wire transfers. So did Nigerian money transfer scammers and, more recently, India-based IRS impersonators and "tech support" scammers.

Elliot Burg of the Vermont AG's office coordinated four multi-state investigations against Western Union and MoneyGram beginning in 2002. The group secured agreements between more than 45 states and Western Union in 2005 and 2017, plus similar agreements with Money-Gram in 2008 and 2016.

When we approached Western Union and MoneyGram in late 2002, both companies claimed they were not legally responsible if criminals sometimes used their wire transfer services to obtain their victims' cash. We countered that our complaint data indicated the frequency of such transactions was more than just "sometimes"; it was "often." MoneyGram protested that they were Western Union's smaller competitor and suggested that we should negotiate with its huge rival first. Whatever solutions Western Union agreed to, they would undertake also.

We subpoenaed Western Union's wire transfer data for seven of our states and surveyed the consumers who had made wire transfers of more than $500 to Canada, a country that was still a hotbed for telemarketing fraud. The survey indicated that an alarmingly high percentage of those wire transfers, around one in four, were fraud-induced. Even more alarming, almost 60 cents of every dollar of these $500-plus wire transfers to Canada appeared to be fraud-induced.[3] The survey data also suggested that the probability of a particular transfer being fraud-induced rose as the dollar amount went up.

We presented our survey findings to Western Union and entered into two years of intensive negotiations, hoping to get them to adopt internal procedures and customer warnings that would reduce fraud-induced money transfers. Western Union and its attorneys spent much of that time contesting both our research methodology and the idea that it could be held liable under any legal theory for our citizens' losses.

The company settled with the states in late 2005. When we took that agreement to MoneyGram hoping that they would adopt similar fraud reduction procedures, they balked. We reminded them that in 2002 they expressed a willingness to enter into something similar to whatever Western Union signed. The two sides then entered into a three-year negotiation which saw turnover in the company's legal and corporate management teams. MoneyGram and the states finally struck an agreement in 2008.

The two hard-fought settlements focused on anti-fraud training for wire transfer agents, proactive steps to root out problematic agents who regularly received fraud-induced transfers for criminals, enhanced internal procedures and technologies to spot and stop fraud, and prominent warnings to consumers about transfers that might be fraud-induced. The settlements funded a special call center staffed by AARP volunteers who contacted people who had been targeted by the elder fraud industry previously and counseled them on how to avoid future fraud attempts.

The agreements also created a procedure through which any state attorney general who believed an older consumer in his or her state was a repeat victim of fraud could secure a "block" on further wire transfers to or from that individual. I used this simple procedure hundreds of times to prevent repeat victims of cross-border scams from wiring any more money to their overseas victimizers.

Unfortunately, those initial settlement agreements with the two major wire services did not cause much of a reduction in fraud-induced wire transfers. We could detect some movement by the scammers from Western Union to MoneyGram and vice versa as each company tweaked their fraud prevention measures, but that was about it. The number of seniors who wired money to overseas scammers appeared to expand with each passing year.

Western Union and MoneyGram, Round Two

By 2011, Elliot Burg of Vermont was leading much more forceful investigations against the two companies, investigations that sought to confirm the suspected high rate of fraud-induced transfers from the United States to other countries where the elder fraud industry had become firmly settled. Those countries included Costa Rica, Jamaica, Nigeria, Spain and the United Kingdom. Wire transfer data from recent years were subpoenaed from one of the companies, samples were drawn, and thousands of calls were placed to the U.S. residents who made those transfers. While many of the transactions turned out to be between family members, a surprisingly high percentage of transfers to each country appeared to be fraud-induced. The average for most of those countries was between 10 percent and 20 percent. Fraud-induced money transfers to the UK, however, were much higher.

Due to the victimization reports they were receiving every hour of every day, the state AGs were not surprised at all by these survey results. The wire service company questioned the findings, however, and tried hard to poke holes in our survey methodology. We challenged them to commission their own independent survey, but they declined. They also claimed that the transfers we surveyed pre-dated reforms that the company adopted in order to reduce fraud-induced wire transfers to these problematic destinations. So we surveyed again, focusing on later transfers. After several months we had the results. The fraud-induced money transfer rate was down but still much higher than that of competing payment systems such as credit card companies and the ACH network, whose rate was less than 1 percent. We settled into another multi-year negotiation with the wire service company. We also turned our attention to surveying the customers of the other wire service company who had wired funds to these same problematic countries.

In 2015, Elliot Burg retired from the Vermont AG's office after a long and distinguished career. The multistate group then was led by Assistant AG Rebecca Pruitt of Illinois and, with respect to one of the wire transfer companies, Esther Chavez of the Texas AG's office. They led the states to multi-million-dollar settlements, signed in 2016 and 2017. Those agreements, one of which was negotiated in tandem with the federal government, saw the companies adopt sophisticated procedures and specialized computer programs that enabled them to bring down their fraud-induced wire transfer rates. Most of those initiatives were implemented by the companies before the settlement documents were signed. How much money each company would pay to defrauded consumers was the issue that drew out the negotiations.

Gift Cards and Other Payment Schemes

Evidence of the success of these drawn-out initiatives with the wire transfer industry is the fact that scammers are moving on to other payment systems. While fraud-induced wire transfers via Western Union, Money-Gram and others have not gone away completely, overseas-based fraud artists are pressing victims to purchase thousands of dollars' worth of gift cards or other prepaid debit cards at a local grocery store, pharmacy or other retail establishment. Then they have their victims read the cards' numbers to them over the phone. Through these techniques, overseas scammers obtain their elderly victims' funds instantly and without detection.

Fraud incidents where the criminals collected their funds through this gift card technique went from 6 percent in 2015 to 26 percent in 2018, according to the Federal Trade Commission.[4] With the encouragement of the National Association of Attorneys General, large retail chains such as Target, Kroger, Apple and Best Buy are training their store managers and cashiers to spot and counsel potential fraud victims who are about to purchase gift cards in large denominations (e.g., $500 to $1000).[5] This is a good start, but more steps might be needed before the scammers abandon the gift card payment technique.

Money Mules

Another technique now being employed by overseas-based fraud artists is to have their victims drive to a nearby branch of a major national bank and then deposit cash into a particular person's account. They name that person and provide his or her actual account number. The account usually belongs to someone in another state or city who the scammers recruited to be their payment processor, or "money mule." Each evening the money mule forwards to the scammers all of the money that has been deposited into the account, minus a commission.

The elder fraud industry sometimes encourages victims to visit their own banks and wire funds to the U.S. bank accounts of money mules located somewhere else in the United States. The money mule then transfers the funds overseas, just like in the previous paragraph.

Both of these techniques are extremely risky for the person serving as the money mule, as they can be identified rather easily and charged with money laundering. Unfortunately, many of these money mules turn out to be seniors who have been duped by the scammers into thinking they are serving as payment processors for important and legitimate international financial transactions.

The "means and instrumentalities" approach still faces challenges. As you probably have noticed, the elder fraud industry is just as nimble and technologically innovative as it is evil. Whenever one payment channel is taken away, it finds and exploits new ones. Still, when it comes to fighting overseas-based fraud artists, the means and instrumentalities approach remains one of the more effective methods. It is not a sexy way for anti-fraud enforcement lawyers to do things—no headline-grabbing court filings, no press conferences by our bosses on the courthouse steps, no televised perp-walks for the overseas-based scammers as they are escorted to jail. In fact, you might have had trouble staying awake as you read this chapter on the subject. But with the continuing globalization of the elder fraud industry, the means and instrumentalities approach to fighting cross-border fraud will become more and more important.

28

Canada Calls—FBI Special Agent Joan Fleming Answers

It was hard to notice at first, but by the mid–'90s Canada was fast becoming a hotbed of international telemarketing fraud. In the late 1980s and early 1990s, aggressive enforcement actions by state and federal law enforcement agencies in the United States caused the mostly Las Vegas–based telemarketing fraud industry to disperse its operations to other states, typically warm and sunny ones. From those locations the criminals resumed their lucrative scams and continued with their pool party lifestyles. As the '90s wore on, follow-up law enforcement campaigns throughout the United States caused communities in Canada—metropolitan Montreal, Toronto and Vancouver in particular—to become major centers of telemarketing fraud.

Except, perhaps, for its limited pool party/suntan season, Canada was an ideal location for the phone fraud industry. Most international telephone calls were quite expensive back then, but not so for calls between the United States and Canada. And because both countries used the same three-digit area code protocol, calling from Canada to the United States was just as easy as calling from one U.S. state to another. It was also easy to process charges to U.S. victims' credit cards in Canada. And if the victims sent checks to Canada via FedEx, UPS or Airborne Express, those checks could be cashed quickly just across the border in Washington State, in northern Vermont or in upstate New York.

Even better for the fraud artists, U.S. authorities had no independent investigative or arrest powers in Canada, and Canadian businesses did not need to honor U.S. subpoenas and warrants seeking call records, bank records or grand jury testimony. Even when American criminal authorities identified and charged culprits located in Canada, there was a lengthy

143

international extradition process to contend with before they could be brought to the United States, and it was never certain that Canadian courts would allow extradition to occur. Compared to how exposed their U.S.-based counterparts were to serious law enforcement action, Canada-based scammers faced little more prospect of punishment in the U.S. legal system than a criminal operating from the other side of the world.

U.S. officials still possessed a few advantages when working cases against Canadian phone fraud groups. U.S. and Canadian law enforcement officials had a long history of working together. Our two nations' legal systems were fairly similar. We all spoke English. Direct commercial flights linked many of our cities. And our favorite professional sports teams played one another regularly. By the second half of the 1990s, many of us were hanging out together at cross-border telemarketing fraud enforcement conferences and becoming fast friends. Most important, we all hated the con artists.

In late 1994, North Carolina attorney general investigator Linda Matthews and I filed one of the first state enforcement actions against a Canadian telemarketing group, Darrin Lake and his company Regent, Inc. Our court pleadings alleged they were running a sweepstakes scam on older U.S. citizens and hitting them for about $500 apiece. A detective in the Toronto police department's fraud unit helped us work up the case, letting us know exactly who ran the scheme, where the call center was located and who the people were who staffed it (young people from a particular south Asian country). He even took our North Carolina summonses and restraining orders down the street and served them on the telemarketers. After the detective "laid papers" on them, Mr. Lake called and assured me that his group would discontinue all calls to numbers with North Carolina area codes, as required by the North Carolina restraining order. Months later, after Canadian officials initiated their own legal proceedings against Lake and company, U.S. consumers started receiving refunds.

Everything about the Regent case just seemed so civilized. My impression of Canada and Canadians had been positive ever since I was a kid and my Boy Scout troop would take long summer road trips to Haliburton Scout Reserve in Ontario and Tamaracouta Scout Reserve in Quebec. The Regent case simply reinforced this pro–Canada feeling.

Regent telemarketers tagged their elderly targets just once and then moved on. In 1995, that seemed tame compared to the repeat victimization scams that the U.S.-based phone fraud groups had perfected.

"This Canada thing will be short lived," I thought to myself. "Scammers up there are nowhere near as ruthless as their American counterparts. Plus, we have excellent cooperation from Canadian law enforcement."

Four months after I made that bold prediction, Cynthia Turner, a loan officer with NationsBank (now Bank of America) in Wilmington, North Carolina, called the AG's office seeking help with an 80-year-old customer. He had just sent checks totaling $64,000 to scammers who phoned and told him they represented the Canadian lottery. Now he wanted to take out a loan for $5,000 so he could send the supposedly final payment needed for the release of his multi-million-dollar prize. According to Ms. Turner, the checks he had written to the scammers could be presented for payment at any moment and NationsBank would have no choice but to honor them if the customer did not have stop-payment orders in place. She and her colleagues could not persuade the customer to take that step. He still believed the scammers. Due to bank privacy laws, she felt she could not give us his name.

"Is he still in the bank branch with you?"

"He's seated right outside my office. Would you like to speak with him?"

"Sure. That would be wonderful."

Investigator Linda Matthews and I quickly confirmed that Ms. Turner's customer was totally immersed in the scammers' narrative about millions and millions of dollars arriving by FedEx or UPS once he paid required fees, insurance premiums and tax bills. All of our claims that legitimate contest companies never required advance payments before releasing a prize went unheeded. So, too, were our claims that overseas lotteries would never reach out to citizens of other countries and tell them they had been entered into their contest "automatically" and without their knowledge.

Because nothing we said registered with this poor man, we decided to link him into a three-way phone conversation with Detective Staff Sargent Barry Elliott of the Ontario Provincial Police. Barry was the founder and director of "Operation Phone Busters" (now the Canadian Anti-Fraud Centre), a specialized anti-fraud unit in North Bay, Ontario, that addressed Canada's growing phone fraud industry.

"Sir, these men are not real lottery officials," Barry told him. "The company names, addresses and phone numbers they gave you are associated with criminal groups that run these scams on citizens of Canada and the U.S. Everything you have sent them will be for naught."

Barry told him how hundreds of seniors had been taken for millions of dollars already. He also offered reassuring comments that we subsequently employed whenever we dealt with repeat victims of fraud: "There is no need to feel any embarrassment. These criminals are very, very convincing and lots of very bright people have been taken in by them. If they call back and press you to send the money anyway, please invite them to call this number and ask for me, Detective Staff Sargent Barry Elliott."

And with that, the customer declared he would forget about the loan and put stop payment orders on the outstanding checks. Ms. Turner immediately carried out those orders.

A week later, Linda Matthews and I filed suit against the lottery group and obtained a restraining order against them. Unlike our earlier case against Mr. Lake and Regent, Inc., in Toronto, these Canadian defendants never responded. When law enforcement officers entered their abandoned office months later, they found our restraining order posted on the wall, along with similar orders and directives received from other U.S. law enforcement agencies. Each document reportedly was scrawled with obscene, mocking comments and cartoons.

By this time, we were receiving numerous reports of North Carolina citizens being victimized by Canada-based sweepstakes and lottery scams. The problem definitely was not going away.

Later that year, a Raleigh-based FBI agent who specialized in white-collar crimes, Joan Fleming, told Jane Feather and me that a 72-year-old Goldsboro, North Carolina, woman had been taken for $102,000 by Montreal-based scammers in a phone fraud scheme.

When Special Agent Fleming called us, she was several years into her second career. She had started her working days as Ms. Marshall, the elementary school music teacher in the small community of Unadilla, New York. Her chosen career path of teaching music to grade schoolers, directing the school chorus and leading the fifth and sixth grade band was challenged one day when she met FBI Special Agent Cheryl Ann Starr. Special Agent Starr's story and accomplishments made Joan want to become an FBI agent herself. With Starr's encouragement, Joan applied to become an agent. That application was rejected. She tried again. She was rejected again. When Joan submitted her third and final application, she was accepted. Off to Quantico, Virginia, she went for training. Ten years later she was calling our office and requesting assistance in her case involving the Goldsboro telemarketing fraud victim.

The woman's plight came to Joan's attention when the wife of a FedEx driver called the Raleigh FBI office to describe a situation her husband had encountered. He had been dispatched to a woman's home repeatedly to pick up and deliver checks to addresses in Canada and upstate New York. He had also delivered several packages to the woman from supposed sweepstakes companies. He could tell from this pattern of pick-ups and deliveries that she was being scammed repeatedly. Even though FedEx was actively encouraging its drivers to report such suspicions back then, the driver worried that his job would be in jeopardy if he went to the FBI. His wife told him, "Well, I don't work for the company. I'm calling the FBI."

The driver's wife gave Joan the woman's name and address, and Joan soon paid the woman a visit.

The victim was very open about what she had experienced. She even let Joan record phone calls as they came in from the scammers. She also let Joan copy or keep all the award notifications she had received in the mail, her FedEx and UPS invoices, and all of the cancelled checks she had made out to the sweepstakes companies. She displayed all the "prizes" she had received from various sweepstakes companies. Many of them were cheap watches and costume jewelry—nothing worth very much. One prize was an inflatable rubber dinghy. She had been told she would be receiving a motorboat as one of her prizes—once she sent money for taxes on the prize, of course. The dinghy was her motorboat. (It lacked a motor.) Most important, she gave Joan her notes from earlier phone conversations with the scammers. They contained call-back numbers, the pitch men's names and summaries of their pitches.

Joan had never worked a cross-border fraud case before, but she took all the right steps. The FBI has special legal attachés, or LEGATs, posted in American embassies around the world. A LEGAT's mission is to serve as a liaison between American law enforcement officials back home and their counterparts in the country where he or she is posted. Joan's first step was to contact the LEGAT posted in the U.S. Embassy in Ottawa. His initial response was "These fraud groups are a big problem here in Canada!" He immediately hooked her up with investigators in Ontario who were working on the problem and with police investigator Mario DuBé in Montreal.

Joan and her Canadian counterparts soon determined that the Goldsboro victim had been preyed upon by a particular group based in Montreal. Even though most of her checks had been sent to locations in that city, some of them had been going to a stereo store in Ontario. Ontario provincial police officers went to the store, interviewed one of the owners and quickly learned that the owners were receiving envelopes from the United States and turning them over to a man who was the father of "Grant," one of the phony sweepstakes officials in Montreal. Soon after that, they arrested Grant's dad when he came in to pick up more checks. Joan and the Ontario officials sent a message to Grant via his father that they would like to speak with him. Not wanting his father to go to prison for these activities, Grant agreed to meet with Joan and her Canadian colleagues in Syracuse, New York.

Grant gave them a detailed description of the organization. The head of it was Boaz "Bo" Langman of Montreal. The organization worked from commercially available lead lists of seniors who liked to participate in sweepstakes and lotteries. Victims who fell for their scams went onto "mooch lists" and were called over and over again. Profiles were created and maintained on each "mooch" so callers could keep track of their past payments and their particular vulnerabilities.

Grant told Joan there were numerous people working the phones and they possessed varying titles and duties:

- "openers" who congratulated victims on winning first prize and spoke of the need to pay taxes or other fees to collect it;
- "closers" who were good at convincing wavering targets they really should send the money;
- "verification callers" who came on the line and tape recorded the details of the transaction after a customer (victim) agreed to send money; and
- "supervisors" who would get on the line and tell the victim he or she would be moving up from first prize winner to grand prize winner because the original grand prize winner had failed to get his tax payment to Canada by the deadline.

Grant named the various individuals who made calls to the United States. What's more, he listened to the recordings that Joan had made of the calls to her Goldsboro victim and he identified the callers.

Later, Joan secured additional recordings of calls made to other U.S. citizens by Langman's organization. She did this by contacting the National Telemarketing Fraud Tape Library, an agency funded by the Federal Trade Commission and the National Association of Attorneys General.

The library compiled recordings of fraudulent phone pitches that had been submitted by law enforcement officials throughout the country, including our office. The library cross-referenced each recording with the names of the pitch persons, the names of the sweepstakes or lottery companies they claimed to represent and the phone numbers they used. Thanks to Grant's assistance, Joan had lots of names and numbers to offer the Tape Library. The result was a substantial cache of damning recordings.

When Joan met with Grant again with these additional recordings in hand, he was able to link specific particular callers with various fraud victims throughout the United States. Joan then contacted the FBI offices where each of those victims resided and got her fellow agents to interview them and take their statements.

Joan also contacted Barry Elliott's group, Operation Phonebusters, and obtained the names of even more U.S. citizens who reported being scammed by Langman's organization.

It was about this time that Joan called our office. She had learned that the North Carolina AG's office was active in trying to address cross-border telemarketing scams and she wanted to know whether we had any consumer complaints listing companies associated with Langman's group, including "Norstarr Industries." We actually had some, and she quickly received copies. This enabled her to identify even more North Carolina victims.

Joan soon learned that many checks sent to Langman's group by U.S. victims were being cashed in a bank in Champlain, New York, across the border from Quebec. Because the bank was based in the United States instead of Canada, she was able to subpoena records from it and learn of even more victims as well as get a handle on how much money Langman's group was raking in.

Joan and the U.S. Attorney's Office in Raleigh did something else that Joan had never done before—they filed an MLAT request with Canadian law enforcement officials seeking their assistance in obtaining business records and witness statements relating to the Langman organization. Many countries have Mutual Legal Assistance Treaties (MLATs) which permit their respective law enforcement agencies to cooperate with one another on cases. In this case, the MLAT request was quickly honored by Canadian officials, and soon Joan was in Montreal with investigator DuBé, obtaining documents and visiting the homes and apartments of Langman's employees. This resulted in even more documentation of the crimes and more statements by insiders explaining how everything worked.

In 1998, Operation Phone Busters alerted Joan that Langman might be headed to Israel. He was an Israeli citizen, and had he departed Canada and made it to Israel, he could not be extradited to North America to face fraud charges. Joan and Assistant U.S. Attorney Scott Wilkinson quickly obtained a federal warrant for Langman's arrest and transmitted it to Canadian officials via the International Division in the U.S. Justice Department. Langman was picked up by Canadian authorities. A Canadian judge refused to order his release on bond, saying that he posed a flight risk. As a consequence, Langman was held in Quebec pending his extradition to North Carolina.

Scott and Joan then obtained federal indictments against 23 individuals allegedly connected to the fraudulent scheme. Court papers spoke of six identified victims in North Carolina plus dozens of others spread throughout the United States. Their alleged losses totaled more than $6 million.

Langman eventually was brought from Montreal to North Carolina to face two dozen U.S. federal criminal charges. On September 14, 1998, pursuant to a plea agreement with the U.S. attorney, he pleaded guilty to one count of wire fraud and one count of conspiracy. Two of his co-defendants, Jeff Szenes and Farbod Mohit-Mafi, pleaded guilty on that day as well. On February 8, 1999, four years after Joan's Goldsboro victim was first scammed, Judge Malcolm J. Howard sentenced Langman to 90 months in federal prison.[1] Mohit-Mafi and Szenes were sentenced to 30 and 36 months in prison, respectively.[2]

Most of Langman's co-defendants, including Grant, were brought to North Carolina, entered into plea agreements and received federal prison sentences. Two named defendants managed to flee overseas before they could be arrested in Canada. Joan and Scott Wilkinson issued Interpol "Red Notices" (international arrest requests) for them, yet another cross-border law enforcement tool she had never employed prior to this case. Approximately two years later, police in Cyprus spotted one of them in their country and detained him pursuant to the Red Notice. Authorities in Germany encountered the other one and did the same. Both eventually were brought to North Carolina to face charges.

The Langman case was a sterling example of a cross-border fraud case done well. It also turned out to be an example of how no good deed goes uncriticized, a phenomenon encountered by many of us who handle elder fraud cases.

While she was in the middle of the Langman case, Joan's office was scheduled for a visit from an outside "review team." Each agent in the office was told to provide the review team with a synopsis of their three biggest cases. One of the three cases Joan summarized was the Langman case. After she circulated her draft synopsis to her superiors, it came back with an interesting margin note from one of them: "Drop these telemarketing cases!" There were those in the FBI back then, and in my agency as well, who thought that phone fraud cases were unworthy of their organization's concern and that greedy older people who got scammed should be left to their own devices. Fortunately, Joan did not view it that way. She could see the special vulnerabilities of those the Langman group targeted. She stayed with the case despite the directive scribbled in the margin of her report. Later, Special Agent Jim Walsh in Charlotte, who oversaw the FBI's white-collar crime efforts in North Carolina, told Joan that the Langman case was one of the finest white-collar crime investigations he had ever seen.

It is interesting that the federal investigations and criminal proceedings against these Canadian defendants started and reached conclusion during the same time period as the House-Mazza home repair fraud cases. It was a nice way to end the millennium. The big question as we reached the year 2000 was this: Will all these prosecutions and hefty prison sentences keep North Carolina seniors from being targeted further by the elder fraud industry? They should know by now that our older citizens are not to be messed with.

Part Eight

Miracles and Grace

29

On a Muggy July Afternoon
... the McPhauls' Case

Certain July days in central North Carolina can be like winter days in the far north when a blizzard is in progress—you don't want to be outside for very long unless you absolutely have to and are properly attired. When they are operating full-bore, the midsummer sun, heat and humidity in the Carolinas can render a person miserable and weak in a hurry and can even pose a health threat. July days make North Carolinians thankful for the development of air conditioning systems for cars, homes, office buildings and public places. Without those wonderful inventions, people might still be fleeing north from states like North Carolina and Florida instead of the other way around.

It was on one of these miserable, muggy July days in 2007 that Dorothy C. Strickland, a telemarketing fraud investigator in our Elder Fraud Unit, alerted me to what would be the most memorable elder fraud case I ever encountered. Dorothy had just returned to the office from the monthly luncheon meeting of the Wake County Paralegals Association. During that meeting she dined with a paralegal from the law firm Cranfill, Sumner and Hartzog who told her of a *pro bono* case they had just taken on. It involved an elderly couple in nearby Wake Forest, North Carolina, Carol and Tommy McPhaul.

Carol and Tommy were retirees who had spent decades running snack bars and cafeterias in state office buildings. Carol had been blind since she was a child and Tommy recently had suffered a debilitating stroke. Soon after Tommy's stroke, and over the course of an entire year, a contractor from Pennsylvania, John Shearer, allegedly took the McPhauls for well over $120,000.

Dorothy put me in contact with her paralegal friend and the young attorney assigned to the case, Dexter "Chip" Campbell III. The Cranfill offices were just two blocks from ours and the sidewalks between our two buildings were shaded by large oak trees, so I managed to walk over without becoming drenched with sweat. Once there, Chip Campbell told me the following story of how Shearer met the McPhauls and eventually obtained their life's savings.

Following Tommy McPhaul's stroke in 2006, he needed 24-hour care. He absolutely did not want to spend the rest of his days in a nursing facility. He just wanted to be in his own home. Carol was determined to honor Tommy's wishes. Her main challenge was the house they had lived in for decades, a 1950s vintage 1200-square-foot brick ranch with three bedrooms and one bathroom. The structure was anything but handicap accessible. The bathroom was not equipped to serve someone with Tommy's physical disabilities and both entrances to the home had steps leading up to them.

One Sunday at church, Carol updated her brothers and sisters in Christ on Tommy's situation and her desire to take care of him at home. She asked about contractors who might make the house handicap accessible. Soon she was approached by Shearer, who told her he was a contractor and could do the remodeling job for her.

Shearer came to the house, did an evaluation, and then told Carol he could perform the needed modifications for around $80,000. It would take him four months. Carol agreed to the deal and a contract was signed. She felt good about Shearer, not just because he seemed likable and competent, but also because he appeared to share her faith.

Shearer was going to build wheelchair ramps for both entrances and make the inside of the home handicap accessible. He would also create a "great room" by tearing down the walls separating the small living room, the kitchen area and the garage. Then he would raise the floor of the former garage area. Once completed, Tommy could easily be wheeled from the couch to the dining and kitchen areas without having to pass through narrow doorways, plus Carol could hear if he needed assistance while she cooked.

While Shearer did tear down walls, pull out kitchen cabinetry and raise the level of the garage floor almost all the way up to that of the living room, he mostly just made up excuses for why he needed far more than the originally quoted price. He repeatedly claimed that newly discovered problems, including damage from a small fire in the home years before, would make the renovations more expensive. Construction experts told us later that such claims were ludicrous. But Carol believed him and kept giving him more and more money. Such "reloading" and repeat victimization were quite similar to what the House-Mazza home repair fraud groups had pulled on seniors a decade earlier. After one year of this, and after paying him over $125,000, Carol ran out of funds. Shearer disappeared from the project. The renovations to the house were nowhere near complete.

Chip's plan was to file suit on the McPhauls' behalf and recoup their lost funds. He worried about others being victimized in the future by Shearer and knew that only the AG had legal authority to ask a court to block Shearer from doing further business in the state. He was thinking that his firm and the AG's office could bring parallel legal proceedings against Shearer. This idea intrigued me.

Chip arranged for us to meet with the McPhauls at their home the following day. I was joined by investigator Linda Matthews, with whom I now worked on home repair fraud cases. When Linda and I pulled up to the McPhauls' home, both of us were stunned. Large swaths of brick cladding had been pulled off the sides of the home, the roof over the front porch was torn open, the former garage had not been fully enclosed, and there were gaping holes in the roof. A flimsy wheelchair ramp had been placed in front of the house, but it lacked proper rails and had a pitch that was too steep. And those were just the problems visible from the driveway.

After Carol welcomed us inside, we noticed that some of the gaping holes we had spotted on the roof extended down through the attic and into the living room itself. One could sit on the sofa and look up at the hot blue July sky above. The air conditioning in the home was running full blast but the living room was still sweltering. In the middle of it sat poor Tommy, immobile, connected to an oxygen tank and sweating. Rolls and swaths of fiberglass insulation material were piled next to him, along with other construction materials. New cabinets had been placed in the kitchen, but they were not permanently connected to the walls or floors, and there were no countertops in most places. Carol's kitchen range was disconnected. She told us she had been cooking meals for months using the crockpot connected to a wall outlet over in the corner.

Shearer had pulled up the floor coverings in the main part of the house. Only the plywood subflooring remained. But the subflooring contained freshly cut holes, some the size of footballs. Carol knew instinctively to avoid them. I, on the other hand, stepped partially into one of them as I examined problems with the ceiling. Looking down through the holes in the floor, one could see the clay soil in the crawl space below the house. The openings were a good way for snakes and rodents to get into the house.

Oddly, the new subfloor of the former garage had been raised to a point two inches below that of the subfloor of the kitchen and living room, creating even more potential for trips and falls, not to mention problems with moving Tommy's wheelchair to and fro.

Shearer had removed all the face plates from light switches and electric outlets, and many of them were simply dangling from the walls with nothing holding them up but the wires, which still carried electricity. Even though Linda and I could see the exposed tips of wires connected just millimeters from the light switches and plug outlets, we were afraid to flip on a light or plug something into one of those outlets. Carol, however, had grown accustomed to doing so without being able to see.

To me, the most outrageous problem we saw that day was the bathroom. Modifications to the bathroom are the most expensive and important part of a project to make a home handicap accessible. Everything else was superfluous in comparison. Carol badly needed the bathroom to be redone so that she could bathe Tommy without resorting to sponge baths, plus get him on and off the toilet safely. After collecting so much money, Shearer had done nothing at all with the bathroom. From what we learned later, he probably lacked the expertise to remodel the bathroom. The only thing he seemed to be good for was tearing down walls and pulling up floor covering.

Carol told us that she was out the $124,000 she had paid Shearer and that she probably would have to pay a similar amount to undo Shearer's "work" and complete the project. That would be a quarter of a million dollars to make a 1200-square-foot house handicap accessible, almost twice the cost of rebuilding the home from scratch.

One of Shearer's workers later told us that Carol and Shearer would pray over each problem he claimed to have found in the home and that afterward she usually authorized the additional "work." The worker told us Carol was also desperate for the project to be completed so her home would no longer be a wreck and she could care for Tommy properly. Forking out a few thousand dollars more to finally obtain that relief seemed like a good trade-off. Shearer reportedly presented her with this trade-off repeatedly.

There was one additional person in the house that hot July day and her presence astounded Linda and me. At first, I thought she was a young social worker or a professional caregiver of some sort. She was one of Shearer's workers! She confirmed that Shearer had scammed the McPhauls for the past 12 months and detailed exactly how he did it. She said that Shearer still thought that Carol would come up with the additional cash he was demanding and told her to be firm and tough with Carol until she relented and paid up. I asked her if she had any prior experience with home renovation work. She indicated that she really did not and explained that she was taking time off from her undergraduate studies at a nearby university. She said she would help us build a case against Shearer.

Another thing that Shearer never did was obtain a building permit for the project. This was illegal and a dead giveaway that everything had been a scam from the outset. Getting a permit requires a showing that the contractor is licensed by the state of North Carolina (Shearer was not), plus it results in regular visits by the local building inspector to ensure that the work is being done in compliance with state and local codes. The inspector would also ensure that important aspects of the project were being performed by properly licensed plumbers and electricians rather than clueless, untrained hacks.

Had a permit been issued for the project, the building inspector probably would have visited and closed everything down in the first week. As a consequence, Shearer would have gotten only a fraction of the originally quoted price from the McPhauls, and he definitely would not have been able to "reload" Carol with claims of newly discovered problems in the house. That is why home repair scammers rarely secure building permits. But Carol said that Shearer claimed he had gotten one. Being blind, she was unaware that a building permit had never been posted outside her home, just as she could not see whether Shearer was lying whenever he claimed to have found more problems with the home after cutting holes in the floors and the walls.

One thing that Carol was *not* was helpless or dimwitted. She was a tall, slender woman with a confident bearing and a gracious personality. She seemed quite sharp, very much in control and in possession of a keen memory. As she showed Linda Matthews and me her home and yard, she pointed out problems that we had not even noticed. Linda and I had to keep reminding ourselves that she was blind. She looked us directly in the eyes as she spoke, then pointed straight at something that was several yards away.

"You see that doorknob over there on the door to the back yard? It's eight inches too low. That's because the door used to be in the old garage. When John [she called Shearer 'John'] raised the floor of the old garage to match the floor inside the house, he was too lazy to raise the door frame with it. He just chopped off the bottom eight inches of the door!" She was right. The door should have been 6½ feet high but now it was much lower than that. The doorknob was situated down toward the floor and the bottom of the door had been sawed off. It was not even a clean or straight saw job.

"Go look under that door, David. You can see the grass in the back yard." I followed her suggestion and knelt down at the base of the oddly shaped door. Then I peered under it.

She was right. She lacked the ability to see what I was looking at, but her description was 100 percent accurate.

Carol knew she had been scammed badly and she was not afraid to say so. Despite her strength of personality, it was still clear that she was in pain from her dealings with Shearer. She spoke of tears and fatigue and despondency. She worried how the ordeal might be affecting Tommy, even though he might not understand everything that was going on. She said that she wanted to help us take legal action against Shearer and keep him from harming others like Tommy and her. "That will be one blessing from all of this." She said she wasn't afraid to talk to the press about him either.

Linda and I took photos, said our goodbyes to everybody and then followed US 1 back to Raleigh. Although we had worked with innumerable home repair and telemarketing fraud victims over the years, our visit to the McPhauls left us stunned. Linda is a person of deep faith, and Shearer's alleged misuse of religion to defraud the McPhauls disturbed her greatly. She is also terribly fond of older folks, and that characteristic alone would have ensured her anger and guaranteed a firm desire to take Shearer down. I was livid as well.

As we negotiated US 1's gauntlet of traffic lights between Wake Forest and downtown Raleigh, Linda and I pondered the best way to handle the case. There were no other victims of Shearer that Linda and I knew of, so it might be difficult to convince the powers that be in the AG's office that we should file a civil suit under the North Carolina Deceptive Trade Practices

Act to shut him down immediately. Usually the court expected us to present the unfortunate experiences of several consumers before it would shut down a business, and the higher-ups might find that concerning. There are few things more embarrassing for an AG than to go to court seeking a restraining order against a business only to be turned down by the judge. ("What? You've got just one victim? Why can't the homeowners file their own suit! Temporary restraining order denied!")

Linda and I felt that this one-victim case was outrageous enough to warrant such an attempt anyway. And besides, Shearer was not even licensed to perform general contractor services in the state of North Carolina. That alone should help us sell it to the higher-ups and to the court. While our civil case was in progress, we could also work with Wake County District Attorney Colon Willoughby and the Wake Forest Police Department to bring criminal charges against Shearer. At the same time, Chip Campbell could file a private suit against Shearer and help the McPhauls collect on any resulting civil judgment if Shearer had any assets. It would be a three-pronged legal attack.

Also during the drive back to downtown Raleigh, Linda and I pondered how best to alert the public to the McPhauls' plight once our case was filed. A general press release, like the ones typically issued by our press office whenever the AG sues to shut down a business, might generate a three- or four-sentence mention during the evening news or in the morning paper. Three or four sentences just wouldn't do the trick. Something more in-depth was needed to show the public just how persistently ruthless home repair scammers could be to decent people like Carol and Tommy.

Linda and I knew reporters at the *Raleigh News & Observer* and at several local TV stations who might run an in-depth story on the McPhauls if it were given to them to work up exclusively prior to the announcement of the AG's enforcement action. Both of us had worked repeatedly with WRAL-TV consumer reporter Monica Laliberte during the preceding 15 years. She seemed like the reporter most likely to do an in-depth story that would portray the McPhauls in a positive and sympathetic light rather than as gullible, cartoonish old people who had ignored the old maxim "If it sounds too good to be true, it probably is!" Moreover, we thought that Carol would take a liking to Monica and do a killer interview on camera, one that would have viewers across central North Carolina clamoring for the heads of Shearer and all the other home repair scammers who preyed upon older people. Linda and I decided to suggest Monica to the higher-ups.

Our plan was already set, and we weren't even halfway back to Raleigh.

30

Miracle Just Off US 1 North

After returning from the McPhauls' destroyed home, Linda and I met with the young head of the Consumer Protection Division, Senior Deputy Attorney General Josh Stein (now the state's attorney general). We recounted the McPhauls' experiences with Shearer, showed him the photographs of their home, and laid out our game plan for addressing the situation. Surprisingly, even though we had only one pair of victims, Josh agreed with our plan in its entirety. The fact that we summarized the McPhauls' experiences as "the most appalling elder fraud incident we have ever come across" might have had something to do with it. Josh knew that Linda and I had dealt with such incidents since long before his arrival. There was a brief discussion of other reporters we might want to pitch the story to as an exclusive, but Josh quickly agreed that Monica Laliberte at Channel 5 could do a compelling news piece on the McPhauls.

Josh spoke to Attorney General Roy Cooper (who is now governor) and he agreed to the plan. I called Monica and she was eager to look into the story. Linda began drafting the affidavits of Carol McPhaul and the young woman we met at the house who had worked for Shearer. That night, I drafted the attorney general's court complaint against Shearer for committing "unfair and deceptive trade practices in violation of North Carolina General Statutes Section 75-1.1" (translation: scamming). Two days later, Linda brought me the signed, notarized affidavits and I attached them to the complaint, together with Shearer's contract and redacted copies of Carol's cancelled checks. Most important, we attached large color photos showing the appalling state of the home while the McPhauls were still living in it. We were confident that as soon as any judge read the complaint and examined the photos, he or she would close Shearer down.

We filed the complaint in Wake County Superior Court. Michelle

Bailey, the assistant trial court administrator, scheduled a hearing in front of Judge Abraham Penn Jones the following afternoon on our request for a temporary restraining order that would put Shearer out of business. When we appeared before Judge Jones, he had already reviewed the complaint and its attachments. Shearer had been notified of the hearing but did not appear. He claimed to be in Pennsylvania.

My pitch for the restraining order lasted only a few seconds. It was, basically, "Your Honor, as you can see from the photos, the affidavits and the allegations in the complaint, this man needs to be shut down right away, before he does this to other seniors."

The judge's only response to my five-second legal argument was "Counsel, do you have a proposed order for me?" As I presented the draft restraining order, Judge Jones observed that many of the civil cases that the AG brought before him involved fraudulent activities that were just as criminal as any that were charged by local DAs, and he asked if we ever coordinated with Wake County DA Colon Willoughby on cases like this. I told him that we did so regularly and that a few years earlier Mr. Willoughby had brought over 125 felony charges against a Rocky Mount–based home repair fraud ring that we had uncovered. I assured him that we were already in conversation with criminal authorities about Mr. Shearer.

After Judge Jones signed several copies of the restraining order, the courtroom clerk stamped them and placed one in the court file. The temporary restraining order shut down Shearer's business in North Carolina and set a hearing date on our request for a preliminary injunction in 10 days. It also required that the proceeds of any sale of Shearer's home, which was for sale in nearby Franklin County, be held in escrow by the closing attorney. At the preliminary injunction hearing, the court would decide whether to extend the terms of the temporary restraining order until the conclusion of the entire case—probably a year or two down the road. We FedEx'd copies of the complaint and the restraining order to Shearer as soon as we got back to the office. Our press officer, Noelle Talley, sent copies to Monica at WRAL-TV.

Monica's story ran on the evening news a day later. She led off by telling news anchors David Crabtree and Pam Saulsby that the story involved one of the worst remodeling jobs she had ever covered, not just because of the awful work but because of the victims involved. Monica masterfully told the story of the McPhauls' experiences with Shearer, and she captured their pain, dignity and current living crisis with skill and compassion. We had been right on the mark with our predictions that she would be quite taken with Carol and that Carol would do a compelling interview.

Monica's video footage of the disabled couple trying to exist in their small, torn-up home was 10 times more shocking than the photos we had provided to Judge Jones. And while our prediction of public outrage against Shearer and his repeat victimization tactics came true immediately, our expectation that other Shearer victims would come forward went unfulfilled. Perhaps we had been lucky enough to stop him on his first set of victims and there were no others out there to be found.

Something then occurred that Linda and I had never anticipated. Viewers of Monica's piece actually organized themselves into a community posse and took matters into their own hands.

I'm not talking about a lynch mob or vigilantes tarring and feathering Shearer and then riding him out of town on a rail, although some of the online commentators reacting to Monica's story might not have objected to that remedy. Instead, individuals, businesses, faith communities and social organizations throughout the WRAL-TV viewing area, and especially in the town of Wake Forest, immediately stepped forward to help the McPhauls. Through social media, they quickly organized a massive effort to undo Shearer's work and turn the McPhauls' home into what had been promised to them.

Licensed general contractor Mike Marguerat of Landmark Construction was so appalled by what had happened to Carol and Tommy that he stepped forward to lead the rebuilding effort. He set up a special phone line for enlisting volunteers. Banks set up special accounts to receive donations to pay for the repairs. Plumbers, electricians, and heating and air conditioning experts volunteered their services or offered them at cost. Stock Building Supply (now Carolina Builders), Lowe's Home Improvement and other building supply companies donated materials and expertise, as did appliance stores, flooring companies, and even curtain installers and fabric stores. The town of Wake Forest waived all permit and inspection fees on the reconstruction of the home.

In all, approximately 100 volunteers worked on the home. Some signed up on their own and others joined with fellow members of motorcycle clubs, veterans' organizations and church youth groups. Motivating the veterans' groups was the fact that Tommy was a U.S. Army vet who had served in several countries, including Vietnam. He was a lifetime member of the Veterans of Foreign Wars. Some of the vets told us they signed up to work because they were incensed over what had been done to their "brother Tommy."

Other individuals and groups volunteered to prepare and deliver meals and refreshments to those rebuilding the home.

Shearer's reactions to both the AG's suit and Monica Laliberte's news stories was to claim "fake news!" Here's how Monica reported his response to both:

> "I'm going to be vindicated from these lies that are being told, and there are many lies being told," he told WRAL in a telephone interview. He blamed the problems on Carol McPhaul, saying she "kept changing the plans." He is, he said, "not being treated fairly" ["Volunteers to Fix Botched Remodeling Job," https://www.wral.com/5onyourside/story/1634633/, posted July 25, 2007].

What happened over the next four weeks resembled a cross between a Habitat for Humanity project and an episode of the television show *Extreme Makeover: Home Edition.* The re-do of the house would take somewhat longer than the 48 hours featured in *Extreme Makeover,* but the spontaneously organized army of good people in Wake Forest, North Carolina, soon pulled off something as stunning as anything the TV pros could accomplish. They quickly descended upon the McPhauls' home and began transforming it.

Shearer's bad work was ripped down and hauled away. Next, subfloors were leveled and covered with top quality wood flooring or carpets. The newly created kitchen and great room were rewired professionally. Carol's kitchen area and laundry rooms received brand new, upgraded appliances and light fixtures. The new cabinets which she had purchased before Shearer quit were still usable, and the volunteers finished them out with high quality countertops and hardware. The HVAC system and water heater were replaced with new systems. Most important, a 570-square-foot master bedroom suite was added onto the back of the home. It featured a spacious bedroom, large closets and an equally roomy, handicap-accessible master bathroom. The small original bathroom at the other end of the house was left as it was.

With the garage area made part of the living room/dining room/ kitchen area, and with the master bedroom suite being added to the back of the house, the square footage of the little house nearly doubled. It would be a home where Tommy could live comfortably and be cared for properly.

During a lunch break one day in late July, Linda and I drove to Wake Forest and visited the house while the volunteers were at work. It was quite the cultural experience. We encountered long-haired, bearded, heavily tattooed motorcycle club members and fresh-faced, well-coifed United Methodist Youth Fellowship volunteers standing shoulder to shoulder. They were sanding drywall joints and painting walls, constructing a large gable above the new front porch, hammering down new roofing shingles, and staining the newly constructed wheelchair ramps. These and other volunteers worked just a few feet from plumbers, electricians and HVAC professionals.

The altruistic buzz in the house was strong.

Monica Laliberte did a second news report on the community's response and the progress on the house. In the meantime, Detective David Richards of the Wake Forest Police Department put together a criminal case against Shearer.

Finally, the big day arrived. In early August, five weeks after Linda and I first visited the premises, Mike Marguerat and the army of community volunteers were ready to present Carol and Tommy with their newly reconstructed home. The event was going to be one gigantic party. Local officials, Attorney General Roy Cooper, and Linda Matthews and I received invitations. The press was there in full force, and WRAL-TV had a mobile broadcast unit on site to live-feed Monica Laliberte's report on the event during the six o'clock news.

Linda, Attorney General Roy Cooper and I each drove separately to the celebration. Once we arrived in the neighborhood, none of us could park anywhere close to the dead-end lane where the McPhauls' home was situated. Cars and vans were parked everywhere in the neighborhood and people were walking toward the house with snack trays, flowers and balloons in hand. As we reached the entrance of the McPhauls' street, Linda and I spotted Carol and Tommy seated in a car. As we congratulated them, Carol told us that the two of them had not been to the house during the reconstruction process and that they were dying to inspect the final product and move back in.

Attorney General Cooper then walked up and introduced himself to the honorees. Carol thanked him for taking legal action against Shearer and for the community outpouring that resulted. Cooper demurred and instead thanked the two of them for telling their story to the people of North Carolina. "So few victims want to come forward and spread the word about these terrible scams, but you had the courage. Your message will have a huge impact for years to come."

Following these brief conversations with the McPhauls, we continued walking toward the house and the large crowd congregating in the front yard. As the house came into view, we were astounded. The torn-up brick masonry on the front and side of the house had been redone completely. The roof was new and glistening in the evening sun. Wooden exterior doors and trim were freshly painted. Smartly constructed wheelchair ramps were in place at both entrances. A gabled roof feature had been added which extended toward the street over a wide new front porch. Shrubbery had been planted. The yard was cleared of debris and sown with new grass, although it was now getting trampled. The gravel driveway had been paved. A condenser unit for the new HVAC system had been installed just outside the back of the house. And those were just some of the features on the exterior of the home. We would have to wait until the homecoming speeches concluded before seeing what had been done inside.

The welcome home ceremony began with Carol and Tommy being driven up the little lane and into the driveway while the crowd cheered and pumped their arms and applauded. As the couple emerged from the car, the cheers and applause grew even louder. Mike Marguerat, the general contractor, welcomed them to their newly renovated home and thanked all the groups, businesses and individuals who contributed to the project. The mayor and other luminaries each spoke a few words.

Finally, it was Carol's turn to speak. She was visibly overcome with emotion, but she kept things together and thanked all the different groups by name and spoke of the joy of receiving so much kindness after hitting a point of deep despair only five weeks earlier. Then she said, "We've just got to go look inside!"

The crowd roared. Tommy was wheeled up the ramp as Carol walked closely behind. The wide new front door was opened, and the couple disappeared inside, followed by a joyful throng of volunteers, friends and neighbors.

Carol had even more words for the crowd once she was inside. Linda, Roy Cooper and I missed them because we were at the back of the long queue waiting to see the interior of the home. When we finally walked inside, we were delighted by the finished product. Not only was the reconstruction work done to near perfection, but people with interior decorating skills had done their magic as well. Walls and furniture were adorned with stylish window coverings or *objets d'art*. The wall paint, wood trim, carpeting and draperies were all beautifully color coordinated. A spectacular bedspread and embroidered throw pillows decorated the large new bed in the master bedroom. The kitchen was stocked with food. The countertops, end tables and bedside tables were adorned with family photos and pots and vases filled with fresh flowers.

The handicap accessible master bathroom was as spacious as any of the original three bedrooms in the house. It was both stylish and fully equipped to take care of Tommy's bathing needs, plus there was plenty of floor space for maneuvering his wheelchair and lifting devices without banging into anything. Even if Shearer had been the best building contractor in America, he never could have converted the tiny original bathroom in the front of the house into something like this. When I asked Carol about the new master bathroom, her response was a happy "No more sponge baths for Tommy!"

I thought the new bathroom would be Carol's favorite new feature in the home, but I was wrong. She told Monica in a follow-up interview that the new kitchen was her favorite. She loved to cook. It helped her to relax. After a long and painful year, she was ecstatic to no longer be preparing meals in a crockpot.

As of the publication of this book, text versions of Monica Laliberte's 2007 news stories on the McPhauls could still be found on the WRAL website. Some of them contained links to the video versions of those stories. All of them are worthy of your attention. Here are the links to those stories:

"Couple Comes 'Home' After Nightmare Remodeling Job," https://www.wral.com/5onyourside/story/2033397/.

"Man Indicted in Botched Remodeling Job." https://www.wral.com/5onyourside/story/2428737/.

"Man Accused of Botched Remodeling Job in Jail," https://www.wral.com/5onyourside/story/1891301/.

"Crews Fix Couple's Botched Remodeling Job," https://www.wral.com/5onyourside/story/1723387/.

"Volunteers to Fix Botched Remodeling Job," https://www.wral.com/5onyourside/story/1634633/.

"States Sues Man Over Botched Home-Remodeling Job," https://www.wral.com/5onyourside/story/1613112/.

31

McPhaul Miracle Postscript

Carol and Tommy McPhaul's story did not end with the homecoming ceremony just described. Chip Campbell filed suit against Shearer on the McPhauls' behalf and eventually obtained a $124,000 civil judgment against him.[1]

In the criminal case worked up by Wake Forest police detective David Richards, Wake County District Attorney Colon Willoughby charged Shearer with feloniously obtaining the McPhauls' money by false pretenses, the North Carolina statutory equivalent of felony fraud. The indictment alleged that he used Carol's Home Depot credit card to purchase tools and supplies, then pawned them. Shearer entered an Alford plea, a guilty plea in which the defendant protests his innocence but acknowledges there is sufficient evidence to convict.

In early December 2008, Shearer appeared before Wake County Senior Resident Superior Court Judge Donald Stephens for sentencing. Stephens was a veteran trial judge with a sharp wit and a wry sense of humor. He could be charming and funny in court, but he could also be tough as nails when the moment called for it. Here is how Monica Laliberte described a key part of the sentencing hearing:

> In court Monday, Shearer apologized for his behavior.
> "I first want to apologize to the McPhauls and thank them for forgiving me. And I want to ask the state of North Carolina to forgive me," he said. "I made some horrible, moral and ethical, poor choices, and for that, I apologize."
> Stephens responded, "The state of North Carolina does not forgive you."
> The judge extended little sympathy to Shearer, who still faces a civil lawsuit from the McPhauls and criminal charges in Durham alleging that he pawned tools belonging to them.
> "There's nothing that I can conceive of that would help me understand how you would commit this crime on these people," Stephens said.[2]

Judge Stephens sentenced Shearer to eight to 10 months in prison, the term prescribed by the North Carolina Structured Sentencing Act for a defendant with his otherwise minimal criminal record. He also ordered Shearer to pay restitution to the McPhauls in the amount of $124,000.[3]

A few months after the McPhauls moved back into their home, Carol invited Linda and me to join them for lunch at the house. We were more than happy to oblige. When we arrived, we noticed that Carol and Tommy had settled into their renovated home rather nicely. It wasn't adorned with fresh flowers anymore, but it still looked gorgeous and new. The meal featured another guest whose identity floored Linda and me. He was another one of Shearer's workers. He, too, regretted what had been done to the McPhauls and had asked Carol's forgiveness. He also asked if he could help with Tommy's day-to-day care.

I never would have allowed this guy to work in my home with a disabled loved one, but Carol is far truer to her faith than I. She apparently forgave the man, accepted his offer to help, and had been employing him for some time. He did seem to care about Tommy genuinely and had put in long days helping him to eat, bathe and use the toilet.

And there we all were—two consumer protection officials, two consumer fraud victims and their victimizer's former employee—all happily breaking bread together and talking about the new home.

Carol continued spreading the word about home repair fraud groups that target the elderly. She eagerly participated in a consumer protection video produced by Attorney General Cooper's office entitled "Stand Up! Fight Back!" It featured actual victims of various types of senior fraud and was distributed to senior centers, churches and other organizations throughout the state. Its purpose was to educate older consumers about the types of scammers who were lurking out there and encourage them to report any suspicious activities to authorities as soon as possible. Carol shared her personal story and made a compelling argument for making a report even if one is embarrassed or scared.

Tommy McPhaul passed away at the age of 81 in June of 2010, almost three years after Linda Matthews and I first met him on that sweltering early July day. Carol fulfilled his wish to live out his final years in his home.

PART NINE

Money Mules, "VAP" and Scam Jams

32

Charles and Miriam Parker

Sometimes the family of a repeat fraud victim concludes that the least-worst option available to them is to step back and just let their older loved one keep dealing with the scammers until his or her life's savings are exhausted and the scammers move on. They find this preferable to endless rows with Mom or Dad over whether they are being defrauded, or whether the children are "sticking their damn noses where they don't belong!" Letting the frauds continue might also seem far preferable to seeking a court ruling that the elderly parent, now irredeemably enthralled with the scammers and their exciting promises, is incompetent to handle his or her financial affairs anymore and therefore requires a legal guardian or conservator to perform such tasks.

The story of Charles and Miriam Parker of Raleigh, North Carolina, is a reminder that fraud artists won't always relinquish older victims from their grips once the money is gone. Their case also shows how local, state, provincial and national law enforcement officials from two countries, with substantial assistance from family members and dedicated elder fraud fighters in the private sector, can bring overseas-based elder fraud criminals to justice here in the United States.

The Parker case started out as a repeat victimization sweepstakes scam out of Montreal, Canada, that successfully targeted two retired professionals and took them for hundreds of thousands of dollars over the course of a couple of years. But after wiping out their savings and putting them deep into debt, the scammers did something else to the Parkers. They turned them into money mules who received cash or merchandise from other elderly victims of the same fraud ring and then forwarded it to Montreal.

Efforts to stop the exploitation of the Parkers and to bring their victimizers to justice lasted from 2004 until 2014, by which time three Montreal men had been sentenced to lengthy prison terms by United States District Court Judge Terrence Boyle in Raleigh, North Carolina. Few people outside of U.S. and Canadian law enforcement knew about the case until Tommy Goldsmith of the *Raleigh News & Observer*, following a last-second heads-up from me, attended the sentencing hearing for two of the scammers in March 2012 and wrote a compelling story about the case that appeared a day or two later. It was an excellent summary of the Parker family's eight-year ordeal, notwithstanding the fact that Mr. Goldsmith had little opportunity to conduct deep research on the case. A few months later, following extensive interviews of Parker family members, law enforcement officials in two countries, and even one of the scammers, Allen Breed of the Associated Press' Raleigh bureau filed a much lengthier account of the case. It was picked up by newspapers and television stations across the country in June of 2012. Breed's newspaper story on the Parker case can still be found with ease on the Internet.

The North Carolina attorney general's involvement in the case began in the fall of 2004, when the Parkers' adult children called to report that their parents had been scammed so badly and for so long that they had very little food to eat. One of our telemarketing fraud investigators, David Evers, met with the Parkers and their children shortly after that. He reported that Mr. and Mrs. Parker were repeat victims of overseas sweepstakes scams. They fit an all too familiar profile: retired professionals with good educations; in their 80s; well respected during their careers; able to acknowledge that they had been defrauded by the phony sweepstakes officials in the past but not able to see that the ones they were dealing with now were also scammers; and showing signs of age-related cognitive decline. Mr. Parker, in fact, showed signs of advanced physical and cognitive decline, so it was Mrs. Parker who was now interacting with the scammers.

Charles Parker was a retired professor who had taught finance at North Carolina State University. Miriam Parker was a former teacher who continued to volunteer as a reading tutor for disadvantaged kids. The two of them had managed their finances and their retirement savings quite well for a long time, and they never involved their children in their financial affairs. The children were fine with that arrangement—until they discovered the staggering fraud losses.

The Parkers' children apparently kept their shock and outrage reasonably in check while discussing the losses with their mom and dad. Despite this restrained response, Charles and Miriam Parker were defensive over what they thought were their children's sudden efforts to meddle in their affairs. They were also defensive about the state attorney general's efforts to intervene, and soon after that, the efforts of FBI Special Agent Joan Fleming.

Joan had learned about the Parkers about the same time we did. A California investment advisor contacted her about a wealthy client of his who had been victimized by Montreal-based sweepstakes scammers. His client had been sending cash and merchandise to the Parkers in Raleigh. More recently, his client had become a money mule for those same scammers, just like the Parkers.

Notwithstanding their annoyance over our mere presence in their home, the Parkers were polite to all of us and agreed to help capture the scammers on tape whenever they called in the future. The fact that they were willing to do that made us hope that they now realized they were being scammed. Voluntarily recording the calls would also be important in the investigation of the scammers. North Carolina is a so-called "one-party consent" state, meaning that a phone conversation can be recorded in North Carolina and later admitted in court if just one party to the conversation consents to it being recorded. (In "two-party consent" states, the general legal requirement is that everyone involved in the conversation must consent to its being recorded.) In the absence of Mrs. Parker's consent, permission from the court would be needed to tap her phone, and that would take time.

David Evers left a simple recording device with the Parkers. It connected to their telephone and automatically started recording as soon as the receiver was lifted. Despite Mrs. Parker's expressed willingness to help with the investigation, we learned later that she disconnected the device and never employed it. Instead, she continued to wheel and deal with the scammers.

What also became evident was that the Parkers thought they were going to recoup their lost savings by helping the supposed Montreal sweepstakes officials collect taxes and fees from other "winners" around the United States. They received cash or personal checks in the mail from those individuals. After retaining a small percentage of the funds per the sweepstakes officials' instructions, the Parkers forwarded the money to Montreal.

Sometimes the other U.S. victims sent expensive merchandise such as computers to the Parkers, who would ship those items to Montreal. Eventually, as we learned in the incident described below, the scammers got those other victims to place two stacks of cash between the pages of a magazine, then send the magazine to Mrs. Parker via FedEx or UPS or the U.S. Mail. One stack of cash would contain 10 to 20 times as much money as the other stack. The smaller stack would be the Parkers' to keep. Mrs. Parker would then repackage the larger stack of cash and forward it to Montreal, again via FedEx or UPS or the U.S. Mail.

An interesting break in the case occurred in the spring of 2006. The Parkers' son, Jim, had come down from Ohio to visit them. One Saturday morning as he was sitting on his parents' porch, a FedEx delivery man pulled into the driveway and handed him a large envelope addressed to his mother. The shaky handwriting on the envelope's labels appeared to be that of an elderly person who lived in Visalia, California. Through the paper outer envelope, Jim Parker could feel what seemed to be a stack of cash wedged between the pages of a magazine. He had already heard that his mom had been receiving money from other victims and forwarding it to Canada. He did not want her to have this package, but he did not want to carry thousands of dollars in cash back to Ohio either. He felt he needed to turn it over to law enforcement.

That same morning, as I was at Chapel Hill's University Mall doing some sort of errand, my cell phone rang. I had trouble at first realizing who Jim Parker was, partly because I had this tendency to push all things Raleigh or AG-related completely out of my mind once I was back home in Chapel Hill at the end of the workday. That tendency was even stronger on weekends. The only Jim Parker I knew in Chapel Hill was the older brother of Patricia, one of those many, many young women in my high school for whom I once held a crush. But it couldn't have been her brother. It had been almost 40 years since he and I had been in school together.

"David, I'm Miriam Parker's son and I'm calling from Raleigh."

Miriam Parker. Raleigh. Now I remembered.

"I've got to see you right away. My mother just received a mysterious FedEx envelope that I know is full of cash. I don't want her to have it and I can't hang onto it. Can I bring it to you right now?"

Jim did not know that I was in Chapel Hill, almost 50 minutes away from his mother's home. I offered to meet him in 25 minutes at a halfway point, a BP gas station just across Interstate 40 from the Raleigh-Durham International Airport.

When we pulled into the BP station, low flying planes were roaring overhead and several people were refueling their rental cars. All of the gas pumps were in use. The place was crowded and chaotic—perfect for exchanging something valuable without drawing too much attention.

Jim handed me the envelope and I gave it a squeeze. "Yeah, there's cash in there, all right. I can see why you didn't want to give it to your mom. I'll have it locked in the safe at the office on Monday and we will film it when it is opened."

"Give me a call, Jim, if you intercept any more packages this weekend. This place is not far from my house."

"Sure thing! I'll be flying back tomorrow, though. Is there a way to cut these courier deliveries off?"

"With FedEx, probably. I know some helpful people in the security department there. UPS might be another story."

And with that, our business was finished.

Even though I doubted anyone even noticed our conversation and package handoff at the BP station, I drove away peering at my rearview mirror far more than at the traffic in front of me. I worried that someone might run me off the road and rob me of the valuable envelope as I made my way home, or that a law enforcement agent hanging out at the BP station observed our suspicious looking exchange and would pull me over. After a few minutes, however, it was obvious that nobody back at the BP station decided to follow me home through the woods of Chatham County.

When I got to the office on Monday, I called Carol Lucchesi with FedEx security in Memphis. Twelve years earlier in 1993, as part of the initiative by several state attorneys general to enlist the business community in the fight against elder fraud (Chapter 27), I had sat with Carol at her desk as she took calls from FedEx drivers who had been dispatched to pick up envelopes from elderly customers and were concerned that those customers might be sending checks to fraud artists. Carol did a great job of counseling the customers about the illegality of requiring contest winners to pay fees and taxes prior to receiving their prizes. She persuaded almost all of them to cancel the FedEx delivery of their check to scammers. During the succeeding 12 years, I often contacted Carol or her boss

Gail Grauer whenever it appeared that FedEx was being employed by scammers to pick up and deliver the checks of North Carolina fraud victims.

When I called them, I would ask, "Gail [or Carol], do you have any recent records of FedEx shipments by or to Mr. So-and-So in Charlotte?" Neither woman could come right out and say yes. Instead, if their computer screens showed information that might be helpful to me, they would reply, "Please send us a subpoena." Upon hearing that response, I would prepare and sign an Attorney General's Civil Investigative Demand, which is a type of subpoena that most state AGs and several federal agencies can issue when they require information from a person or company. I would then fax the Investigative Demand to FedEx's general counsel, with a copy to Carol or Gail. By 11:00 the next morning, I would receive—via FedEx, of course—a print-out detailing all the shipping transactions involving the FedEx customer named in the Investigative Demand. It was a really nice arrangement.

I was shocked when I saw Carol Lucchesi's printout of all the FedEx shipments to and from Mr. and Mrs. Parker. Miriam Parker had been receiving packages and envelopes from people all over the country for a long time, far more than I had anticipated. Many of the senders had first names that had not been bestowed on newborn babies since the early 20th century. The FedEx shipments from Miriam Parker to Montreal were just as numerous, and the records usually showed one outgoing shipment by Mrs. Parker less than 24 hours after she received an incoming shipment.

A Raleigh-based local supervisor for FedEx called our office the same week that these data arrived from FedEx headquarters. He was totally unaware of our dealings with FedEx higher-ups in Memphis regarding the Parkers. He wanted to report that his drivers were alarmed by the pattern of shipments going to and from the Parkers' home. They suspected what was up but could not get much out of Mrs. Parker when they inquired.

Thanks to the records that Carol sent to us and the comments of the local supervisor, we were able to get FedEx to suspend all shipments to or from the Parkers. We also shared the records with Joan Fleming at the FBI, who shared them with Canadian law enforcement and with FBI colleagues throughout the United States.

After FedEx put the Parkers off limits, the scammers just switched to UPS and continued exploiting them.

What about the package that Miriam Parker received from the lady in Visalia, California, the one that Jim Parker handed over to me out by the airport?

We opened that package during a videotaped gathering in the financial services office of the North Carolina Department of Justice. Joan Fleming was present along with telemarketing fraud investigator Dorothy C. Strickland of our office. NCDOJ financial officer Mark Brinson was there to count and deposit in the bank any cash that might be in the envelope. The AG's media specialist, John Bason, showed up with his video camera.

As John recorded, I introduced the parties present, discussed how I had come into possession of the FedEx package, and described how I had stored it since that date. Then I asked Mr. Brinson to open it. He slit the package open and pulled out a rather ancient edition of a *Martha Stewart Living* magazine. Then he opened the pages of the magazine to reveal the source of the bulges that we felt whenever we touched the outside of the envelope. It was $5,725 in cash wrapped in two bundles. The smaller bundle contained only $725, and that probably was the bundle that Miriam Parker was supposed to retain after forwarding the rest to Montreal.

Brinson counted the cash in both bundles, recited the total sum, and announced that he would deposit the money into a special account that held victims' recovered funds. He then stated he would cut a check in the same amount payable to the woman in Visalia, California.

Shortly after we opened the FedEx envelope, I received a call from a man purporting to be the California victim's son. He described how his eighty-something mother had fallen for sweepstakes scams repeatedly and had just sent money to Mrs. Parker. When he contacted FedEx to try and recover the package, they advised him to contact me directly. He was eager for us to send the money back and invited us to wire it directly into his bank account or send a check directly to him.

The problem with the son's call was that he could have been one of the scammers, and he might have tricked FedEx into telling him what had happened to the package. It was not unusual for the scammers to call victims minutes after they had dispatched the money and get them to read back the number on the FedEx airbill (invoice). Then the scammers would go online to track the package's progress. Equipped with that same invoice number, a scammer in Montreal could have called FedEx, pretended to be the elderly Visalia victim's son, and learned what happened to the package.

Now, I will grant you that I might have been overly dramatic and paranoid when I worried about being followed out of the BP station a few days earlier. But this was different.

A couple of months earlier, I had a series of phone conversations with a woman in Franklin, North Carolina, a beautiful mountain town in the far western tip of the state. She was about to make a $30,000 bank-to-bank wire transfer to a supposed sweepstakes official in Canada who told her it would be the last payment she needed to send in order to obtain her multi-million-dollar sweepstakes prize. The teller at the bank persuaded her to contact our office and learn whether we had any complaints against this sweepstakes company before completing the wire transfer.

When the woman was put through to me, we discussed her dealings with the supposed sweepstakes company. I asked her to let me check the computer for any reports of improprieties by the company. As we chatted briefly about the goings-on and the weather in Franklin, I logged onto Consumer Sentinel, a Federal Trade Commission consumer complaint database that also receives fraud reports from businesses and law enforcement agencies throughout the world. It documents hundreds of thousands of consumer fraud incidents each year. Only law enforcement agencies have access to its data.

I had heard the name of that so-called sweepstakes company before. It was a generic name that lots of scammers used. Just as I expected, Consumer Sentinel listed page after page of troublesome reports on the company, some only hours old.

"Ma'am, there are scores of serious complaints here alleging fraud by this sweepstakes company. Here's one from a man in Montana who sent them $27,000 last week and received no prize, and another from someone in Arizona who sent a similar amount, plus other reports from Missouri, Florida..."

I told her that she definitely would not receive any prize money if she wired the $30,000 and the supposed sweepstakes officials would only press her for more if she did. I gave her my direct phone number and asked her to have the supposed sweepstakes official call me if she heard from him again. In the meantime, I would be mailing her more information on the scam.

The woman thanked me profusely and promised not to wire the $30,000. After she hung up, I entered the information on the scam attempt into Consumer Sentinel. As soon as I finished, my phone rang. The caller I.D. screen flashed a Montreal area code.

"Is this Alice's Ice Cream?"

"Sorry, we're not an ice cream shop."

"Who am I speaking with then?"

"You've reached the North Carolina Attorney General's Office."

"Can you please look up the number of Alice's Ice Cream in Raleigh?" I pulled out my Raleigh phone book and started thumbing through it. As I did so, the man apologized for the inconvenience and then engaged me in conversation about the weather in our respective cities and the Montreal Canadiens' victory over the Carolina Hurricanes a few nights earlier.

"I don't see them listed in the phone book, my friend. If they exist, you probably can find them on the Internet."

"Good idea. Thanks."

I felt kind of sorry for the guy calling all the way from Montreal and getting the wrong number. Then I went back to whatever I was doing just before the woman from Franklin called.

After a few seconds, a small voice called to me from the recesses of my brain. "Moron! That guy was the damn scammer."

I grabbed the phone and quickly dialed the woman in Franklin. I did not know what the scammer was going to tell her after talking with me about "Alice's Ice Cream," but I knew it would not be anything good. She answered and said she was headed to the bank to wire the $30,000.

"Ma'am, please don't!"

"Mr. Kirkman, you are really confounding me! Fifteen minutes ago, you told me this was all a scam, so I phoned the sweepstakes man and told him I would not send the money. Then a couple of minutes ago you called me back, apologizing profusely and saying you were wrong. You told me I should go ahead and send the money. Now you are telling me once again not to do it?"

"I called you a couple of minutes ago?"

"You most certainly did!"

"Did it sound just like me?"

"It sure did! The attorney general's name and number even came up on the caller I.D. You told me you had checked further and found that the sweepstakes company was legitimate, that some scammers had been using their name, and that was why there were complaints."

I then explained to her what had happened, that the scammer had just called me from Montreal in order to get a feel for my voice and speech patterns and then called her back impersonating me. I also told her how they could "spoof" caller I.D. numbers to make it appear that I was calling her. She seemed to buy what I was saying.

She also agreed that I could send an AARP senior fraud prevention volunteer to speak with her. I knew that if there were a live person in the community to help her whenever the scammers called again, she would be far less likely to send them money. As things stood at that moment, she probably would follow the advice of the last person to speak with her over the phone. The volunteer, Hugh Moon, called her immediately and they met for lunch. From that day forward, she ran all sweepstakes transactions by Hugh before sending money to anyone. She suffered no further losses.

So, getting back to the Parker matter, that is why I distrusted the caller from Visalia, California, who claimed to be the son of the victim who had sent $5,725 to Mrs. Parker. He very easily could have been one of Mrs. Parker's scammers, and the bank account where he wanted us to wire the $5,725 could have belonged to someone who had agreed to forward the funds to Montreal. You just never know.

I called and told the man that the North Carolina attorney general would send a check for the $5,725, payable to his mother, in care of the Visalia Police Department. The Visalia Police Department would be instructed to turn the check over to his mother and him only if the two of them showed up together, presented acceptable identification and signed a release, which someone in the police department would then sign as a witness. I also told him I would email the name of a specific officer to contact there. That plan worked for him.

The woman had her $5,725 back a few days later. The Visalia police reported that she and her real son showed up at the station and that the son appreciated my paranoia about him possibly being one of the scammers who had ripped off his mother.

About this same time, Joan Fleming and Assistant U.S. Attorney Gaston Williams obtained court authorization to put a PIN register on the Parkers' phone line. This allowed them to track all calls to or from Mrs. Parker, although they could not listen to those calls. They were able to identify each cell phone number the scammers used to speak with her. Joan and her FBI colleagues around the country also began working with other victims they had identified from subpoenaed FedEx, UPS and Airborne Express records. The same cell phone numbers used to call those victims were being employed to call Mrs. Parker. Joan and her colleagues also began collaborating with federal, provincial and local law enforcement colleagues in Quebec, just as Joan had done in the Langman case a decade earlier.

33

VAP and the Retired Fortune 100 Company Exec

Back in the 1960s, in an instance of public-private foresight and collaboration that continues to pay astounding dividends for the people of North Carolina, the Research Triangle Park (RTP) was established in the pine forests of the north-central part of the state. It was to be similar to an industrial park, but its focus would be research and development. After IBM opened a large research campus there in 1965, a steady stream of major corporations from around the world followed suit. So did the U.S. Environmental Protection Agency. So have countless smaller start-up companies that develop new medicines, electronic devices, computer programs, chemicals, etc. Since then, Research Triangle Park–based companies have collaborated closely with the major universities at the three corners of the Triangle, the University of North Carolina at Chapel Hill, North Carolina State University in Raleigh and Duke University in Durham. In addition, employees of those companies and agencies have been able to witness and enjoy decades of national championship college basketball, thanks to teams from those three universities plus North Carolina Central University in Durham.

Once the RTP got off the ground, its thousands and thousands of newly arriving engineers, scientists and business execs had to live somewhere. Tiny nearby hamlets experienced explosive growth. Cary, North Carolina, a humble village in the woods that my high school football, basketball and track teams regularly journeyed to for games, quickly evolved from a jumble of crisscrossing railroad tracks into a huge, upscale RTP bedroom community. It is now the seventh largest city in North Carolina.

Similar RTP-fueled growth caused a tiny railroad crossing known as Morrisville to morph into a large, thriving RTP suburb. Other small towns like Apex, Fuquay-Varina, Garner, Wake Forest and Clayton exploded from the influx of RTP talent, and larger nearby municipalities like Chapel Hill, Durham and Raleigh also grew rapidly.

By the year 2005, thousands of employees who came to work in the RTP during the '60s and '70s had retired. Many of them were in their late 70s and early 80s. Quite a few ended up on our Elder Fraud Unit's roster of repeat victims and super victims. One man, a prominent executive and community leader who had a municipal park named after him, lost hundreds of thousands of dollars to Nigerian 419 money transfer frauds. More than one former higher-up at IBM paid hundreds of thousands to overseas sweepstakes and lottery scammers. The same was true for former staffers at the massive GlaxoSmithKline pharmaceutical research facility in RTP. These and other victimized former RTP employees had been high-functioning individuals throughout their adult lives. Their natural skepticism and penchant for testing assumptions and results had been keys to their successful careers. Those traits and skills notwithstanding, the elder fraud industry feasted on them.

One such RTP retiree was a former corporate executive whose work repeatedly took him to cities across the globe. Upon his retirement, he was a daily regular on the golf course, a weekly regular at the local Rotary Club, and a guy whose cautious, no-nonsense demeanor in almost every situation made it seem like he was still helping to run a Fortune 100 company.

This man's wife called the AG's office one day in 2006, begging us to stop him from wasting money on overseas lottery scams. She told Telemarketing Fraud Investigator Dorothy Strickland that he had sent at least $125,000 to criminals in the Philippines and other countries, that he was on the phone with them constantly, and that he just would not stop. He would not even go play golf with his friends anymore. She worried endlessly about his mental health and their financial future.

Upon Dorothy's invitation, this gentleman (we will call him Mr. S) visited our office with his wife. Joan Fleming of the FBI came to help us pry him away from the scams and learn more about the people behind them. A couple of minutes in, Mr. S seized control of the meeting and told all of us, including his wife, that his dealings with the overseas folks were none of our damn business. He was quite experienced with overseas financial transactions and knew what he was doing. He also knew that overseas transactions, especially in places like the Philippines, where much of his money had gone, often required one to grease the palms of greedy local officials if anything was going to get done. That was all that he was up to, and soon his multi-million-dollar prize would arrive.

"Then you'll feel stupid for inviting me here."

Nothing that Joan, Dorothy or I said in response fazed Mr. S in the least. We cited the experiences of others who had lost thousands to similar entities. That failed. We pointed out that no overseas national lottery and no legitimate sweepstakes company ever required payment of taxes or administrative fees prior to delivering a prize, that they simply deducted those charges from the prize itself. That did not faze him either.

"It's different in the Philippines. They put me in contact with a lawyer there, and he explained why they had to do it that way." We told him stories of how overseas scammers frequently posed as lawyers or barristers to convince victims that the scam was real. That did not sway him.

At one point, I noted that Joan Fleming had helped put several overseas lottery scammers in U.S. prisons and that she knew what she was talking about. His response was "So, if these guys are such crooks, why haven't you put them in jail yet?"

"Well, sir, the names and addresses they are using with you are bound to be fake, so the warrants would be worthless. Plus, we have no independent authority to investigate and make arrests overseas. We have to coordinate with officials there…"

He terminated the conversation and walked out of the room. Mrs. S remained behind.

"This is what I put up with all the time. Those criminals have him thinking he is the go-to man in a multi-million-dollar international deal, just like when he was with the company. I can't counteract it. They've also convinced him that law enforcement here in the U.S. is crooked, that you are just going to seize his prize."

Mrs. S gave us copies of Western Union, MoneyGram and FedEx records from her husband's transactions with the scammers. One of those documents showed a FedEx delivery from her husband to our Raleigh super victim turned money mule, Miriam Parker.

"Does he ever send cash between the pages of a magazine using FedEx or UPS?"

"Yes, he does."

Small world! Miriam Parker was the money mule for Mr. S's scammers in the Philippines too.

I was frustrated that a skeptical, high functioning individual like Mr. S could be so taken in by blatant con artists. Sure, the scammers probably were exploiting a strong desire in Mr. S to be an important, central figure in a high-stakes transaction, probably making him feel like he was the go-to guy again, but that did not explain it. He also seemed to have an obsession for lotteries that the scammers were exploiting. But that did not explain it either.

I fired off an email to Drs. Peggy Noel and Virginia Templeton at MemoryCare in Asheville. It described Mr. S, his behaviors and his background, then asked what might be going on with him. Part of the reason I did this was because Dr. Templeton and I had been making joint presentations to lawyers, Alzheimer's caregivers and the general public on elder fraud, and we were about to publish an article on the topic in the medical journal *Alzheimer's Care Today*. Those presentations and the article utilized actual "case histories" from the files of MemoryCare and the North Carolina Attorney General's Office to illustrate various victim vulnerabilities and scam techniques. Mr. S could be a very compelling case history, if only we could figure out what was going on with him.

Dr. Noel shot an email right back. "He seems high functioning in almost every respect, but his *judgment* is terribly impaired."

My AG colleagues and I had encountered innumerable fraud victims whose judgment in excited situations was impaired due to age-related cognitive decline. The fraudsters were always looking for such people. We also knew from the research literature that as some people age, they become more credulous, believing things that are told to them no matter how implausible the statements might be. There were also the studies suggesting that as people aged, they missed or ignored warning signs about dangerous situations that younger people would not. But Mr. S seemed too unflappable, too cynical, too cool under pressure to possess any of those vulnerabilities. Squaring off with an assistant attorney general and a white-collar crime expert from the FBI had not caused him to panic or suddenly accept something he normally would not believe. If my understanding of what Dr. Noel was saying is correct, she was referring to deterioration or damage to the part of Mr. S's brain that controls judgment.

This explanation was the only way that Joan, Dorothy and I, with our laypersons' understanding of cognition and aging, could make sense of Mr. S's behavior. That key and very complex faculty of his probably was now impaired, even though the others were operating just fine. His short-term memory was excellent, he still processed information quickly under pressure, and he certainly did not suffer from a lack of skepticism.

Mr. S continued to surprise us.

Our Elder Fraud Unit at that time was collaborating on the Victims Assistance Project (we called it "VAP" for short) with the Aging and Adult Services Division of the North Carolina Department of Health and Human Services. Donna White and Debbie Brantley of the division worked with county social services departments across the state to identify and recruit older volunteers who were willing to work with repeat victims of elder fraud in their communities. Dorothy Strickland would perform background checks on the recruits and, if they passed, she, Carissa Burroughs and I would work with Donna to train them and pair them with elderly victims of fraud—assuming, of course, that each victim was willing to accept such a volunteer.

The VAP volunteers learned all of the ways that scammers would engage and re-engage with older consumers and repeatedly defraud them until their money was gone. They learned the 12 main elder fraud victim vulnerabilities and how the scammers tailored their scams to the specific combination of vulnerabilities that they detected in a particular target. They learned all of the "reload" techniques that accompanied the sweepstakes scam, the lottery scam, the sweetheart scam and more. They learned which mailings or phone calls would be preludes to a fraud attempt. They learned that many older fraud victims were looking for telltale signs that the offer or promise being made to them was legitimate, even though in their younger years, just like the Baby Boomers, the Generation Xers and the Millennials of today, they would have looked for telltale signs of its illegitimacy and then stopped as soon as they noticed one.

We then taught the VAP volunteers how to get victims to revert to their former skeptical ways of evaluating an offer and into the habit of running the offer by the volunteer before deciding whether to respond. For victims who were obsessed with the imagery of a large prize slowly making its way to their front door, we showed the volunteers how to flip the obsession around and get them fixated on spotting and reporting details of the scam attempt so that other targeted seniors might be protected.

This peer-to-peer counseling program posed several challenges. It was rather time consuming to organize and operate, and often the victim would not consent to being assigned a volunteer. We wanted to place a particular Raleigh-based VAP volunteer with Mr. S because the two of them had such similar professional backgrounds and we thought they would work well together if Mr. S simply gave the volunteer a chance. As we had witnessed in our abbreviated meeting with him, however, Mr. S probably would not give this VAP volunteer the time of day. We asked him about it anyway. He was impressed by the volunteer's resume and agreed to meet with him.

The VAP volunteer and Mr. S got along spectacularly well. The volunteer soon reported that Mr. S was beginning to perceive how the scammers were making him feel important again by placing him in the midst of a huge, expensive and entirely fictitious transaction. Mr. S was angry once he finally accepted what was being done to him, and soon he was obsessed with foiling the scammers and protecting others from their frauds. He opened up to us and provided a wealth of information that was helpful in the investigation of the Canadian scammers who had turned Miriam and Charles Parker into money mules.

The VAP volunteer program worked perfectly in this instance. Mrs. S reported that the losses stopped and that her husband no longer was diving for the phone whenever it rang. He was back to playing golf with his buddies, the retirement funds were no longer draining away, and now she had the house to herself again.

Mr. S's VAP volunteer also helped us with a $100,000-plus victim in Chapel Hill whose heavy losses were reported by Art Southard, the head of security at the Carol Woods retirement community. Chief Southard had tried without success to get the retired New England businessman to stop dealing with overseas sweepstakes officials. So had I. Southard and I met with the victim at his cottage in Carol Woods and introduced him to the VAP volunteer. The volunteer's ability to relate to him businessman to businessman created an instant rapport. That rapport and the volunteer's skillful work soon resulted in a complete cessation of interactions with the scammers.

A young VAP volunteer who worked full-time at SAS Institute, the enormous business software company in Cary, North Carolina, was placed with several repeat fraud victims in the Raleigh-Durham-Chapel Hill area. She, too, was quite successful in breaking the cycle of fraud that had ensnared those victims. A Wilmington VAP volunteer was able to stop two retirees in the coastal town of Shallotte, North Carolina, from sending any more money overseas after they had wired or mailed away over $100,000. This was after their adult children and several parties in town had tried in vain to get them to stop.

In the western part of the state, a VAP volunteer in the Asheville area worked with several repeat victims and got them to stop dealing with their victimizers. In a county just east of Raleigh, Donna White herself worked with one of our repeat victims for whom elder fraud investigator Margrita Harrison of our office and Angela Ellison of the U.S. Postal Inspection Service had intercepted and recovered about $40,000. In the process, Angela and Margrita learned that the scammers had converted that victim into a money mule, just like Mr. and Mrs. Parker of Raleigh. Donna was able to persuade her to stop sending money to the scammers—both her own money and the funds of other fraud victims.

There were times when no VAP volunteers were available in a victim's community, so we improvised. In Greensboro, a former finance office employee at one of the universities in the area lost all of her savings to sweepstakes scammers. She also had run up enormous credit card debts in order to send even more payments out of the country. These debts she could not repay, and the North Carolina bank that issued the credit card had obtained a court judgment against her and was about to have the sheriff auction off her home to pay that judgment. She had no spouse or siblings or living children to bail her out either, just some nieces and nephews who lived on the other side of the country. She was an "elder orphan" fraud target, just like Lewis who once lived one county away.

This Greensboro victim was still dealing with the criminals, desperately clinging to their latest promise that just one more payment was needed to get her multi-million-dollar prize delivered. In the absence of any VAP volunteers in Greensboro at that time, Dorothy Strickland of our office worked hard to help this victim, but the scammers would not give up. As soon as Dorothy got off the phone with her, the scammers were placing calls to the victim and winning her over yet again. Dorothy described both the victim and the situation as "desperate."

For years, we had helped Helen Savage of AARP North Carolina to train "AARP Senior Fraud Fighter" volunteers to give elder fraud presentations to the community. A good number of her Fraud Fighters were from Greensboro. So, because there were no available VAP volunteers in that area, we called Helen and asked her if she had an AARP Senior Fraud Fighter in Greensboro who might help us. She said she had someone who was a perfect fit—Marie McCandless. Dorothy Strickland and I contacted Ms. McCandless and she quickly agreed to try to help. She, like the victim, had a background in finance. After some quick VAP "training" over the phone on techniques for breaking an older victim out of the cycle of fraud that the criminals create, Dorothy arranged for Marie to meet with the victim. We also contacted the victim's bank, explained her situation, and got them to hold off on the foreclosure sale for the time being.

Here, too, the results were quite positive, even though it was not a true VAP placement. Marie McCandless built a rapport with the victim and got her into the habit of calling whenever the scammers contacted her. Upon receiving such a call, Marie would talk her through the reasons why she might not want to send more money. She also got the victim to change her phone number, something we seldom could persuade a victim to do. The money transfers stopped. In addition, Marie reviewed the victim's finances and concluded that she had a large amount of equity left in her home. Most of that equity would evaporate if the sheriff's sale of her home went through.

Even though reverse mortgages sometimes are bad deals for seniors, Marie made a compelling case for this victim obtaining one in order to pay off her fraud-induced debts and end the foreclosure. The plan would enable her to stay in her home for the rest of her life. Additional proceeds from the reverse mortgage would also supplement her monthly retirement income from the state, which had not increased in several years. There was no one to inherit her home once she died, so a reverse mortgage made sense for her. Within a few weeks, the reverse mortgage was in place and the debts were paid off.

Two final things about this Greensboro victim and Marie McCandless. First, the victim initially and repeatedly told Dorothy and Marie that she would commit suicide if the foreclosure sale took place and she was rendered homeless. She was saved from all that. Second, Marie McCandless later received AARP of North Carolina's Legacy Award for her efforts in the case.

The VAP program ended about five years after it began. Volunteers moved on to other things, in large part because we had trouble getting victims in their communities to accept a volunteer. We also had a vexing supply and demand problem. In certain communities, Charlotte, for instance, we might have several victims but no volunteers. In other communities we had lots of volunteers but rarely any victims—or victims willing to accept their help. There were additional problems with possible legal liability for the volunteers' acts or omissions, and we had no funds to reimburse volunteers for basic expenses like gasoline. That was a big issue in areas of the state where a volunteer might need to cross two or three counties to meet with a client. On top of all that, there was the enormous amount of time and human resources that went into recruiting, screening, training and supervising the volunteers. Dorothy, Debbie, Donna and I were trying to run the VAP program as a part-time, uncompensated side venture to our regular work for the state of North Carolina and we often lacked sufficient time to do the program justice.

Still, whenever the VAP program placed a trained volunteer with an older repeat victim of fraud, the results usually were remarkable.

34

Justice for the Parkers?

As Joan Fleming and her FBI colleagues around the country developed information on scores of other U.S. victims of Miriam and Charles Parker's scammers, law enforcement officials in Quebec worked to identify those scammers. The shipments of money and merchandise were tracked to a David Stewart of Montreal. The phony sweepstakes official who constantly called Mrs. Parker used disposable track phones and the pseudonym "Howard Clark," so he was hard to identify at first. Eventually the Canadians learned who "Clark" was: Clayton Atkinson, also from Montreal.

After Stewart was identified and questioned by Canadian law enforcement, Atkinson allegedly recruited someone else in the Montreal area to receive cash and merchandise from the group's U.S. victims: Jamaal McKenzie. The switchover appeared to be rather seamless, and Atkinson allegedly continued to defraud U.S. seniors after Stewart was out of the picture.

Meanwhile, back in Raleigh, Joan Fleming and company had obtained permission to record Miriam Parker as she spoke with Atkinson ("Clark") on the phone. In one conversation, Atkinson scolded her for the way she had shipped one of the packages to Montreal. Apparently, that method had not been speedy enough. He sounded more like an angry boss than a scammer trying to sweet-talk his target. She seemed unfazed by the abuse, however. It was as if she really viewed herself as his employee at this point. The fact that he was giving her a small cut of everything she reshipped to Montreal probably made her more amenable to his criticisms and his harsh tone.

Because the FBI could now listen in on her conversations with Atkinson, they and their Canadian colleagues devised a plan to catch him in the act. Through one of Atkinson's track phone signals and some pretty sophisticated tracking technology for that time, Canadian officials pinpointed the apartment from which he was calling Mrs. Parker. As she and Atkinson were having another one of their regular conversations, and as the FBI was recording it in North Carolina, Canadian officials stationed themselves just outside his front door. They could actually hear him as he spoke to Parker, and he was still speaking to her when they burst into the apartment pursuant to a warrant. Atkinson then reportedly tried to pull the SIM card out of his phone and destroy it. He was unsuccessful. The Canadian-American law enforcement team had him dead to rights.

Formal U.S. charges of wire fraud, money laundering and conspiracy were lodged against Atkinson, Stewart and McKenzie in 2008. Although the three men's victims were located throughout the United States, the case was brought in the U.S. District Court for the Eastern District of North Carolina in Raleigh.[1] Raleigh had been selected as the court venue because so much of the merchandise and cash that had been collected by the defendants had been processed in Raleigh by Miriam Parker. Gaston Williams was the federal prosecutor and Joan Fleming was the lead agent in the court proceeding.

Due in part to a lengthy international extradition process, Stewart and Atkinson were not brought to North Carolina to face trial until 2011. McKenzie did not arrive until almost two years later.

During the five years between Jim Parker's handing me that package full of cash at the BP station in 2006 and Stewart and Atkinson's arrival in North Carolina, a lot happened with Charles and Miriam Parker. The early-stage dementia that Frank seemed to be experiencing in 2004 had become pronounced by 2008. He and Miriam continued to be targeted by other sweepstakes scammers, not just as easy marks who would send money to collect a prize but also as reliable money mules who would collect and send the money of other victims. Atkinson or his associates must have shared the Parkers' names and their money processing skills with others in the industry.

The money mule services the Parkers provided for others in the fraud industry no longer entailed receiving cash or merchandise via overnight courier and forwarding it overseas. Instead, we got word that they were receiving large sums of cash via Western Union or MoneyGram, then immediately re-wiring 90–95 percent of those sums to parties in other states or outside of the country. We utilized the attorney general's recent agreements with those two companies to secure blocks on wire transfers to or from the Parkers, which seemed to stop the craziness once and for all.

Throughout this time period, the Parkers' children struggled to keep their parents above water financially. Charles still had a decent monthly retirement income from the state and both of them were drawing Social Security, but the couple otherwise appeared to be deeply in debt and without funds because of all the fraud committed against them over the years. And they fiercely resisted their children's attempts to learn more about their financial affairs.

Their daughter, Donna Parker, finally petitioned the state court to appoint her financial guardian (the term "conservator" is used in some states) for her parents. They resented it. After the court granted her petition, she was able to obtain a complete picture of her parents' financial mess. Savings were gone. Credit cards were maxed out. Personal loans had been taken out to pay the scammers. Insurance policies were cashed out or borrowed against. Medical bills were piling up for her dad. There were no assets besides the equity in the house.

Donna Parker took out a 30-year mortgage on her parents' home and used the proceeds to pay down their bills and debts. She also put her parents on a strict monthly allowance, one that was big enough to let them to cover groceries, gas and other day-to-day expenses but too small to allow them to respond to sweepstakes or lottery offers anymore.

The pain of having to take such steps weighed heavily upon Donna. Her parents blamed her and her siblings (and our office and the FBI) for preventing them from collecting the sweepstakes prizes they had been promised so long ago. Even after Atkinson, Stewart and McKenzie were charged with fraud, they reportedly held out hope that large prize awards finally would come their way.

Stewart and Atkinson pleaded guilty to some of the charges. They were scheduled for sentencing before the Honorable Terrence O. Boyle on March 15, 2012. Gaston Williams and Joan Fleming invited me to attend and I did. Also in attendance were Yves LeBlanc and Yvan LaPierre of the Royal Canadian Mounted Police in Montreal.

During the sentencing hearing, Joan testified about the nature of the fraudulent scheme, how it was investigated, and how Stewart, Atkinson and McKenzie were identified and apprehended. She described how Atkinson always used the name "Howard Clark" when he called victims throughout the United States, how the initial payment he sought from them was always $1,800, and how he would reload and re-victimize his targets by saying the that prize award had increased and that more taxes and fees were required. She recounted how he told victims throughout the United States to send required payments, or in some instances merchandise, to Mrs. Parker in Raleigh. Joan stated that 38 elderly victims throughout the United States had been identified and interviewed by the FBI and that there likely were many more. Collectively, the 38 victims had lost $900,000 (an average loss of just under $24,000). She testified that most had been victimized several times.

Joan also testified that the defendants would not tell authorities where the victims' money might be, which would make it difficult to secure any restitution for them.

Donna Parker was allowed to read a letter into the record detailing her family's experiences at the hands of Atkinson, including the fact that her parents blamed her and her siblings for keeping them from collecting their big prizes. She also told Judge Boyle that her father had died the previous month.

Gaston Williams then played the recording of Atkinson browbeating Miriam Parker over the way she had sent a package up to Montreal. Judge Boyle's immediate reaction to the recording showed that he was quite attuned to the age-related vulnerabilities of older adults. That awareness is captured in the following passage from the hearing transcript:

> THE COURT: Well, in the unconscionability of the preying on vulnerable victims you have elderly people living on marginal means and being coaxed and teased into thinking that this—and this is so typical, that this is why collection agencies shouldn't have access to elderly people who have some level of dementia or Alzheimer's and misapprehend the situation and how serious or unserious it is. I mean, this is just really shameful. Really shameful. I mean, everybody's had parents since Adam and Eve, so you've had parents. I don't know what their condition is. I don't mean to be personal about it, but can you imagine if somebody like you was doing this to your family? Could you imagine how shocked and outraged you would be?
>
> THE DEFENDANT: (No response).
>
> THE COURT: Answer me.
>
> THE DEFENDANT: Yes.
>
> THE COURT: Don't you think?
>
> THE DEFENDANT: I would.
>
> THE COURT: Listening to it, it's just shameful that you would do this to these people.

THE DEFENDANT: I can't sit in front of you and give an excuse for it.

THE COURT: No, it's just greed and an unwillingness to be decent. I mean I guess if you had the telephone numbers of all the people in nursing homes that would have been even an easier target, you wouldn't have stopped. You were going to the point of least resistance. You think you would have gotten away with it if you called their adult children and said I'd like to deal with you rather than your parents?

THE DEFENDANT: Perhaps not.

THE COURT: Your success rate would be zero [Atkinson Sentencing Transcript, page 20, line 17 to page 22, line 12.[2]

A few minutes later, Judge Boyle pronounced Atkinson's sentence. Atkinson was to serve five years on the count of Conspiracy to Commit Wire Fraud, Mail Fraud, and Interstate Transportation of Stolen Property and 12 and a half years on the count of Mail Fraud and Aiding and Abetting. He ordered that the two sentences be served concurrently. He also ordered Atkinson and his co-defendants to pay $840,000 in restitution to specific victims.[3] Judging from his statements during the conversation set forth above, and the look in his eyes as he made them, Judge Boyle might have been straining not to impose an even harsher sentence.

Earlier that afternoon, Judge Boyle sentenced Stewart to five years and six and a half years, respectively, on those same two counts, with the sentences to be served concurrently.[4] Two years later, Jamaal McKenzie pleaded guilty and received sentences identical to Stewart's.[5]

Following Atkinson's sentencing hearing, I got to chat with the two RCMP officers in Gaston Williams' office. The Mounties seemed well pleased with the afternoon's proceedings, noting that such charges could have resulted in far, far shorter prison sentences in Canada.

The Parkers and the other victims never received restitution. Miriam Parker passed away in July of 2019 at the age of 95.

35

What Are Scientists Saying About All This?

For years, scientists have studied how the human brain changes over time—how it develops, when it stops developing, how many of its functions start to decline ever so slowly once we cross over into our 30s, etc. Some of their recent research suggests how changes in or damage to specific areas of the brains of older individuals can make them more vulnerable to frauds and scams.

That our brains eventually lose processing speed and some of their other abilities should come as no surprise. Other systems in our bodies do the same. For instance, most middle-aged people experience dismay over pesky age-related physiological changes or declines, such as

> difficulty reading small print, especially in low-light conditions;
> declines in one's leaping ability or quickness on the basketball,
>   volleyball or tennis court;
> slower and slower speeds in 5K races as the years roll by;
> once-smooth skin that becomes wrinkly, thin and less attractive;
> hair, especially on guys, disappearing from the top of one's head
>   and, all too often, showing up in other unfortunate places; or
> dental work becoming more frequent and more expensive.

Whether and when each of these abilities and physical attributes starts to fade varies from individual to individual.

Our brains are not immune to such changes. Fortunately, most of us are blessed with so much excess brain capacity that the effects of those changes are not noticeable until we reach an advanced age. That could be a key reason why the elder fraud industry lays off people in their 40s and 50s.

Scientific studies have documented interesting changes in behavior as we age, even though the reasons for those changes remain mysteries. One such study suggests that as many individuals grow older, their cautious approach to financial decisions grows less risk averse. Basically, they become less sensitive to the prospect of financial loss (Samanez-Larkin, G.R.; Kuhnen, C.M.; Yoo, D.J.; and Knutson, B., "Variability in Nucleus Accumbens Activity Mediates Age-Related Suboptimal Financial Risk Taking," *Journal of Neuroscience*, 2010, 30[4] 1426–1434). Another example is a 1990s study suggesting that as individuals grow older they tend to look for signs that an offer or pitch is legitimate rather than a scam. Younger individuals look for the opposite (Princeton Survey Research Associates, *Telemarketing and Older Americans: An AARP Study*, AARP [1996]).

Brain imaging technologies have enabled scientists to link damaged areas in older individuals' brains to certain surprising behaviors. A study conducted at the University of Iowa College of Medicine suggests that older patients who have suffered damage or deterioration to their brains' ventromedial prefrontal cortex have problems with credulity, experience a "doubt deficit" and will believe representations that few of us would consider plausible (Asp, E.; Manzel, K.; Koestner, B.; Cole, C.; Denburg, N.; and Tranel, D., A Neuropsychological Test of Belief and Doubt; Damage to the Ventromedial Prefrontal Cortex Increases Credulity for Misleading Advertising," *Frontiers in Neuroscience*, July 2012).

A similar study performed at UCLA's Geffen School of Medicine suggests that patients with damage to their brains' anterior insula lose the ability—or "gut instincts"—to recognize dangerous individuals or risky situations (Castle, E.; Eisenberger, N.; Seeman, T.; Moons, W.; Boggero, I.; Grinblatt, M.; and Taylor, S., "Neural and Behavioral Bases of Age Differences in Perceptions of Trust," *Proceedings of the National Academy of Sciences*, October 2012).

Research also indicates that the ability to manage one's financial affairs in one's own best interest (including the ability to avoid scams) declines early in the Alzheimer's disease progression and appears about a year before "mild" Alzheimer's has developed (Triebel, K.L.; Martin, R.; et al., "Declining Financial Capacity and Mild Cognitive Impairment: A 1-Year Longitudinal Study," *Neurology*, September 22, 2009, 73[12] 928–934. Widera, E.; Steenpass, V.; and Marson, J., "Finances in the Older Patient with Cognitive Impairment: 'He Didn't Want Me to Take Over,'" *JAMA*, February 16, 2011).

On April 16, 2019, researchers at Rush University Medical Center in Chicago published the results of a long-term study involving more than 900 participants that measured the association between "low scam awareness" in seniors and the onset of Alzheimer's dementia. "Low scam awareness" was defined as reduced "knowledge of tactics used to deceive older persons and a willingness to engage in behaviors that increase chances of financial exploitation." After adjusting for differences in age, gender and education, the researchers concluded: "Low scam awareness is a harbinger of adverse cognitive outcomes and is associated with Alzheimer disease pathology in the brain" (Boyle, P.; Yu, L.; et al., "Scam Awareness Related to Incident Alzheimer Dementia and Mild Cognitive Impairment," *Annals of Internal Medicine*, April 16, 2019).

Research is continuing in these arenas. What is already out there suggests a neuro-biological component to the problem of repeat victimization. It further debunks the stubborn yet commonly held belief that older victims of fraud are scammed because they grew up in a "kinder, more trusting time."

One thing is certain. A scammer, be he a 17-year-old sipping tea at a computer terminal in Pakistan or a thirty-something good ol' boy knocking on an elderly homeowner's door in Richmond, Virginia, does not need a Ph.D., an M.D. or an MRI machine to identify and exploit older individuals suffering from any of these changes in cognition. He just needs to spot the outward signs of these changes and have the audacity to exploit them.

36

We're Scam Jammin'!

Some of the most effective elder fraud warriors are people who warn older consumers about the frauds and scams that are out there and explain how those consumers can protect themselves. For instance, in 2019, Michael and Camryn Friedman, two high school students from Cary, North Carolina, put together a presentation called "Goats & Musical Notes." This brother and sister and their friends visited area senior centers and retirement communities and presented petting sessions with their baby goats, performed on the piano and did presentations on the latest senior scams. They also distributed printed materials on other scams. Their presentations were both fun and informative.

In the 1990s, senior fraud awareness events tended to be anything but lively or fun. Back then, many of the law enforcement fraud fighters featured in this book regularly gave presentations at live senior fraud prevention programs held throughout the state. These were fairly basic productions, with speakers delivering short lectures on what they had encountered in their fraud cases and what seniors should look out for.

Before PowerPoint gave those rather dry presentations some multimedia pizzazz, speakers' "visuals" were little more than simple props, such as worthless watches and costume jewelry or tiny—as in four inches across—electric pianos that consumers finally received as "grand prizes" after paying thousands of dollars to sweepstakes scammers. We held up those cheap items as we spoke and sometimes circulated them around the room. The liveliest things ever got was when Consumer Protection Division Investigator Jane Feather would bring an old telephone to the podium and use it as a prop to reenact phone conversations with pesky, fraudulent telemarketers. It was a hysterical routine that rivaled the 1960s phone conversation monologues by comedians Lily Tomlin and Bob Newhart.

The highest-tech features of my presentations back then were audio cassette recordings of criminals trying to defraud seniors over the phone. I would play them on a tape recorder that I held up to the microphone. I might also bring old-fashioned color transparencies and project them on a screen using an overhead projector as I discussed home repair fraud techniques. Very low tech.

Attendees of these programs claimed that they learned a lot about the scams that were out there, but they also told us the subject matter left them feeling dispirited and hopeless after an hour or two.

We were bumming out our audiences.

Beginning in the late 1990s and very early 2000s, producers of these events started making them far more enjoyable. In 1998, the state director of AARP of North Carolina, Bob Jackson, and his team helped form the North Carolina Senior Consumer Fraud Task Force, a coalition of government officials and private nonprofit employees who were dedicated to fighting senior fraud through a collaborative approach. In addition to coordinating anti-fraud investigations, Bob and members of the task force began conducting "Senior University" and other events around the state that focused on elder scams. Jackson, quite the comedian himself, required that all speakers bring humor, energy and color to their presentations, along with useful takeaway points that empowered attendees to fight the scammers. Refreshment breaks and prize drawings were incorporated into the agenda to keep attendees' energy levels high.

The Senior Consumer Fraud Task Force member most responsible for advancing this new type of anti-fraud event was Maryanne Dailey, the vice-president of the Better Business Bureau in Charlotte. She called the events she organized "Senior Scam Jams." It was a catchy name that rolled off the tongue and evoked thoughts of fun and fellowship.

Maryanne always invited a mix of local, state and federal law enforcement officials, and sometimes area congressmen, to make presentations at her Scam Jams. She, too, encouraged them to use humor wherever possible and to stress things attendees could do to foil the scammers. Her events also featured a local group called "The Senior Cheerleaders." Clad in '50s-style cheerleader uniforms and armed with pom-poms, these 70- and 80-year-old women would perform dance routines and lead cheers that highlighted speakers' key takeaway points. The Senior Cheerleaders always got the audience rocking.

Another one of Maryanne's brilliant innovations was to recruit a popular local TV or radio personality to serve as the master of ceremonies. Not only did these charismatic professionals keep the events lively and fast-paced, but they also hyped them for days or weeks on their own shows or newscasts. It was free publicity that otherwise would have cost a fortune. And if the MC was a consumer reporter or TV news anchor, the event often was featured on the evening news afterward.

Maryanne recruited sponsors for the events she produced. They paid for door prizes and free meals for attendees. The meals enabled these events to be expanded to half-day affairs. The sponsors also helped pay for buses and vans to transport attendees from all over the Greater Charlotte area.

Maryanne's Scam Jam events quickly outgrew their original venue, the Charlotte Senior Center on Tyvola Road, and had to be held in larger places such as the Merchandise Mart on Independence Boulevard or some of Charlotte's enormous mega-churches.

Starting about the same time as Maryanne's first Scam Jam, and apparently without any familiarity with her events in Charlotte, Judy Baker Estridge, the vice-president for security at First Bank in Troy, North Carolina, staged a large senior fraud forum in that small community in the south central part of the state. Except for the absence of the Senior Cheerleaders and the name "Scam Jam," it was almost the same as one of Maryanne's programs. The MC was the popular consumer reporter for Channel 2 News in Greensboro. Judy and First Bank later produced similar events in other communities in the bank's four-state territory. She also recruited some of the law enforcement presenters to come back and train bank employees on how to spot, interrupt and report senior fraud events in progress. First Bank was the first banking chain in the state to do this, and Judy and the bank later received the North Carolina Senior Consumer Fraud Task Force's annual award for that initiative.

Meanwhile, in the mountains of western North Carolina, the doctors and staff of Asheville's MemoryCare signed up as elder fraud warriors. They organized a large public forum at the University of North Carolina at Asheville on the relationship between cognitive aging and senior fraud. That was the first of many collaborations that I had over the years with Dr. Virginia Templeton and her MemoryCare colleagues—and it was also my first presentation using PowerPoint. Together, Dr. Templeton and I addressed the phenomenon of senior fraud from both the medical and the law enforcement perspectives. We illustrated our key points with actual cases from MemoryCare and North Carolina Department of Justice files. Attendees were able to learn not only about the senior scams that existed, but also about the scammers' carefully crafted tactics and the ways in which those tactics exploited certain cognition issues that were being experienced by many older consumers.

That presentation at the MemoryCare forum is one that Dr. Templeton (and many times Dr. Templeton's MemoryCare colleague, Dr. Tom Kaluzynski) and I perfected, updated and reprised many times over the next 15 years. A 2007 article that Dr. Templeton and I had published in the journal *Alzheimer's Care Today*, titled "Fraud, Vulnerability and Aging: Case Histories,"[1] was one of the outgrowths of that forum. So is this book.

Back to the Scam Jams. They are still being presented throughout North Carolina and around the country. The current, very charismatic co-chairs of the North Carolina Senior Consumer Fraud Task Force, Stephanie Bias of the North Carolina Department of Insurance's Seniors Health Insurance Information Program (SHIIP) and John Maron of the North Carolina Secretary of State's Securities Division, have been participating together in Scam Jams all over the state for the past decade. Caroline Farmer, also quite the crowd pleaser and currently head of the AmeriCorps program in the North Carolina Governor's Office, traveled with Stephanie and John for most of that decade and did presentations as well. Greg Tanner, former assistant director of AARP of North Carolina, and Maryanne Dailey organized and presented Scam Jams throughout the state for years and years.

Scam Jams remain one of the most effective vehicles for educating seniors about the scam groups that are operating out there and the best methods for foiling them.

PART TEN

King Tommy Won't Relinquish His Throne

37

Tommy C, King of the Driveway Paving Scammers

The members of the elder fraud industry who have been doing their dirty deeds the longest are driveway paving scammers. For the better part of a century they have traveled from town to hamlet to isolated farmhouse, telling older property owners that they have "a load of leftover hot asphalt from a big job just down the road" and can pave their gravel driveways for next to nothing. In the earlier years, they might also scare homeowners into buying unneeded lightning rods for their homes or barns or fool them into paying for "low cost" paint jobs for those structures. The paint they quickly sprayed on the barns and houses and the tar-like substances they applied to the gravel driveways usually washed away in the next rainstorm. By that time, the culprits were a hundred miles down the road, seeking out and defrauding other elderly property owners.

To this day, many driveway paving scammers still apply mysterious tar-like concoctions to their elderly victims' gravel driveways. Some simply roll asphalt shavings (a byproduct of removing and grinding up old asphalt road surfaces—black sand, basically) onto their victims' driveways, tell them it is fresh asphalt pavement and warn them not to drive on it for five days so that it can "cure." As soon as rainwater or a vehicle passes over the surface, it crumbles away. Most modern-day paving scammers, however, lay and steamroll hot asphalt that is fresh from the asphalt plant. They might even do a passable job of it. But it is anything but cheap.

What is intriguing about driveway paving scammers is that so many of them reportedly are descended from landless groups from the British Isles or eastern Europe. Before some of them came to America, those groups reportedly made their livings by traveling from town to town and repairing things—and occasionally scamming the locals.

206

A good thing about driveway paving scammers is that they and their equipment are easy to spot when they work in an area. In addition, they seldom victimize the same homeowner more than once or twice. But that's where the positives end. Modern-day driveway paving scammers are audacious and efficient. A skillful paving fraudster can scam several homeowners in a day and pocket $20,000 to $30,000 before suppertime arrives. In North Carolina, we went to court against several such pavers.

Maybe it results from running the same old scam all day long for years and years and years, but driveway paving scammers, more so than other fraud artists, seem to find great sport in defying and confounding the law enforcement officials who take them on. When you serve them with a judge's restraining order limiting or outlawing their activities in your state, they might feign contrition and cooperation, but what they are thinking probably amounts to this: "Game on! Let's see how many times I can violate your little restraining order!"

Being served with a judge's restraining order and promptly violat-ing it must elevate them to superhero status in the eyes of their families and their paving scammer peers. After a while, whenever I obtained and served such an order on a paver, I assumed that I would be back in front of the same judge a few months later, asking him or her to hold the paver in contempt of court and throw him in jail for scamming more homeowners in the state.

There was one paving scammer, let's call him "Tommy C," against whom I obtained four contempt citations signed by three different judges. He was from Sanford, a town located in the geographic center of North Carolina. During the six years that I dealt with him, Tommy C also appeared to have homes in Landfall, a pricey gated community near Wrightsville Beach, North Carolina; in Grandover Resort, a posh golf course community just south of Greensboro; and on White Lake in a blue-collar vacation community near the coast, where he and his men reportedly would convene on Friday afternoons, have a big cookout, and divvy up all the cash that had been collected from elderly property owners during the week. During the final months that we dealt with Tommy C, he and his family resided in an expensive rental property near Myrtle Beach, South Carolina. He always seemed to be living the high life.

One of the reasons Tommy C could live like a rock star was the amount of money he could obtain per victim. Whereas most driveway scammers might score $1,000 to $5,000 per scam, Tommy could haul in four to five times that much. His basic technique was the same as the others: claim to have leftover asphalt, offer to pave their gravel driveway at cost and immediately lay down the asphalt with very little prep work to the existing driveway. But then, with incredible audacity, he would demand $8,000 to $15,000 from the startled homeowner.

What also differentiated Tommy C from the others was his charm and his research. Before striking a particular property owner, he might learn who her late husband or his late father might have been. "I was so sorry to learn that your father passed, sir. He was a very good man. We were very close. I worked for him back in…" It did not matter where the deceased loved one had worked or lived, Tommy had been his employee or colleague back in the day or had done a lot of paving work for his business. His sales pitch reportedly was loaded with contrived but seemingly sincere empathy and fondness. If the homeowner began telling a story about the deceased loved one, Tommy reportedly would insinuate himself into that story and ad lib: "Oh yes, he was like that! He and I used to have fun doing…"

Tommy would promise the best work plus free follow-up repairs if anything with the driveway job proved deficient. He would promise a special deal on the price "because your [father/brother/husband] meant so much to me." He barely gave the poor homeowner a chance to say no before directing his men to commence work.

Once the work was done, Tommy would spring his outrageous price on the victim. The homeowner would express shock and the crew members standing in the yard often would pretend to be angry or agitated. According to his victims, Tommy could switch from ingratiating charmer to terrifying menace in seconds. He never made direct threats, as far as we knew. Gesturing toward his angry crewmen was about as far as he went. But his sharp change in demeanor and appearance convinced many a frightened homeowner to issue him a check for $8,000 or $12,000 for a paving job that should have cost only a fraction as much.

Tommy usually showed only charm and contrition when he dealt with investigator Linda Matthews and me, but soon I learned what his victims meant when they claimed that he had spooked them into meeting his outrageous payment demands even though he never uttered a threat. Once, after I had filed a motion to hold him in contempt for violating a court injunction, his conversation with me veered into a discussion of my home in rural Chatham County. "Mr. Kirkman, that's such a beautiful home you have out near Jordan Lake. Beautiful wooded lot. Huge wrap-around porch with a big hammock hanging at the far end..." He described the outside of my home to a T. And he did it long before one could go on the Internet and find images of people's homes using programs such as Google Earth. He had driven 1.3 miles up our dead-end road and cased my place!

Tommy could deny that anything he said about my home was sinister or threatening, but his comment had its intended effect. It was as creepy and worrisome as the explicit death threats I received from certain other fraud artists over the years. I notified my superiors and my federal and state law enforcement colleagues of Tommy's comments so that they might know who to call upon if something ever happened to me, our house, its other occupants or our dogs. The one person I did not tell was my wife. She is a medical anthropologist with a Ph.D. She is also from the Missouri Ozarks, is an expert marksman and might have taken Tommy C on for making such a creepy comment about our home. You just don't mess with people from the Ozarks.

Jane Jones with the Cape Fear Valley Area Agency on Aging brought Tommy C to our attention in the spring of 2007, a couple of months before Linda Matthews and I learned about the horrific home repair scam against Carol and Tommy McPhaul described in Chapter 29. For years, Jane had been a key member of the previously mentioned North Carolina Senior Consumer Fraud Task Force. If a senior was defrauded in the Wilmington, North Carolina, area, Jane knew about it, and she knew which local law enforcement officials or district attorney needed to address it. She could get results for her people. She also was very active in educating local seniors about the many types of frauds and scams that were targeting them. She organized forums on senior fraud for businesses, law enforcement and the general community, and she did radio, TV and newspaper interviews on the topic. Jane also helped create a local theater group called The Rocking Chair Players that performed for older audiences, bringing the scams to life. (In the opposite end of the state, there is a similar group affiliated with the Asheville Community Theater known as The Autumn Players. Its senior fraud presentations are coordinated by Roger Bargainnier.)

Jane called one day to report that deputies in Wilmington had charged Tommy with approximately two dozen counts of failing to notify homeowners of their unconditional three-day right to cancel a door-to-door sale. That legal requirement is found in Section 14-401(13) of the North Carolina criminal code.[1] The statute also requires that both a verbal and a written notification be given to the buyer so that he or she might cancel the deal easily and without penalty. The statute further requires that two copies of a simple-to-execute Notice of Cancellation be attached to the contract, together with the seller's business address, so one can communicate the cancellation decision to the seller. Violations of that statute are misdemeanors.

Like practically every other driveway paving scammer, Tommy never gave the three-day cancellation notices to his customers back then. Giving them and then waiting three days to start paving would have totally defeated the sales pitch, which involved urgency ("the hot asphalt will cool and go bad soon"), a rushed decision by the homeowner, quickly laying down the asphalt, and immediately receiving and cashing the customer's check. The statute was drafted with driveway paving scammers in mind and its whole purpose was to give customers a three-day cooling-off period during which they could get bids from other companies and make a final decision without the pressure and drama of a pushy salesman.

After bringing the two dozen misdemeanor charges for violating the three-day cancellation statute, New Hanover County sheriff's detectives Craig Springer and Craig Bredenbach secured warrants for Tommy's arrest and had him detained by authorities in Florida. They drove to the Sunshine State, took him into custody and transported him back to Wilmington. The two dozen homeowners, most of them from the same neighborhood, confronted Tommy C in New Hanover County District Court. They claimed they had been overcharged for the paving work. Many of the newly paved driveways allegedly violated local codes because of the way they connected with the public streets. In addition, some homeowners complained of defects and deficiencies in the work.

The court found Tommy guilty of multiple counts of violating North Carolina General Statute § 14-401(13) and had the bailiff escort him away for a brief visit to the New Hanover County jail. The judge also ordered him to make restitution to the homeowners. Tommy would not be coming back to scam seniors in New Hanover County, North Carolina, thanks to detectives Springer and Bredenbach. But that meant absolutely nothing for elderly homeowners in North Carolina's other 99 counties.

When we learned about these Wilmington charges, Linda Matthews searched for complaints against Tommy that had been filed with the

Attorney General's Office. She found a few, including one from 2004 where investigator Jane Feather had mailed Tommy a copy of North Carolina General Statute § 14-401(13) together with a cover letter warning him to give the required three-day cancellation notices in all future transactions with homeowners. Not surprisingly, Tommy C had ignored Jane's warning.

Because he had been put on notice of the statute and had repeatedly violated it when he went through that neighborhood in Wilmington, the attorney general had statutory power[2] to seek an order from a Superior Court judge requiring Tommy C to pay a penalty of up to $5,000 for each subsequent violation he committed anywhere in the state. Such an order could also require him to refund the payments made by those other North Carolina homeowners since 2003 and to go to jail if there were any future violations. We quickly obtained the go-ahead from Attorney General Roy Cooper to file suit against Tommy C and ask the court to do just that.

Linda collected sworn affidavits from several homeowners around the state describing their treatment at the hands of Tommy. I drafted a deceptive trade practices lawsuit against him and attached the affidavits and copies of the 24 misdemeanor warrants that had been issued against him in Wilmington. Then we filed it at the Wake County courthouse.[3] Assistant Trial Court Administrator Michelle Bailey scheduled a hearing in front of Judge Donald Stephens the next day on our request for a temporary restraining order. I then faxed a notice of the hearing to Tommy.

Tommy's lawyer quickly called and said that his client would consent to the entry of a preliminary injunction requiring him to give homeowners the three-day cancellation notices and to comply with other conditions designed to prevent deception and to ensure all paving jobs were performed correctly. Judge Stephens then signed and entered the agreed-upon injunction. Its requirements would remain in effect until the completion of the trial, probably a year or two later. Attorney General Cooper's press officer, Noelle Talley, issued a press release concerning the case and the preliminary injunction and it made the six o'clock evening news on television stations throughout central and eastern North Carolina.

As usually happened when we filed such a case, defendant Tommy C and his attorney soon showed up in our office seeking to negotiate terms of a final settlement that would not be too onerous. The attorney was an older gentleman from Whiteville, North Carolina, whose first reaction to

Linda when he shook her hand was a penetrating stare and the flirtatious comment "Y'ur purdy!" She never got over that sexist declaration.

Linda never got over her initial impression of Tommy C either. He was obsequious, deferential and fairly charming during the meeting. He repeatedly told us how much he respected our office and the work that it did, how terrible he felt because so many people thought he had deceived or pressured them, and how he would be glad to refund their money and do whatever it took not to get sideways with our office in the future.

Linda was not buying any of it. Someone who made his living scamming seniors was never going to have her trust.

"I despise that man!" she told me during a break. "He's trying to butter us up so he can go out there and scam older folks all over again. That's probably the same phony sweetness and charm that he uses on them."

Linda's assessment of Tommy proved to be right on the money.

As often happens with driveway paving scammers when the attorney general sues them, Tommy claimed he did not have records of other North Carolina property owners whose driveways he had paved. I cannot recall what his excuse was exactly. Usually a fire or computer crash is the supposed culprit when a defendant maintains his business records are lost. Nor could Tommy recall off the top of his head doing business with any North Carolina homeowners *other* than the individuals who signed affidavits for us. That, too, is a common claim whenever one goes after a driveway paving or home repair scammer ("Oh, I think you've done a good job finding all my customers!"). Since he was not going to help us locate additional victims, Linda and I decided we would wait to see how many of them came forward as a result of all the news coverage. Then we would demand that Tommy C make them whole as well.

The main thing we insisted be included in the final settlement was a requirement that Tommy C and his men always give the verbal and written three-day cancellation notices that are called for in the statute. We had no choice but to demand that, since neither the attorney general nor the court can allow a defendant to ignore the mandates of a statute. Tommy understood we could not relieve him of his statutory duty. He went even further, telling us, "I cannot do business in North Carolina if I have to follow the three-day cancellation law. Too many customers will cancel on me. I will simply leave the state and probably go down to South Carolina when the injunction gets signed."

That suited us just fine. Bye, Tommy!

It was not too much later that the case was settled with the help of a court-appointed mediator. Tommy agreed to be bound by a court injunction compelling him to give all the disclosures and forms called for in North Carolina's three-day cancellation statute. He would also pay civil penalties and make restitution to homeowners who had registered complaints with the attorney general. This financial obligation would be satisfied via monthly installment payments made to the attorney general over the course of a year.

Sure enough, Tommy C and his family moved to South Carolina. Reports of him operating in our state ceased. I received a check from his wife each month in the amount of the agreed-upon installment payments. Linda and I concluded that we had rid North Carolina seniors of Tommy C and his driveway paving scams and that he would now be the problem of authorities in South Carolina.

38

Tommy C Is Back

About 18 months after we thought we had rid North Carolina of driveway paver Tommy C, news arrived that he was back in the state and running his paving schemes just like before. This time, however, he was actually disclosing to homeowners that they had three days in which to cancel the contract, and he was giving them the printed notifications and cancellation forms that were required by statute and by the court's earlier injunction. The problem was that he reportedly failed to provide those documents and disclosures until after the driveways were paved with freshly rolled, steaming asphalt. Plus, he was still commencing work immediately rather than waiting three days. Once the asphalt was down, homeowners reasonably assumed that they could not cancel. The way the statute was written, however, they could still cancel, and any contractor who commenced work on a job solicited at the customer's home before three days had passed did so at his financial peril. But Tommy was not going to suggest that to the homeowners.

Linda Matthews and I notified Tommy C's attorney that we would go back to court and ask the judge to amend his injunction to include a provision requiring him to wait until the fourth business day before commencing any work on a homeowner's driveway. No more paving right away and making homeowners think they had waived their right to cancel. We would also ask the judge to order restitution for the homeowners in question. As our appointment date with the judge drew closer, Tommy and his attorney agreed to those conditions, and we were able to get the injunction changed without a hearing.

Tommy told us that this time he really, really would be pulling out of North Carolina. These newest conditions were way too onerous for him. He congratulated us. I thought that two years of annoyance and frustration with this clown had concluded on a positive note.

Linda Matthews' reaction to this turn of events, however, was the same as when she first met Tommy. "I despise that man! He'll violate this new court order too."

As it turns out, Tommy C's paving practices got him into trouble with authorities in South Carolina. That must have been why he had returned to North Carolina. After tangling with us that second time in 2009, he moved his paving business to Maryland and quickly faced legal problems in Ann Arundel County. Unlike North Carolina, which allows any crook or yahoo to perform work on somebody's property without a state contractor's license so long as he does not charge more than $30,000, Maryland's law required that Tommy have a state contractor's license regardless of the costs of his paving jobs. He never obtained one. His problems in Maryland were heavily covered by the local press and caused him to flee that state for a while. I do not know whether Virginia's large colony of paving scammers or laws governing paving contractors discouraged him from setting up shop there, but he avoided Virginia and headed straight back to North Carolina for a third go at our citizens.

We learned of Tommy's reappearance in early 2010. Linda Matthews fielded four complaints against him that were registered by homeowners in Harnett and Johnston counties, both just east of Tommy's hometown of Sanford. He did not wait until the fourth business day before he paved those elderly homeowners' driveways, which was what the latest North Carolina court injunction required. Linda also learned from local law enforcement officials in Sanford that Tommy's vehicles and paving equipment were being stored there at night and on weekends.

Based upon these four complaints, we persuaded Superior Court Judge William Pittman to cite Tommy C for civil contempt of court. Judge Pittman's contempt citation required Tommy to appear on May 24, 2010, to "show cause" why he should not be put in jail for violating the injunction. Tommy hired a Raleigh attorney and that attorney got the contempt hearing postponed until June 7 so he could finish a trial that was already on his schedule and then get up to speed on Tommy's case.

The problem that caused for me was that June 7 would be my first day back from a 10-day trip to Italy with my wife and our two lovely nieces. I would have to do the witness preparations and draft all my trial briefs before leaving, and when I got back, I would just have to wing it on any developments that had popped up in the case while I was living "la dolce vita" over in Italy. Mainly, I was annoyed that I might fret over the hearing while I was on vacation due to the expected presence of TV news reporters and their cameramen in the courtroom.

The good thing about obtaining a "show cause" order against a defendant is that the court already has made a preliminary determination that the defendant has violated one of its orders. Most judges do not require further evidence from the party seeking punishment for contempt. Instead, as the phrase "show cause" implies, the judge gives the offending party an opportunity to explain himself. If that party cannot provide proof that he never knowingly violated the order, he goes to jail. Contempt of court hearings are about vindicating the court's authority and powers, and most judges conducting a contempt hearing are going to guard that authority and those powers jealously. Tommy C was going to have a hard time showing that his violations of the court's injunction were unknowing or unintentional.

Whenever worries about the upcoming contempt hearing crept into my consciousness while I was away on vacation, I told myself that I would merely be a jet-lagged spectator at that proceeding, that there was nothing more for me to do or stress over. In those instances where I just could not persuade myself to stop worrying about it, I would fire off an email to Linda seeking updates on the four victims' ability to come to court the morning of the 7th, just in case the judge wanted us to put them on the stand and take their testimony. Linda would reply promptly, assuring me that each victim was going to make it and that each was looking forward to telling the judge their story.

If I had been a private attorney preparing for the upcoming contempt hearing during my vacation, I could have billed my client hundreds of dollars per hour for those efforts. That would have taken some of the sting out of having to work on the damned Tommy C case while hanging out in Rome or Florence. As a government attorney, however, I was entitled to no compensation for those spoiled vacation moments.

I arrived in the courtroom on the 7th so jet lagged that I could barely put together a thought. Tommy and his new attorney were there. So were the victims and their families. And so were the TV cameras. Presiding that morning was Judge Robert Hobgood, a calm, experienced jurist from nearby Vance County who was as decisive as he was low-key. I knew from previous cases that violations of court injunctions displeased Judge Hobgood greatly. For these reasons, I was relieved to see him up there on the judge's bench.

It was also a relief *not* to see a certain judge who regularly presided in Wake County Superior Court. That judge was no fan of the state or the Attorney General's Office. I had lost several hearings in front of him that would have been easy victories if the presiding judge had been anyone else. Part of what worried me so much during the Italy trip was the substantial possibility that we would draw that other judge. With him on the bench, I probably would be humiliated in court that morning with all the Raleigh trial lawyers looking on, then humiliated again that evening when the story aired on the local TV news. Plus, Tommy C would feel he had a free pass to scam anyone in North Carolina.

Judge Hobgood heard a few motions in other cases, then called our case for hearing. The TV cameras sprang to life. Tommy's counsel and I introduced ourselves and stated that we were ready to proceed. Judge Hobgood replied, "Thank you, counsel. I have read the pleadings, the homeowners' sworn affidavits and Judge Pittman's contempt citation. Mr. Kirkman, is there anything further you would like to add?"

That question was a relief. It was courtroom code for "I just want to hear how the other side is going to explain all this." I would not have to spend the morning examining witnesses, making and meeting objections, and going through the series of court orders and injunctions that Tommy had violated, all while my jet-lagged brain was stuck in low gear.

I thanked Judge Hobgood and took a moment to introduce our four sets of victims seated in the back of the courtroom. Two of them were Patricia Odom and her husband, who had paid Tommy $11,000 for a driveway paving job that quickly began to deteriorate. I told Judge Hobgood that all of the victims were happy to answer any questions he might have. Then I sat down and settled in for the show.

The proceeding was fun to watch. Judge Hobgood greeted each of the homeowners and thanked them for their affidavits and their presence in court. He said he did not need for them to take the stand. Tommy was visibly nervous at this point and so was his attorney. The attorney collected himself and launched into his pitch, quickly acknowledging the obvious fact that the injunction had been violated. He offered to have his client refund the victims' money in order to "purge" himself of contempt.

In civil contempt proceedings, the person being punished can get out of (or stay out of) jail by "purging" himself of the contemptuous conduct that violated the court order in the first place. If he had violated an order to turn over property or disclose information, he could "purge" himself of contempt by finally complying. If he refused, he or she could just stay in jail indefinitely. The only way one might purge himself or herself after violating an order not to enter into certain types of transactions with consumers is to give the consumers all of their money back. Tommy had collected just under $28,000 from the Odoms and the other three victims, and he was offering to pay it all back.

Tommy C's attorney asked that he be given 60 days to come up with the money and repay the four victims. His client probably had the ability to repay the money then and there, but I had no way of proving it. I urged Judge Hobgood to give him only 10 days to repay, hoping that he would compromise at 30. That is exactly what he did.

I also asked Judge Hobgood to ban Tommy permanently from offering or soliciting to perform residential driveway paving jobs in North Carolina, since he had ignored the conditions placed upon him in earlier court injunctions. Judge Hobgood agreed to that, too, and dictated his order into the record right there on the spot. Tommy could never again offer or perform residential driveway paving services in North Carolina, and he would pay the $28,000 into the Clerk of Court's Office for the benefit of the homeowners on or before July 7. Violation of either requirement would result in his imprisonment in the Wake County jail.

Linda watched as Tommy C and his wife left the courtroom. She was happy with Judge Hobgood's ruling but not at all charitable about Tommy's intentions to comply.

"I bet he violates that order too."

Patricia Odom was more positive about the outcome. She told the TV reporter from WTVD News, Diane Wilson, "I'm very happy with it and if he doesn't pay, he gets jail time."[1]

On the date by which Tommy C was supposed to pay the victims' money to the clerk of court, a deputy clerk called me. "Mr. Kirkman, one of Mr. C's men is down here attempting to pay the money for those homeowners, but Judge Hobgood's order explicitly states that Tommy C must pay it by today or go to jail. I don't think I have the option to accept the money from a third party."

I thought about how Tommy had prided himself on defying the law, multiple court orders and the standards of human decency in order to scam all those older North Carolina property owners. I remembered his creepy comments about my home in the woods near Jordan Lake and the disruptions he had recently caused to my much-needed overseas vacation. I knew that what I said next could result in Tommy being picked up and taken to the Wake County jail for not obeying the latest court order.

Then I thought about the homeowners who needed their money back.

"Please go ahead and accept the funds from Mr. C's employee. I will take the heat from Judge Hobgood if that displeases him."

The money was accepted by the clerk of court and promptly disbursed to the victims. Judge Hobgood never registered any displeasure with the arrangement. With equal promptness, Tommy violated the ban on his performing or soliciting any more driveway paving contracts in North Carolina by paving the narrow 35-foot driveway of one of my elderly neighbors, Mrs. R. He charged her $8,000. It would be several months before that "in your face, Mr. Kirkman" paving job would come to our attention.

39

Cat and Mouse with Tommy C

By early 2011, Tommy C was facing trial on serious felony charges in both Maryland and South Carolina. In addition, a task force of state and federal officials in North Carolina was working to bring serious criminal charges against him. That North Carolina federal-state initiative began in 2007, shortly after I sent Kevin Anderson of the IRS' criminal division photographs of one of Tommy's Friday evening cookouts near White Lake. This was where he divvied up shares of his weekly cash haul to his men. The initial focus of the task force was whether Tommy was declaring all of this cash income on his income tax forms.

There were scores of cases during my career where my North Carolina AG colleagues and I would put fraud artists out of business quickly with civil restraining orders and court injunctions while criminal authorities built their own cases. Eventually, sometimes months or years later, the criminal investigations would result in the defendant being taken to prison. During most of the months and years that I dealt with him, my enforcement actions against Tommy were intended to shut him down and recover money for his North Carolina victims before the federal-state task force put him away.

Kevin Anderson couldn't tell me exactly what was happening with the task force's investigation because I was not one of the criminal prosecutors assigned to the case. Federal investigators are like that. They must adhere to strict confidentiality rules, especially when it comes to evidence and charges being considered by a grand jury. Even though I was a state official handling a parallel civil case against Tommy, I was not entitled to know what was going on with the federal criminal case. Nevertheless, Kevin repeatedly made it clear that Tommy was in big trouble and that charges would come soon. So, throughout the 2007 to 2010 time period,

I operated under the assumption that Tommy would be in federal prison any week now.

But here we were in 2011 with reports coming in that Tommy C recently had ripped off a retired college professor in Greensboro for $78,000 as well as my neighbor down the road, Mrs. R, who paid him $8,000 just weeks after Judge Hobgood banned him from offering or doing paving work in North Carolina. The professor's job involved a driveway over a hundred yards long, while Mrs. R's driveway was only a few yards long.

I petitioned the state court to issue another contempt citation against Tommy C. Superior Court Judge Michael O'Foghludha signed the contempt citation and ordered Tommy once again to "appear and show cause" why he should not be punished for violating the statewide driveway paving ban that Judge Hobgood had ordered the previous June.

When the show-cause hearing commenced, our two victims, Tommy's lawyer, and Linda Matthews and I were present. Unlike the previous summer's contempt hearing, Tommy was a no-show. After hearing the evidence against Tommy, Judge O'Foghludha not only found him in civil contempt for violating Judge Hobgood's statewide paving ban, but he also found him in criminal contempt for not showing up that day. He ordered Tommy's immediate arrest. The pick-up order was entered into criminal law enforcement databases and probably would result in Tommy's arrest the next time he returned to North Carolina to escape problems in other states.

The order also required that Tommy be held in jail on the civil contempt finding until he could "purge" himself of his misconduct by refunding $86,000 in damages to our two victims. The additional punishment for criminal contempt would be determined once he was brought before the court.

With an order for his arrest hanging over him, North Carolina then experienced another multi-month lull in Tommy C scam activity. The action shifted back to Maryland where Tommy's criminal trial was underway. Maryland prosecutor Marot Hoskins kept us posted on events in that case. She called one day to report that Tommy had been found guilty and sentenced to two years in prison. He probably would be freed after serving one year. Upon hearing that news, I was ready to close our file on Tommy C. After all, the feds here in North Carolina likely would be charging him with some pretty serious stuff before he ever got out of prison in Maryland.

Tommy C did, in fact, get out of prison in Maryland about a year later and he did return to North Carolina. And sure enough, he was picked up in late February of 2012 pursuant to Judge O'Foghludha's arrest order. I heard about the arrest one Monday morning as I arrived at work and received a call from one of the local assistant DAs.

"We've got this guy Tommy C in the Wake County jail. He's scheduled to appear this morning before Judge O'Foghludha pursuant to your 2011 contempt order. Since this is an attorney general case and not one of ours, you'll have to handle it."

"No problem. When does Judge O'Foghludha start court today?"

"He calls his calendar at 10."

"We'll be right there."

I swung by Linda Matthews' office and interrupted her. "Tommy was picked up last night and will appear before Judge O'Foghludha in 45 minutes. Let's go!"

Linda was only too happy to oblige. She was ready to see Tommy squirm.

I also placed a quick call to Kevin Anderson of the IRS and told him what was up. He said, "That's great. Our case against him should move real soon."

"How soon is 'real soon'?"

"A few of weeks at most. I think his scamming days are finally over. Wish I could tell you more."

I had no reason to doubt Kevin, despite the incredibly drawn out nature of the federal investigation. Previously, whenever he told me that charges were coming against other suspects, the charges came down fairly quickly. It had been explained to me that everything in Tommy's case had to go through special vetting in Washington, D.C., due to the fact that tax charges were involved and tax prosecutions were under heavy scrutiny in Congress. Had the case arisen a few years earlier, charges would have come quickly. Tommy had been the beneficiary of an anti–IRS frenzy that had gripped the nation's capital.

When Judge O'Foghludha saw Linda Matthews and me enter his courtroom with Tommy and his attorney, he flashed a grin.

"What brings this fine group back before me? Has Mr. C shown up in North Carolina again?"

I responded, "Yes, Your Honor. He was picked up on your contempt order last night. The clerk is sending the file down from the eleventh floor."

Judge O'Foghludha did not need to review the file. He seemed to remember everything about the case and Tommy's no-show at his show-cause hearing 10 months earlier. His readiness to punish Tommy's contempt was unmistakable.

Tommy's attorney stated that he needed to confer with his client and then with me. Judge O'Foghludha obliged this request and proceeded to deal with other cases on his calendar.

After conferring with his client, Tommy's attorney summoned me into the hallway.

"Tommy is willing to accept his punishment on the criminal contempt. By statute, it can't be more than 30 days. But he does want me to ask the court for some additional time to collect the $86,000 so that he can purge himself of the civil contempt. If he can't purge the civil contempt, he'll be in jail indefinitely. Basically, we want a postponement of today's hearing. Are you okay with that?"

"Not really. How much of a postponement is he talking?"

"A month. He needs to sell some property and call in some loans. With the IRS all over his butt, that kind of stuff takes a lot of time."

I thought about our two victims and the $86,000 they had lost. It would be so sweet if Tommy paid them back just before the feds arrested him. On the other hand, if he were to go to jail now on Judge O'Foghludha's contempt finding and then get hammered with federal indictments before he could pay, our victims would never see a cent.

"If you want to propose that to the judge, I won't oppose it."

When we went back into the courtroom, Judge O'Foghludha summoned us to the bench and asked if we were ready to proceed. Tommy's attorney made his proposal for a continuance. Judge O'Foghludha winced and looked at me.

"You really think he's going to repay those people?"

"Oh, I will, Your Honor!" Tommy replied.

His lawyer chimed in. "There's a lot going on in the background here, Your Honor. My client has every reason to comply."

"What say you, Mr. Kirkman?"

It took me several seconds to respond. "The State doesn't oppose the request, Your Honor. I will leave it at that."

"This probably is a mistake, but okay. Madame Clerk, the defendant's unopposed request in case number 07 CVS 07752 to postpone this hearing for 30 days is hereby granted so that he can arrange payment to the victims. Defendant is released from custody upon his cash bond of $30,000. All prior orders and injunctions remain in effect, including the injunction against offering or performing residential paving services in the state of North Carolina."

"Do you understand those conditions, sir?"

"I do, Your Honor. Thank you! Thank you! And thank you, Mr. Kirkman. Thank you, sir!"

As we headed back to the office, Linda's displeasure was written across her face. She knew Tommy had gotten over on the court and me. But she was not going to say anything.

I just kept telling myself, "There's no downside to this. Tommy C's butt will be in federal custody soon enough."

40

Famous Last Words
About Tommy C

"Tommy C's butt will be in federal custody soon enough."

Soon after I uttered those words of assurance to myself in the spring of 2012, Tommy C wrought his revenge upon the good people of North Carolina.

It took us a few weeks to find out, but soon after Judge O'Foghludha freed him so he could arrange to repay our two victims (with my ill-advised acquiescence), Tommy began running his driveway paving scams on older homeowners in the towns of Zebulon, Knightdale and Wendell, just outside of Raleigh. We first learned of it from employees at the State Employees' Credit Union (SECU) who had attended our training sessions on how bank personnel could spot and interrupt elder fraud incidents in progress. We had employed photographs and court documents from our case against Tommy C during those SECU trainings, so those employees were primed to respond if and when he showed up to cash his victims' checks.

"David, Tommy C was just in our branch trying to cash two checks from one of my elderly members. The total amount was $10,000. The notations on the checks said 'paving.' I told him I would need to speak with our member before cashing the checks and I immediately walked back here to my office and called you."

"Is Tommy still there?"

"No. He bolted."

SECU saved that particular customer from losing $10,000, but they soon determined that Tommy had managed to scam four of their other customers. First Citizens' Bank called and reported that one of their older customers had been taken as well. That was six new violations of Judge Hobgood's ban on further paving activities in the state.

One of these elderly homeowners paid Tommy $18,000 for paving a relatively small driveway. He felt he needed to pay that amount after Tommy and his men suddenly grew angry at him for questioning the $18,000 figure after earlier being told the job would cost next to nothing.

Another of these homeowners did not have enough funds in his bank account to pay the price that Tommy had sprung on him after laying down the asphalt. Tommy was unfazed by this. Noticing a nice motor home in the customer's back yard, Tommy told him he would accept that as payment for the paving job until the customer could come up with the cash. The homeowner obliged, gave Tommy the keys, then watched him drive away with his $35,000 motor home.

Linda Matthews immediately set to work interviewing the half-dozen new victims and drafting their written affidavits. I drafted a motion asking Judge O'Foghludha to revoke his order releasing Tommy and to hold him in contempt yet again for these six new violations of the court's orders. When it came time for her to type, copy and go file the motion and supporting documentation with the court, my longtime legal assistant, Kittrell Hinton, asked me, "Is it ever going to end with this man? I've been typing his name on court papers for five years now."

A few days later, I found in my mailbox a notice that Tommy C had filed for bankruptcy protection in the United States Bankruptcy Court for the Middle District of North Carolina. The notice warned that any attempt to collect money from him outside of the bankruptcy court would be punishable under federal law. Tommy's bankruptcy lawyer had also filed a copy of that notice with the Wake County Superior Court in the civil case where we were asking that he be held in contempt and jailed until he repaid all those homeowners.

I contacted Tommy's bankruptcy attorney and reminded him that bankruptcy laws did not prevent a state law enforcement official like the attorney general from enforcing the laws of the state and that we still intended to punish his client's contempt of court. He suggested that our proceeding further against his client would be punished by the United States Bankruptcy Court.

Judge O'Foghludha was holding court in a different county when our state court motion came on for hearing. Superior Court Judge Paul Ridgeway, a relatively new judge with years of experience as a trial lawyer, was assigned to hear our request. Judge Ridgeway knew that the federal bankruptcy laws did not prevent the state of North Carolina and judges like him from punishing violations of state statutes or state court orders banning certain conduct.

To be on the safe side and avoid entanglement with the federal bankruptcy court, however, Judge Ridgeway chose to treat the latest violations as six acts of criminal contempt of court rather than pursue them as civil contempt. The latter might cause the bankruptcy court to view the entire exercise as nothing more than an attempt to collect a civil debt from Tommy outside of the bankruptcy proceeding—a violation of federal bankruptcy laws which would trigger severe sanctions. The downside of treating Tommy's violations as criminal contempt of court rather than civil contempt, however, was the fact that only civil contempt allowed the state court to hold Tommy in jail until the consumers were repaid. Criminal contempt would simply punish each violation of the paving ban with 30 days in jail.

After citing Tommy C for criminal contempt, Judge Ridgeway reordered his arrest. Once again, I made sure that the order was "in the system" so that law enforcement could detain him. Then we waited.

In the meantime, Linda Matthews received word from one of her law enforcement contacts in Tommy's hometown of Sanford, North Carolina, that our victim's motor home was parked there. She arranged for the victim to go pick it up. When he did so, he noticed that it had been filled with food and other provisions, children's toys, flat screen TVs and a wooden sign proclaiming Tommy's family name and hometown. The vehicle appeared totally prepped for a tour of America's RV parks.

The homeowner drove the vehicle straight to the Attorney General's Office. Linda, Bill Bennington and I unloaded Tommy's belongings from the motor home, then cataloged them and placed them in storage. Then Linda arranged for Mrs. C to come and retrieve it all. According to Linda, Mrs. C was not exactly smiles and kisses when she arrived. According to other AG employees who were there for the handover, Linda held her tongue nicely, but she definitely won the brief battle of contemptuous stares.

As the weeks went by, we noticed that no further reports of Tommy C paving scams were coming in. We were hopeful that he had once again left the state or was otherwise lying low. Perhaps he and his family had acquired another RV and were camping in an RV park in another state.

Then Linda received a call from a South Carolina police official in a coastal community just below the North Carolina line. He told her that

Tommy C was residing in a rather nice piece of rental property there and doing paving jobs in the area. He even sent us a picture of the rental property. It seemed far nicer than any resort rental property that one of us government employees could ever afford—even if just for a week. Linda told him about the pick-up order that was outstanding in North Carolina, and she also told him that his counterparts just a couple of counties over were asking if we knew of Tommy's whereabouts, that he was soon scheduled to appear in court in a case involving elderly South Carolina homeowners—a case first filed after our efforts caused him to leave North Carolina in 2008. Tommy apparently had not been reporting his whereabouts to South Carolina court officials as required and they had been looking for him.

Both the South Carolina law enforcement agency that had found Tommy and the one that was looking for him were happy when Linda put them in contact with one another. She was happy with herself, too, and justifiably so.

And then the happiness grew and grew. Kevin Anderson called to give me an update on the efforts of his IRS, U.S. Justice Department and North Carolina State Bureau of Investigation task force. "Hey, Dave, Tommy is in federal custody. The charges are bank fraud, tax evasion and 'structuring.' He's facing some serious prison time."

It was now August of 2012. Almost six whole summers had gone by since Linda and I first went to court to get Tommy C to clean up his act. We had expected the initiative to conclude quickly and successfully. But unbridled audacity mixed with contempt for court orders and injunctions had enabled Tommy C to keep preying on elderly homeowners throughout that five-year period.

In April of 2014, Tommy C was sentenced to 66 months in federal prison.[1] He was released in the spring of 2018. In August of 2018, I received word that Tommy C had approached one of his former North Carolina customers about paving his driveway—another apparent violation of Judge Hobgood's June 2010 order banning him from offering or performing such services in North Carolina ever again. It also appeared to violate the terms of his federal probation. State and federal investigators sprang into action. State criminal charges were filed against him by the Wake County DA. The feds moved to have his probation revoked in their case.

On March 13, 2019, I received the following email from the IRS's Kevin Anderson:

FYI

[Tommy C] was sentenced today to an active prison term of 20 months to be followed by 40 months of supervised release for violating the terms of his supervised release from the first Federal charges.

KA

PART ELEVEN

More and More

41

Romance Scams:
What Percy Sledge Said

Not all senior scams target individuals who are 75 or older. Take romance scams, for instance. Most of the romance scam victims that my colleagues and I worked with ranged in age from 60 to 75. Few of the 12 common vulnerabilities that fraudsters look for in older individuals were present—usually just loneliness and a healthy retirement fund.

Homer's Greek epic *The Odyssey* featured numerous passages about Odysseus' wife Penelope having her home and her personal life overrun by a horde of ill-intentioned suitors after her man failed to return from the Trojan War. The suitors were so out of control that Odysseus had to sneak into his own home and slay them once he finally returned from his years of travel and travail. Homer's tale suggests that well-to-do widows—or thought-to-be widows, in Penelope's case—were prized targets of schemers even 3,000 years ago. Since the days of Homer, innumerable books, plays, television programs and movies have featured stories of older individuals losing their mates and being preyed upon by younger pseudo-suitors ("gold diggers") intent upon separating them from their property and savings.

In the North Carolina Attorney General's Elder Fraud Unit, romance scams were the toughest of all to deal with. A key reason for this was the six to seven figure losses our victims often incurred. The main reason, however, was the Herculean struggle necessary to separate those victims from their phony love interests and halt the loss of money and personal dignity.

We were not alone in feeling frustrated. Family members, close friends, clergy, banking and financial professionals, local law enforcement officials and others who cared about those victims were stymied

232

and flabbergasted by their tenacious loyalty to their victimizers and by their refusal to heed perfectly reasonable warnings about romantic relationships with total strangers, some of whom seemed to exist only on the Internet or over the phone. The victims often responded to everyone's well-intentioned pleas and warnings with hostility, resentment and the abandonment of long-established personal relationships. Singer Percy Sledge described this victim behavior in a verse of his 1966 classic "When a Man Loves a Woman": he is blind to her motives and does not believe anyone when they try to tell him she's not what he thinks she is.

Investigator Dorothy Strickland of our office once worked with a romance scam victim from a small county not far from Winston-Salem, North Carolina. Let's call her "Mrs. L." A widow, Mrs. L was befriended by her victimizer when she went on a dating website for single seniors. The victimizer claimed to be from Texas and told her he was a contractor heading up a huge construction project in Nigeria. He sent her several pictures of himself, his overseas friends, his dog, his boat and his fabulous flat in the capital, Lagos. He regaled her with stories of how he had traveled the globe working on big projects. The online friendship quickly morphed into a romance. Soon Mrs. L was engaged to be married to this man with whom she exchanged photographs and romantic emails night and day. He promised her he was coming to North Carolina to marry her just as soon as the current construction project was done.

Then, as always happens with these frauds, the drama began. Mrs. L's fake fiancé told her that the Nigerian bank his business was using had frozen his accounts and was not processing payroll checks for his employees. He begged her to wire him $60,000 right away so he could meet his weekly payroll, otherwise his workers would walk off the job and the entire construction project would fail, leaving him bankrupt. He promised to return her $60,000 as soon as the mess with the bank was resolved.

Once the $60,000 was wired, the fake fiancé contacted Mrs. L claiming the bank account would remain frozen until he paid a bribe of $50,000 to the crooked bank official behind it all. Could she wire him that amount, please? The $50,000 would be returned along with the earlier $60,000 once the crooked banker was paid off. There were millions of dollars in the account, so immediate repayment would not be a problem. Mrs. L, now viewing herself as the heroine in a complicated international drama, was happy and excited to come to the rescue of her beloved yet again.

The drama didn't let up. Next, she learned that her fiancé was in a hospital in Lagos due to a serious auto accident. His injuries were severe, according to his assistant, and his doctors needed to be paid if he was to receive treatment. "Can you forward $75,000 to the doctors right away? Obviously, he cannot go to the bank and withdraw the money himself." She complied gladly. She felt needed and vitally important. Then came word that her fiancé had been charged with manslaughter in connection with the auto accident. "Can you send more money so we can hire him an attorney and post his bail?" Again, she complied.

As one calamity after another befell her beloved, Mrs. L complied with each urgent request for more funds. Suspicious about her wire transfer behaviors, the two major wire service companies and her bank of many years eventually stopped transferring money for her. Her new bank eventually took the same stance, as did the one after that. At that point, the scammers needed a new way to receive her funds. And they found one.

When Dorothy Strickland first learned about Mrs. L one April morning, it came in the form of a phone call to the Attorney General's Office from one of Mrs. L's friends. The friend said that Mrs. L had lost over half a million dollars already and was just now beginning a plane trip on U.S. Airways that would take her to meet her fiancé in Toronto, Canada. She was carrying $27,000 in cash in a carry-on bag. She had taken little else with her, not even a jacket or sweater.

Dorothy often worked with law enforcement officials in Toronto to fight sweepstakes and lottery scammers there, so she immediately contacted those officials in an effort to stop Mrs. L from being defrauded once again.

My response was to reach out to Deborah Thompson, a U.S. Airways executive from Winston-Salem who had worked with me on a case a year earlier. An older friend of hers who was in the early stages of dementia spent over $30,000 buying the same items of merchandise over and over from two prominent cable television sales networks. Deborah and I were able to recover most of her friend's money and get her blocked from making further purchases from the networks. When I told Deborah of Mrs. L's situation, she alerted U.S. Airways officials in Toronto to ensure that Mrs. L was met by them when she got off the plane.

Thanks to Dorothy and Deborah's efforts, Canadian passport control and customs officials were ready when Mrs. L deplaned with her $27,000 in cash. The U.S. Airways officials put her on a return flight to Greensboro and warned her against bringing such a large amount of cash on an international flight again. They also informed us that Mrs. L would not have lasted too long outside of the airline terminal dressed as if she were enjoying her garden in the sunny Carolinas. It was still rather cold in Toronto.

Mrs. L was not to be deterred from saving her man, however. Days after her Toronto rendezvous was spoiled, she embarked on a U.S. Airways trip to London. There she would meet her fiancé and hand him the cash he desperately needed to address the latest calamity. Her friend called us again. Dorothy, a London native, reached out to law enforcement contacts there, while I called Deborah Thompson once again. Fortunately, Mrs. L had only made it as far as Philadelphia, and Deborah got U.S. Airways officials to send her and her $27,000 in cash back home to North Carolina.

Mrs. L remained determined to help her man. A few weeks later we learned that she had left again for London the previous evening. Dorothy immediately called passport control in London, but Mrs. L had already passed through and was somewhere in the city. She never checked into the hotel listed on her visa entry card.

What probably was going to happen once Mrs. L got to wherever she was staying was this: one of the scammers would meet her in the hotel lobby or hotel restaurant and announce that her fiancé would be arriving later due to a flight delay or some other scheduling problem; then the scammer would ask for the money and tell her he was heading across the street to deposit it in her fiancé's bank account and the fiancé would be along any minute; then he would disappear with the cash and Mrs. L would be left alone until she figured out that the fiancé was never going to show. Nigerian scammers, a group to which these perpetrators belonged judging from Mrs. L's many, many wire transfer receipts, often resorted to this hotel lobby disappearing trick when their victims brought cash across the Atlantic.

Mrs. L returned to North Carolina a few days later, her carry-on bag still filled with the $35,000 in cash she had stuffed into it when she left home. No one ever met her at the hotel as promised. We do not know why. Whatever transpired, it seems that it burst the romantic narrative with which she had been totally obsessed for almost a year. Mrs. L realized, finally, that her fiancé never existed, that she had not been heroically coming to the rescue of her man and that she had been defrauded.

This was not the only time we contended with a repeat victim of romance scammers who flew overseas to meet the guy who had been professing his love for her. The year before we dealt with Mrs. L, elder fraud investigator Margrita Harrison worked with a woman, whom we shall call "Ms. W," who lived three or four counties west of Mrs. L. She had lost over $300,000 to a romance scammer based in Ghana. He, too, connected with her through a senior singles website and pretended to be a wealthy American businessman working in that country. The fraud narrative and the repeat victimizations unfolded just as they had in Mrs. L's case, and eventually Ms. W's banks and the two major wire service companies were refusing to send money overseas for her anymore.

But that is about as far as it went. Mrs. W finally figured out that her friends and family were right and that she was being played. She acquired evidence that her supposedly older, handsome, globetrotting American businessman fiancé was actually a Ghanaian university student.

So what did Ms. W do? She got mad, flew to Ghana, moved in with some missionary friends who were working there, and persuaded Ghanaian officials to bring charges against the student. After a few months, Ms. W needed to go home to North Carolina. Because her live testimony was vital to a successful prosecution, the prosecutors dropped the charges and released the student.

The following year, Margrita Harrison worked with a woman who had lost $1.2 million in a romance scam that lasted two years. She was our first $1,000,000-plus victim of any type of senior fraud. Her victimization had unfolded just like those of Mrs. L and Ms. W, only she never got on an overseas flight. She was a retired bank executive who thought she was romantically involved with an accomplished fellow American bank executive working on a huge project in the Middle East. He was charming in his emails and phone calls, looked handsome in his photographs and, most important, quite conversant in bank procedures, regulations and terminology. She mortgaged her home, drained her retirement and savings accounts, and maxed out her credit cards, all in the hopes of saving her imaginary fiancé from various catastrophes. When her money ran out, the phony fiancé disappeared from her life.

When Margrita first made contact with this poor woman, she was about to lose her home and was threatening suicide. Margrita did an admirable job of calming her down, helping her to save her home from foreclosure and helping her realize that many other bright and accomplished women had been taken in the same way. The suicide threats subsided. As you will learn later, we even recouped some of her losses.

One of the best ways to break female victims out of the powerful, romantic narratives in which they are ensnared is to acquire a copy of their fake fiancé's photo and run it through an online photo matching program like Google Images. Such programs often reveal that the photo was copied from an advertisement, a magazine feature on a French movie star or the Facebook page of a happily married guy who is not living or working overseas. Gently revealing the photo's origin to the victim often does the trick.

Before you conclude that only women fall for this crime, please know that large numbers of romance scam victims are men. Their losses are just as huge and their families are just as alarmed when they realize what is happening. The male victims are also every bit as uncooperative and resentful, if not more so, whenever someone tries to intervene and stop the never-ending cycle of fraud. The only real difference is that male victims tend to be defrauded by romance scammers face-to-face rather than online or over the phone.

There are actually organized groups that seek out and exploit widowed men just like there are for widowed women. Often, they are affiliated with the same itinerate groups that that pass through an area doing paving and other scams. Usually, however, a lone scammer will operate without much of a support network. Younger women who carry out these scams, and their collaborators, spot and befriend their targets by lurking on senior singles websites and chatrooms and by poring over obituary notices in newspapers. Sometimes they will spot potential targets at public libraries, senior centers or bars. They initiate friendships with their targets, then feign romantic feelings toward them, and eventually become engaged to them. Sometimes marriages even result.

Fairly quickly these male victims start lending money to, buying cars for, or transferring real estate to the younger female scammers. Handing over credit cards and cash is quite common. Sometimes the younger woman claims to have an investment or finance background and she persuades her mark to let her manage his assets and increase his investment returns. Then the assets start draining away.

Sex resolves any doubts that the target might entertain about the younger woman's true intentions and affections. Female scammers often employ sex early in the process. The fact that the scammer attends family gatherings and interacts with his adult children further reinforces his belief that she wants to be a part of his life. The family's assertions that she is not sincere just rile him up, causing him to disengage from them and resist with even more vehemence their warnings and predictions. The younger woman thereby achieves what all repeat victimization con artists strive for: separation of their marks from their support networks. She becomes the victim's one-person support network.

It is often said that, due to the chemicals it prompts the human body to produce, a newfound romance can be as powerfully satisfying and addictive as cocaine. In addition to the wisdom imparted earlier by Percy Sledge as to why victims of sweetheart scams resist the advice of friends and family members, in his 1986 hit "Addicted to Love," the late rock 'n' roller Robert Palmer added his own insights into the physical and emotional state of a male sweetheart scam victim: he is blind to what's going on. Palmer went on to describe the male sweetheart scam victim's usual fate in the refrain to his 1988 hit "Simply Irresistible": he is powerless to do anything about the situation, her power is that great.

The fact that several prominent older men have irresistible young girlfriends or wives makes it even harder for the targets of these frauds to accept what is really going on. Men with beautiful, much younger women tend to be powerful politicians or quite wealthy, or they may be stars in the fields of television, cinema, music or sports. None of our male victims fit those profiles. While some had good retirement savings and nice homes, none were anywhere close to landing on *Forbes* billionaires list or being elected to the U.S. Senate. That did not matter. They just knew that other older guys had acquired young wives or girlfriends, so who was to say that they were not virile and charming enough to do the same?

The few times that we succeeded in breaking up face-to-face romance scams involved fairly common situations where the female scammer also maintained her relationship with her actual boyfriend, who was totally in on the fraud. Helping the victim to learn about the boyfriend usually brought back the needed skepticism and awareness that he had so happily set aside when the hot young sweetheart came into his life. Sometimes private investigators hired by the adult children ferreted out the existence of those boyfriends. Sometimes local law enforcement knew that the younger woman lived with her boyfriend because they were both involved in other crimes, such as drugs or larceny. In a couple of cases, the young women's social media sites made it abundantly clear—even to the victims—that they were in romantic relationships with men their own age.

Letting a victim know that that his newfound girlfriend or fiancée had other older gentlemen boyfriends also did the trick. Accomplishing this usually required the assistance of private detectives, Adult Protective Service officials or local law enforcement officers who were onto the woman's other fake romances. In one instance, a credit union employee told us about a young woman coming in with two different older men on the same day to withdraw large sums of cash from their accounts. That information was put to good use.

Like their counterparts who scam women over the Internet, these face-to-face romance scammers seldom employ their real names. That hampers investigators. The scammer's photo is all they have to work from. Recently, some law enforcement agencies and private detectives have begun subscribing to services that can run a suspect's photo through powerful search engines and provide the identity of that individual in a matter of seconds. Such services also produce the individual's criminal record and aliases, links to his or her social media sites, full employment and education histories, and a wealth of other personal information. Currently, such services are not cheap. Nevertheless, in the coming years they may prove instrumental in persuading older men that their sexy young sweethearts are not the real deal after all.

In most of the cases that my staff and I handled, however, there was little that we or anyone else could do besides document the sweetheart scam. That information might prove helpful if and when another report came in against the same woman. Trying to convince the male victim that his relationship with the young woman was a sham on her part was like arguing with a political or religious extremist. They just were not going to believe us. They always had a comeback. And they would just get madder and madder the more we tried.

42

Threats

We now know that the elder fraud criminal's key tool is the exciting or alarming statement. It taxes the impaired abilities of some older individuals to process information quickly or make sound decisions under pressure. Threats, whether expressed or implied, can tax those impaired abilities to the fullest. The only question for the criminal is when to employ threats.

The phony IRS agent robo-calling from South Asia typically opens his scam with a threat. "A warrant for your immediate arrest for nonpayment of taxes has been issued. You will be taken to jail and your home and property seized. To avoid such proceedings, press 1 to speak with an agent..." With online sweetheart scams or over-the-phone grandparent scams, the threats to imprison or re-imprison the victim's loved one usually come after the first two or three payments have been made. Grandparent scammers, for example, might pretend that they are jailers. They will threaten to let other inmates beat, rape or kill the grandchild if more money is not wired immediately. The pretend grandchild can be heard in the background screaming and wailing as if being struck or strangled. With online sweetheart scams, a phony foreign government official will threaten to imprison the victim's online fiancé forever if thousands of dollars are not wired in the next couple of hours. It's powerful stuff.

Nigerian 419 money transfer scammers will employ threats once a victim is hundreds of thousands of dollars into a scam. They will lure victims overseas to "finalize the transaction," hold them against their will, then warn them they will never be allowed to return home unless even more money is transferred over from their U.S. accounts.

With traditional lottery and sweepstakes scams, direct threats often are employed when the victims begin to balk, either because they are growing wise to the fraud or because they have run out of money. The phony government lawyer might warn that the government will assume that the victim was participating in illegal money laundering—and will need to be arrested immediately—if she or he refuses to pay an additional $10,000 for a "money laundering audit" of the multi-million-dollar prize award.

Quite often, however, lottery and sweepstakes scammers pretend that they themselves will lose their jobs or their personally invested funds if the latest make-believe fee or tax is not paid. They express great anger at that prospect and threaten the victim with violence if they do not pay more.

Below is a partial transcript of a 15-minute phone conversation between a Carrboro, North Carolina, woman and an overseas sweepstakes scammer in 2009. She had already wired him thousands of dollars but was refusing to send him more. He then threatened to have her killed if she did not comply. She called the FBI and Special Agent Joan Fleming arrived in time to record the next call. The name "Mrs. Shaughnessy" is used in the transcript, although that is not the victim's real name. "Mrs. Shaughnessy" addresses the scammer as "Mr. U" in the actual recording because she could not pronounce his real name. Joan Fleming and I have played this recording while training law enforcement officials, bankers, doctors and other professionals on the tactics of the elder fraud industry. See what you think.

> [Mrs. Shaughnessy] I can't use the phone! It rings all the time. Your calling me's a scam. You've already told me they're out to murder me—they're gonna shoot me. And you told me you'd locked them up today, that I'd be safe…
>
> [Mr. U] Well, I'm gonna let them out. Yes. Listen, I'm gonna let them out.
>
> [Mrs. Shaughnessy] You're gonna let them out?
>
> [Mr. U] No. Listen! Those are my murderers. Whenever I tell them to go and murder someone they will go and murder them. I *pay* them. I have to give them lots of money.
>
> [Mrs. Shaughnessy] Sorry, I didn't understand that…. Oh, you *pay* them?
>
> [Mr. U] Yes. I can give them money to kill anyone I want to kill—anybody at all.
>
> [Mrs. Shaughnessy] How much money did you use?
>
> [Mr. U] Well, I can give them at least $30,000 U.S.
>
> [Mrs. Shaughnessy] Thirty thousand! Mr. U, you know you didn't!
>
> [Mr. U] Yes. They will kill you.
>
> [Mrs. Shaughnessy] Oh, mercy! No wonder my life's in danger.
>
> [Mr. U] Yes, they will kill you because I pay people to kill people. That's how I'm rich.

[MRS. SHAUGHNESSY] Oh, you paid that to get them to kill me, Mr. U?

[MR. U] Yes. I will pay them if you don't listen!

[MRS. SHAUGHNESSY] And you want me to do business with you when you've already threatened my life?

[MR. U] No ... if you don't listen ... if you do good business right now, they will not come after you. But if you do not, they gonna come after you.

[MRS. SHAUGHNESSY] All right, thank you, Mr. U, for the warning. I hear you. I heard you loud and clear. Thank you for the warning.

[MR. U] So, what I'm saying now, if you do the business and do the business right, so we can help you, everything will be fine. But if you do not do the business ...well.... I'ma have to give them thirty thousand to come and get you. And then...

[MRS. SHAUGHNESSY] ...You're going to give them thirty thousand to come get me and take my life?!?

[MR. U] Um ... yes. Because you...

[MRS. SHAUGHNESSY] ...Oh, Mr. U, I wish I'd never gotten involved in the scam. I've never had anything to upset me like this. Now I've got to go. I've got to go...

[MR. U] No!

[MRS. SHAUGHNESSY] I'm so nervous.... I'm so nervous. I've got to go see a doctor.

[MR. U] If you go, I'm sending them over to your house now if you go right now! Listen to what I have to say! If you listen, I will not make anything happen to you. But if you don't listen to me and hang up the phone, I'm gonna send them over right now! So it will be best for you to listen to what I have to say. Okay? All right?

[MRS. SHAUGHNESSY] I'm listening, Mr. U.

[MR. U] Just listen...

[MRS. SHAUGHNESSY] ...Save my life! Please, I beg you! Save my life!

[MR. U] All right, I'm going to save your life if you do what I said. But if you *don't* do what I said ... [*other men's voices audible*].... You hear that? You hear that?

[MRS. SHAUGHNESSY] What about what God said? You said you're a Christian. God tells me to get out of this mess!

[MR. U] All right, you want to talk to one of my murderers? He's right beside me right now.

[MRS. SHAUGHNESSY] No, I don't want to talk to anybody but you, Mr. U.

[MR. U] Okay.... I'm gonna let you hear his gunshot. Don't worry ... don't worry. He's got a big gun in his hand right now.

[MRS. SHAUGHNESSY] Well, goodbye, Mr. U.

[MR. U] No! If you hang up, he's going to be rough on you. I tell you before ... okay?

[MRS. SHAUGHNESSY] Well, I'm sorry you ever called me ... my life's before me. I'm shaking in my boots...

[MR. U] ...No!...

[MRS. SHAUGHNESSY] ...I'm a nervous wreck...

[MR. U] No, just listen. Here it is. Here it is. Listen to this.

[The sound of repeated gunfire can be heard. Then Mr. U resumes his threats to kill Mrs. Shaughnessy. More gunshots can be heard. She appeals to Mr. U's Christianity, which he professed during earlier, more cordial conversations.]

[MRS. SHAUGHNESSY] You told me you're a Christian! Mr. U, if you are a Christian, you'll hear God...

[MR. U] ...I'm a Christian! But I waste my money.... I waste my money on people...

[MRS. SHAUGHNESSY] ...I don't want to talk anymore...

[MR. U] ...So I've got a killing spirit. And I've got [*inaudible*]...

[MRS. SHAUGHNESSY] I don't want to talk any.... Mr. U, I've got to go sit down. I'm shaking. I don't want to talk...

[Mr. U calms down and proceeds to discuss how she simply needs to wire a few hundred dollars more to his company overseas, and then he can show up at her house in a few minutes and deliver her multi-million-dollar sweepstakes prize. Eventually, Mrs. Shaughnessy refuses to pay him anything, complaining that the money is "not blessed by God," whereupon Mr. U threatens again to send his murderers after her. She tells him she is headed to the Carrboro police station for safety.]

[MR. U] Okay, I can pay.... I can pay even the police in Carrboro in the police station to come and kill you tonight. I can *pay* them!

[MRS. SHAUGHNESSY] You can tell the Carrboro police to come and kill me tonight? I don't think so!

[MR. U] Yes! Yes! I ... you want to bet? You want to seek a bet?

[Mrs. Shaughnessy] No, it won't be them. It'll be you, Mr. U.

[MR. U] No! You want to seek a bet? You want to seek a bet and see?

[MRS. SHAUGHNESSY] The Carrboro police people are not going to come kill me, Mr. U. You're going to kill me.

[MR. U] I never said the Carrboro police people would come and kill you. I said my killers would come in the Carrboro police station and shoot up that. Because the Carrboro police station is not...

[MRS. SHAUGHNESSY] ...Oh, I pray you won't shoot up the Carrboro police station! Surely you wouldn't do that!

[MR. U] So, you want to do that? You will see who...

[MRS. SHAUGHNESSY] ...I didn't think you would shoot up my police station.... They're my security. And your security. And *your* security!

[MR. U] Well, if you don't.... If you don't make that payment today, I'm telling you, I'm gonna shoot ... shoot up the Carrboro police station. And I'm also gonna come at your door, and I'm gonna knock that door down.

[MRS. SHAUGHNESSY] Oh, Mr. U, I can't deal with a man like you...

[MR. U] ...I'm serious...

[MRS. SHAUGHNESSY] ...You're a crook and I can't deal with a man like you. I gotta go. Goodbye.

[MR. U] I'm gonna.... I'm gonna prove it! If you go...

[*Mrs. Shaughnessy hangs up. Recording concludes*]

This particular recording—and I have heard similar recordings involving other victims—illustrates more than just the depravity of some of these criminals and the power of their death threats. It also explains why your older client, customer, patient or loved one might be so reluctant to open up about the peculiar financial transactions he or she has engaged in. Or their nervousness. Or their inability to sleep. The scammers have already coached them not to talk to you or anyone else about the transactions. When they pull out the threats, they again remind the victims not to talk to anybody, not to go for help. In the case of Mrs. Shaughnessy, the criminal threatened her even harder when she said she was so nervous she needed to go to the doctor. And he made it abundantly clear that involving the police would subject her, and them, to unspeakable violence.

43

"Bahkah?"

During my three decades in the North Carolina Attorney General's Office, one of the things that pained me greatly was checking my office mailbox and finding another Record on Appeal in a criminal case. By statute, the Attorney General's Office is responsible for all criminal cases once convicted defendants have filed their appeals with the North Carolina Court of Appeals in Raleigh. It does not matter whether you are an environmental lawyer, a lawyer who represents a state hospital or a lawyer who handles election law issues. If you work in the Attorney General's Office, you must handle three or four appellate cases a year. An appellate case and all of its strict filing deadlines begin the moment you are mailed the book-like Record on Appeal.

Appellate cases can be extremely time consuming. They require the attorney to become totally familiar with printed trial transcripts that can run into the thousands of pages, plus all the exhibits admitted at trial. Then the hard part begins: researching cases and drafting a legal brief of up to 35 pages rebutting the defendant's arguments that he or she is entitled to a new trial, if not an outright acquittal, because of some supposed misstep by police, the trial judge, one or more jurors, or the local prosecutor. And if one is particularly unlucky, the Court of Appeals will require both sides to appear before it and present oral argument—a mind-boggling and ego-destroying exercise where three judges pepper each lawyer with tough questions as he or she tries to debate the opposing lawyer's legal points.

The appellate cases that I handled over the years ranged from a probation revocation matter (my very first appeal, which I believe I lost) to child molestation, homicide or sexual assault cases. The majority of my appellate assignments during the final decade of my AG career fell into the latter two categories. Those cases were gruesome and featured lengthy trial transcripts.

I seldom had time to work on my appellate cases during office hours. Consequently, whenever another Record on Appeal package landed in my mailbox, I immediately pondered with great resentment the upcoming weekends and innumerable evenings that the newly assigned case would take from me. I also resented how the appellate assignment meant putting my elder fraud cases on hold.

One day in late July of 2014, I pulled a Record on Appeal from my box and actually said to myself, "Cool! This one is from Orange County." If a case was from Orange County, my longtime home, I probably knew the judge, the attorneys and the law enforcement officers involved. Sometimes I knew a witness or two, and maybe even a couple of the jurors. In one case, I actually knew the defendant. Knowing the players definitely made an appellate case more interesting to work on.

Then I looked at the name of the defendant in this newly assigned case, "Gary Anderson Barker."[1]

"Bahkah?"

My thoughts immediately turned to our late colleague, Will Garrett, the Richmond FBI agent who took down key members of the House-Mazza home repair fraud group in the late '90s. Gary Anderson Barker was the name of one of his informants. Will referred to him often during our law enforcement task force meetings, always using only the last name and pronouncing it with no "r's."

"He's probably not the only Gary Anderson Barker out there," I thought to myself.

I opened the Record on Appeal and skimmed through the indictments near the front. They spoke of obtaining money or property by false pretenses (fraud), home repairs and elderly victims. Hmm. Still, this just could not have been Will's guy. "Bahkah" had gone off to federal prison for such activities and could not possibly be stupid enough to engage in them again.

Then I flipped to the sentencing documents near the end of the Record on Appeal. It showed that the defendant had been sentenced to prison for wire fraud in 1997 by a federal judge in Richmond, just like "Bahkah" had been when the House-Mazza group went down.

It was Will's guy "Bahkah," all right. And yes, he had been that stupid.

I vowed right then and there that I was not going to lose the Barker appeal. My only problem was that my upcoming court schedule already was poised to overwhelm me. A couple of my consumer protection cases were coming up for trial in state superior court, plus there was a make-or-break hearing in one of my federal court cases, *US v. Dish Network*, coming up in Springfield, Illinois, in October that I had to prepare for and attend. *US v. Dish* was the largest, longest-running telemarketing do-not-call enforcement case ever brought by government officials, and North Carolina, Illinois, Ohio, and California had joined the federal government in filing it five years earlier. It was going to be a tough few months.

Barker's case in Orange County was investigated by Carrboro Police Detective (now Captain of Operations) Chris Atack and prosecuted by a young assistant district attorney named Byron Beasley. My efforts in defending Barker's appeal were easy because they did such a sterling job meeting the state's heavy burden of proving to the jury that Barker's misstatements, errors and omissions when he ripped off his victims were not the result of inadvertence, incompetence or the intervention of factors outside his control but instead the result of a calculated plan to deceive and defraud. And while the charges against Barker only involved two victims, Mrs. N and Mrs. H, the trial also highlighted the experiences of three other older homeowners—two of whom resided just blocks away—who were scammed by Barker during roughly the same time period.

According to the trial testimony, the first incident began when Barker pulled into 85-year-old Mrs. N's driveway on Hillsborough Road and claimed the metal roof on her house needed painting. Even though she had not experienced any problems with her roof, he persuaded her to let him paint it for $2,000. He then applied black barn paint to the roof. That type of paint was never intended for a metal roof. It absorbed heat, which would cause the metal roof panels to expand and contract, causing leaks that would bring water into the house during the next rain. It also would not stick to the raw metal for very long. Soon it would be bubbling and blistering and need to be scraped off.

Before she realized there might be problems with the roof of her house, Mrs. N told one of Barker's helpers that some metal roofing on the corner of a shed in her back yard needed nailing down. This was a shed in which she kept and operated her laundry equipment. Barker told her the entire roof of the shed needed to be redone. She approved the work and Barker and his men rebuilt the roof. They also applied untreated siding to the shed that touched the ground, which would eventually draw termites into the structure.

After collecting $7,300 for these supposed repairs, Barker and his crew left the premises without hauling away the construction debris.

Mrs. N proudly showed Barker's work to her friend and former neighbor, contractor Dennis LaRue. She told him, "I didn't even have to call you, Dennis. I did this all on my own." LaRue immediately noticed the problems with her painted roof and with the structural and wiring modifications that had been made to her laundry shed. He wondered how he was going to break it to her that she had been "taken."

Mrs. N summoned LaRue when the next rain fell. When he arrived, he found her "falling apart." Water was dripping from the interior ceilings throughout her house and the paint on the metal roof above was already blistering. The rebuilt roof on the laundry shed had burst open and drenched her brand-new dryer with water. When Mrs. N proudly displayed Barker's work days earlier, LaRue wondered whether the rebuilt roof of the shed would hold up during a heavy snow or rain. Now he knew.

LaRue scraped the peeling barn paint off the roof and applied "cold seal," a reflective, elastic coating designed for metal roofs. He also helped Mrs. N buy a new, prefabricated shed to replace her destroyed laundry shed. While he was able to get her the contractors' rate on materials, plumbing and electrical work, and while he charged her nothing for his own labor, Mrs. N still had to pay an additional $8,000 to correct Barker's "work" on her shed and remove all the construction debris.

Around the same time that he was collecting $7,300 for this "work" on Mrs. N's property, Barker pulled up to Mrs. H's home on nearby Oak Street. He told Mrs. H, who was sitting on her porch, that he had spotted a small problem on her roof that he could fix for $40. He sent one of his workers up to fix the supposed problem, and when the worker came down, Barker reported that the man had found chimney problems and rotted roof decking that would require extensive repairs. He told her the total costs of the repairs would be $7,700, $4,000 of which would be due immediately and the balance upon the completion of the work. She agreed to the deal.

A day after she paid him $4,000, Barker told Mrs. H that he needed the balance right away so he could go to Lowe's Home Improvement and preorder the white shingles needed for her repair job. She took out a loan at the State Employees' Credit Union and paid him the balance. Barker never preordered the shingles.

Barker and his men pulled two to three rows of shingles off of the perimeter of Mrs. H's roof and covered the exposed wooden decking with roofing felt. Then they left. The roofing felt eventually blew off in several spots. The next time it rained, water came into the house through the ceiling. Barker told her over the phone that he would return and finish repairing her house once the white shingles arrived at Lowe's. He also asked for and received an additional $200 to complete the work. Weeks later, he left a note informing Mrs. H that he was still waiting for the shingles and that his aunt had suffered a stroke. He never returned to finish the work.

Detective Atack of the Carrboro PD could find no problems with the roof decking on Mrs. H's home, other than a perfectly sound roof decking board that appeared to have been split down the middle with a hammer recently.

The 86-year-old Mr. G lived a few blocks away on Dillard Street in Carrboro. Barker had contracted to replace the "flat" roof on his home. Barker began installing the new rubberized roof fabric, stopped work for several days, and then demanded the balance of the payments under the contract, even though they were not due until work was complete. Mr. G refused, saying a deal was a deal and that Barker would only get paid once the work was completed in a satisfactory manner. Barker responded that he had just returned from Mrs. H's house nearby and that she had just paid him the balance due even though her project was incomplete. He questioned why Mr. G could not do the same.

Mr. G's son was a contractor. He summoned Detective Atack and showed him that Barker had totally botched the work already performed. The rubber roofing fabric had not been fastened down around the skylights. Overlapping edges of the fabric had not been sealed together. Edges along the perimeter of the roof had been nailed down with interior sheetrock nails which would quickly rust in the rain and cause the fabric to pop loose. These problems quickly resulted in edges of the roof fabric pulling up in the wind and rain. Water came into the house. Even though those conditions were corrected by the son, Barker's new roof continued to fail and had to be replaced three years later.

That same month, Barker approached Mrs. Z, an older homeowner who lived just a few blocks from Mrs. N, Mrs. H and Mr. G. He told her some flashing on her chimney had come loose and that he could repair it for $40. She authorized him to proceed. When he came down off of the roof, he reported that it had extensive damage and needed $350 in repairs. After he repaired this supposed damage, he told her that there was even more damage, caused by hail, and that the roof would need to be replaced.

Mrs. Z called her insurance company, which sent out an adjuster. He found no hail damage. She then called the man who installed the current roof. He, too, said there was no damage to her roof, only normal wear and tear. He said that Barker had not repaired anything on the roof, just tacked down some new shingles near the chimney flashing, shingles that were not even the correct color. He also found a large, brand-new nail driven partway through the center of some metal flashing immediately below the chimney. He said that the only thing this nail would do was cause rainwater to leak into the interior or the house.

Prosecutor Byron Beasley also presented testimony from Mrs. O, a woman in her early 80s who lived in Greensboro. Nine months before these Carrboro incidents, Barker and another man approached her and said that they could see a problem on her roof and that they could fix it for a small fee. After completing this small repair, they claimed there was extensive damage on her roof. Barker presented her with contracts for $2,525 in repairs. She quickly paid him these fees, plus more for other problems he claimed he was finding. She testified, "He just wanted more and more money." Barker opened a large hole in her roof and covered it with roofing felt. As happened with Mrs. H in Carrboro, the felt blew off during the next storm and allowed water to enter the interior of the house. She tried to repair this hole herself but failed. She could not get Barker to return and finish the work.

The jury found Barker guilty of two counts of obtaining property by false pretenses—commonly referred to as fraud. He then pleaded guilty to being a habitual felon, based upon his prior convictions. That enhanced the amount of punishment he could receive. The trial judge sentenced him to a minimum of 96 months in prison and ordered him to make restitution to Mrs. N and Mrs. G.

I managed not to lose the case in the North Carolina Court of Appeals. The main issues before that court were Barker's claim that the wording of the indictment did not match up with the evidence introduced at trial (which can void the conviction) and his claim that the testimony about the experiences of Mr. G, Mrs. Z and Mrs. O was inadmissible. Barker had only been charged for the incidents involving Mrs. N and

Mrs. H, and he argued that evidence about what he did to the other three homeowners was irrelevant and unduly prejudicial. Prosecutors are not allowed to prove that a defendant committed a crime by introducing evidence that he had committed other bad acts elsewhere. I argued that the testimony about those three other incidents was relevant and admissible under Rule 404(b) of the North Carolina Rules of Evidence. Rule 404(b) states that evidence of "other bad acts" is admissible if it tends to show that the charged offense was intentional or part of a common scheme and not the result of mistake or inadvertence. Both of Barker's legal claims were rejected by the Court of Appeals.[2]

44

Barker Wasn't the Only One

In my personal opinion, Gary Anderson Barker probably went back to scamming elderly homeowners following his conviction in the '90s because he did not know any other way to earn big bucks. He had gotten out of prison and was no longer on probation. The House-Mazza law enforcement task force that sent him and so many of his buddies off to prison had been disbanded for a dozen years, so no one was on the lookout for him anymore. Why not start scamming old folks again?

As it turns out, Barker was not the only member of the House-Mazza home repair fraud group to resume his pre-prison ways. In early 2013, Cary, North Carolina, police detective Jim Grier contacted the Attorney General's Office to report that several older homeowners in his city had been defrauded to the tune of $100,000 to $200,000 apiece by contractors based in the Rocky Mount, North Carolina, area. When I asked Grier the names of some of the suspects, many possessed the same family names as members of the old House-Mazza group. Some, in fact, were members whom we had sent off to prison in the late '90s. Like Barker, they had gotten out of prison, were off probation and were raking in the cash again by defrauding older homeowners.

It struck me as quite odd that the group was active in the city of Cary. In the '90s they avoided Cary. Back then we thought it was because of Cary's notoriously strict building inspections department, a department which struck fear in the hearts of legitimate and illegitimate contactors alike. So why would these scammers be targeting that municipality now?

Over time, Cary became the perfect place for home repair fraud groups to seek out their prey. Its older neighborhoods were now full of homes that were over 40 years old—about the age when a contractor can say with some credibility "this needs fixing" or "that needs replacing." That was not the case in Cary when we took on the House-Mazza group in the mid–'90s. Moreover, by 2012 many of the thousands of the high-income Research Triangle Park employees who settled in Cary's newly built neighborhoods during the second half of the 20th century had become retirees in their 70s and 80s.

Jim Grier learned that a home repair fraud inter-agency task force led by our office took many of these same criminals off the streets in the 1990s, and he wondered whether the same could be done now. I told him that most of the members of that task force had retired or had passed away but that there were still a few of us left. Jim said, "Well, let's see if we can put together another task force. These guys are going wild."

Linda Matthews and I convened a meeting at the Attorney General's Office in response to Jim's suggestion. Wake County District Attorney C. Colon Willoughby, whose office had prosecuted so many members of the House-Mazza group on state felony charges 13 years earlier, showed up. So did Kevin Anderson of the IRS Criminal Investigations Division. I was the third and last attendee who had worked on the old House-Mazza law enforcement task force. Mike East, the current head of the State Bureau of Investigation's Financial Crimes Unit, attended with Special Agent Heather Stroud. They proudly recalled their office's key role in prosecuting the House-Mazza group and seemed gung-ho on the idea of taking on these guys again. The rest of the law enforcement attendees were from area police and sheriff's departments from Burlington to Raleigh to Wilson.

Grier gave a PowerPoint presentation on the scammers his department had investigated, their techniques and their victims. His case summaries, photos and victim profiles took Anderson, Willoughby and me right back to 1996. The others in attendance quickly shared their experiences with the suspects Grier had just mentioned. Kevin Anderson and I offered some deep background information on the group, its structure and its techniques. Willoughby then recited what a prosecutor would need in order to bring cases against them successfully. Because the city of Cary was in his prosecutorial district, and mainly because he was appalled that this same group was back at it, Willoughby expressed his eagerness to bring charges again.

While a huge multi-agency task force like the one we put together in the '90s was never assembled, the group did add other law enforcement agencies to its roster. Two newly hired white-collar crime attorneys from the North Carolina Conference of District Attorneys, Tammy Smith and

Kim Overton, also joined us in the meetings that followed. So did representatives of the North Carolina Licensing Board for General Contractors and several local building inspection departments. These professionals would provide their services to any local district attorney willing to prosecute the scammers.

The group was able to avoid some of the blind alleys that took up so much of the earlier Task Force's time and energy, like trying to build cases based upon the recollections of elderly victims whose memories were not that sharp anymore. Instead, it built the cases from within, using insiders' recollections of who was scammed and how. Criminal information databases had become much more sophisticated and nimbler in the intervening years, allowing Heather and her colleagues to quickly find incidents and pending charges in communities where law enforcement and prosecutors had no idea that they were dealing with an organized home repair fraud network.

In August of that year, the law enforcement agencies in our little group jointly announced "Operation Nail It," 75 felony charges against 10 suspects in six counties. Attorney General Roy Cooper, District Attorney Willoughby and Special Prosecutor Tammy Smith were the featured speakers at the press conference announcing the charges. Also featured was retired professor and swing band leader Leon Jordan, a recent victim of an expensive roofing scam involving both his home and a small downtown Raleigh building he owned. That building housed Poole's Diner, operated by James Beard Award–winning chef Ashley Christensen.

State charges against several other defendants followed. Coincidentally, perhaps, the U.S. Attorney's Office for the Eastern District of North Carolina brought federal charges against home repair contractor James Dino Wills, a former higher-up in the House-Mazza group who went to prison in the late '90s. The new 2013 case against Wills was investigated by Kevin Anderson of the IRS and prosecuted by Thomas Murphy, the same assistant U.S. attorney who brought the first charges against members of the House-Mazza group 16 years earlier. Wills was not charged with home repair fraud, however. He eventually pleaded guilty to "structuring" in 2015 and was sentenced to just over eight years in federal prison.

In all, dozens of felony convictions resulted from Operation Nail It. While it was frustrating that remnants of the House-Mazza home repair group had once again wreaked havoc on older homeowners, it was gratifying to see them defeated.

45

Retired Fortune 100 Exec: The Rest of the Story

Earlier we discussed Mr. S., the seemingly high-functioning former business executive who was victimized repeatedly by overseas lottery scammers based in the Philippines. Although Dorothy Strickland, Joan Fleming and I totally failed to get through to him, one of Donna White's VAP volunteers did. Mr. S soon stopped sending money to the scammers and instead helped us build cases against them.

That success was not everlasting.

Mr. S's son contacted me a few years later and reported that his father had "fallen off the wagon" and was wiring cash to the same types of scammers all over again. The family was at the end of its emotional rope and had hired an attorney. Nothing and nobody could stop their father from sending money to the scammers. He was totally engrossed in their vivid tales of a huge fortune winding its way to his front doorstep, and he was just as resistant to loved ones' words of caution as he had been when we met him at our office years before.

Mr. S's physician had evaluated him and determined that, while he remained competent to handle most of his daily affairs, his repeated dealings with con artists revealed an inability to manage his financial affairs in his own best interests. That finding squared with definition of financial incompetency. Equipped with the doctor's finding, Mr. S's son and wife petitioned the court to make the son Mr. S's financial guardian so that he could take control of his finances and property before it all evaporated.

The son and the family's lawyer wanted me to testify at the guardianship proceeding about Mr. S's history with the scammers over the years. I invited them to send me a subpoena and assured them I would be there.

In North Carolina, the local clerk of court serves as the judge of probate and presides over guardianship proceedings. Usually, in a large metropolitan area like Raleigh-Wake County, a senior assistant clerk of court handles such proceedings full-time. On the date of Mr. S's hearing, I worried whether the assistant clerk of court would find that Mr. S lacked financial competency.

Personally, I was totally convinced that Mr. S lacked capacity to handle his financial affairs anymore and that a limited financial guardianship was vital for his protection. There were clerks of court around the state, however, who felt that our super victims' months and years of slavish devotion to obvious scammers, and the resulting devastation to their life's savings, did not warrant a financial guardianship. My personal assessment was that they considered general competency and financial competency to be one and the same. But they are not. General competency includes important day-to-day functioning skills such as bathing, grooming and feeding oneself, shopping, driving, planning one's day or making important medical decisions. Financial competency is basically a subset of the personal skills that constitute general competency. Because financial skills and financial decisions are more abstract and cognitively complex, financial incompetency can show itself well before general incompetency does. In such situations, the court can enter a limited order that only gives the guardian authority over the person's finances and property.

Whatever caused clerks of court to decline financial guardianship petitions in those extreme instances, their decisions certainly were not in the best interests of the victims. Nor were those decisions going to maintain the victims' dignity and financial independence for very long. Soon they would be too broke to be personally or financially independent and their dignity would take a severe hit.

My worries about the assistant clerk of court in Mr. S's case evaporated as soon as he called the proceeding to order. As we went around the table and introduced ourselves, he noted that he was familiar with the article that Dr. Virginia Templeton and I had written in *Alzheimer's Care Today* on the topics of elder fraud and repeat victimization. He also noted that the many, many fraud incidents detailed in both the petition and the doctor's statement raised serious concerns about Mr. S's financial competency and that most of the morning's discussions would center on those incidents.

He also noticed that the respondent, Mr. S, was not present.

"Where is Mr. S this morning?"

"He refuses to leave the house. He's waiting on more calls from the scammers," replied his son.

Looking at Mr. S's attorney, the assistant clerk asked, "Did your client get a notice of this morning's hearing?"

"He did," replied his attorney. "I even called him this morning to remind him."

"I reminded him too," added Mrs. S. "He still thinks he's one last wire transfer away from receiving his multi-million-dollar prize."

"There's no talking to him," said the son. "He's always been proud of his abilities as a businessman, and he will suffer no comments or warnings about being defrauded."

The clerk asked a few more questions of the son and Mrs. S. Then he announced that Mr. S was no longer able to conduct his financial affairs in his own best interests, that a limited guardianship protecting Mr. S's property and finances was necessary for the protection of Mr. and Mrs. S and their ability to live independently and comfortably, and that he was appointing the son as financial guardian for Mr. S.

With several certified copies of the limited guardianship order in hand, the son began a quick tour of Mr. S's banks, brokerage services, insurance companies, etc., and let them know that he was now in charge of Mr. S's finances and property. He was not looking forward to meeting and speaking with his dad once that tour was done.

We never heard further from the family. We did, however, read Mr. S's obituary in the *Raleigh News & Observer* about four years later. Just like the obituaries of our other super victims, his spoke of being raised by loving parents in the first half of the 20th century, of hard work in college, of a lengthy career full of accomplishments and accolades. It also described his falling in love, getting married and being a devoted spouse and parent for decades and decades, his years of contributions to his church and his community, and the large, multi-generational family that loved him, had received many valuable lessons and insights from him, and would miss him terribly. Like many of those other obituaries, this one closed with a few words about the valiant battle that Mr. S waged against the medical condition that eventually took his life, and it conveyed the family's gratitude to all of the doctors, nurses and other caregivers who had helped and comforted him during that battle.

As with so many other victims we dealt with, no one reading his obituary would have detected that Mr. S had been defrauded for years by the elder fraud industry. Such truths are closely guarded by the families.

Conclusion: The Rewards of Fighting Elder Fraud

Most of the elder fraud warriors mentioned in the preceding chapters told me that fighting the criminals and protecting the victims from further harm was the most gratifying thing they had ever done during their careers as bankers, doctors, retirement community security officers, prosecutors, law enforcement officers, senior care specialists or nonprofit officials. And it is easy to believe. You should have heard the happiness and pride in the voice of North Carolina Attorney General elder fraud specialist Margrita Harrison as she forwarded a phone message from an extremely grateful (and, at one time, suicidal) sweetheart scam victim after we recouped $41,000 of her losses in the 2016 MoneyGram settlement. Or seen the tears welling in former FBI agent Joan Fleming's eyes in October 2018 as she recounted the lengthy prison sentences imposed against Boaz Langman and his Montreal colleagues after one of her superiors told her to "drop these telemarketing cases!" You would have felt it had you seen investigator Linda Matthews bow her head and clasp her hands as Carol and Tommy McPhaul entered their home after a contractor wrecked it and took $124,000 from them and then an outraged community rebuilt it for them. Or heard banker Cynthia Turner's voice after we and (mainly) Barry Elliott of Canada's Phone Busters anti-fraud law enforcement task force convinced her older customer to stop dealing with his victimizers north of the border.

As for me, there were hundreds of satisfying outcomes going all the way back to the older consumers whose homes we saved from auctions on the courthouse steps when I was a rookie attorney (Chapter 2). Most of those successful outcomes over the years involved simply breaking up the cycle of fraud being experienced by particular consumers and preventing further losses. Such results never make the headlines. They might not even prompt a congratulatory email from one's boss.

There is really no way to put a dollar figure on such outcomes, as no one can ever predict how much a repeat fraud victim truly would have lost but for our efforts. All we can point to is the amount of money that was demanded in the scammer's most recent "reload" attempt, which we foiled. But we have always known, based upon experience, that the losses we prevented would have continued on but for our efforts to protect that consumer.

Some of my college buddies and law school classmates regularly are written up in lawyer magazines due to the impressive verdicts and settlements they and their private law firms obtain in multi-million-dollar personal injury and business dispute cases. I have obtained some multi-million-dollar settlements and verdicts against major companies myself, but public sector attorneys seldom are celebrated in those publications. I really do not care. The letters and phone calls we in the Attorney General's Office received from grateful older consumers and their families were far more satisfying. I still treasure a scratchy, wrinkled photocopy of a handwritten thank-you note from a $28,000 victim of several sweepstakes scams for whom we were only able to recover $7,000. It reads:

July 27, 1994

Dear Mr. Kirkman,

At this time, I wish to thank you so very much for recovering the $7,000 from Consumer Protection Network.

I would assume that you put in much time to convince them to "turn over" this prodigious amount.

Again, many thanks to you for helping me.

Sincerely,

[T.R.]

Re: File # 9403501, Consumer Protection Network.

One of the first elderly consumers that I helped after I arrived in the Attorney General's Office in 1987 was a Moore County, North Carolina, farmer in his mid–80s who had been taken for $6,000 in an invention marketing scam. After collecting regular payments from him for four years through false and repeated promises to find a purchaser for his invention idea (an idea that had been developed, patented and manufactured by others decades earlier), the invention marketing company sent him the type of form letter that invention scammers eventually send: "We regret to inform you that, despite our repeated and diligent efforts, we were unable to sell your invention idea."

I recovered this gentleman's $6,000 by sending the invention marketing company a couple of fiery letters threatening suit by our office. Weeks after I forwarded the $6,000 check to him and closed his file, the old guy sent me a note. I did not save a copy of it, but I will never forget it. He told me, essentially, "I am dying of colon cancer. That $6,000 was all the savings that I had, and without it I would have had to burden my family with the costs of my funeral. Thanks to you, I can cover them myself and die in peace."

That note, more than anything else, set me on the course of helping older consumers throughout my career in the Consumer Protection Division. That career ended in January 2017 when I retired. My final two years there were consumed by management duties and several non-elder fraud trials and investigations, including the trial in the previously mentioned case involving Dish Network and millions of alleged Do Not Call and robocall violations. My opportunities to fight the elder fraud industry were few and far between during that period, but I tried to make good use of them.

A few weeks before my final day in the office, consumer protection specialist Maria Harkley brought me a troublesome consumer complaint submitted by an older couple in Hillsborough, North Carolina. A door-to-door salesman sold them what probably was a $400 room air filtration device for just over $2,000. With financing, the total costs would be $3,000. His main pitch to the couple was that the wife, who suffered from respiratory issues and had dementia, would benefit medically from the device. The day after the salesman completed the transaction and left the device with the couple, the husband sought to cancel the deal because the wife, in her demented state, kept attacking the menacing looking, noisy contraption. He had a legal right to cancel without penalty during the statutory three-day cancellation period. Instead of retrieving the device, the salesman showed up and sold them a second one.

Now the total payments were almost $6,000. The husband tried to cancel the following day, just as he had attempted before. Neither the salesman's company nor the Minnesota firm that financed the transaction would honor the husband's cancellation attempt.

By means of a pair of letters that I composed during a lunch break,

I introduced myself as the head of the AG's Elder Fraud Unit and demanded that the salesman's employer and/or the company that financed the transaction cancel it and refund any payments that had been made so far. The stated legal reasons for my demands were the sales company's liability for not honoring the three-day cancellation attempt by the husband, plus the false health claims the salesman had made concerning the wife's medical conditions. The finance company told me to stick it, but the sales company agreed to cancel the deal. That was a lunch break well spent.

Soon after that, and just as my days in the AG's office were dwindling down to nothing, consumer protection specialist Billie Rouse brought me a similar complaint involving an 80-year-old woman in Winston-Salem, North Carolina, who had been pressured into buying an unneeded and very expensive water filtration device. She was told that her water was unhealthy and dangerous. The door-to-door salesman never told her of her three-day cancellation rights, as required by law.

The company maintained she was on the hook for $4,000 for the purchase, installation and finance charges. She probably could have purchased such a device at Lowe's or Home Depot for a fraction of that cost. I only had a few minutes to devote to the matter, so I pulled up the letters I had sent on behalf of the Hillsborough couple, changed the names, company addresses and merchandise descriptions, and fired them off to the finance company and the water filter sales company. The water filter was retrieved and the woman's finance contract was cancelled three days later, just as I was clearing out my desk and heading off to retirement.

I bring up these two small cases for a couple of reasons. The first is to point out that those final cases of my legal career were not terribly different from the cases of the Charlotte space heater salesman and the Stanly County remodeling contractor 35 years earlier when I was a mere boy lawyer (see Chapter 2). People who are low enough to scam vulnerable seniors will always be with us.

The other reason I bring them up is to point out how, despite how busy you might be with other matters, it is important and personally rewarding to muster up whatever time and energy you can to fight those who would prey on vulnerable older adults.

It matters not whether you are in law enforcement, the medical field, the financial industry or the glorious days of retirement. You can have an impact. Strike up a conversation with any senior you spot in a store purchasing multiple gift cards or prepaid debit cards, then gently shift to a discussion of how the only people who want to be paid in gift cards are scammers. Write the heads of retail chains that sell such cards and encourage them to put limits on the amount of money that a customer can put on them or, at the very least, to train their employees on how to persuade older customers never to use such cards to pay a debt or a bill. Let the manager or check-out clerk at your favorite store know how much you appreciate their following Western Union, Walmart or MoneyGram protocols whenever an older customer approaches and wants to wire money, even though it might be awkward for the store employee to do so. Sign up with your state AARP chapter to become a fraud watch volunteer and learn how to go out and do presentations on senior fraud. Attend campaign events and ask each candidate to make elder fraud a priority, especially if the candidate is running to be the local prosecutor, sheriff or state attorney general.

If your job brings you into contact with older adults, ask your employer or professional association to develop staff training and continuing professional education programs on the best ways to spot and interrupt elder fraud incidents in progress. If you are a family caregiver for someone with dementia, share with younger professionals your knowledge of the early and middle stages of age-related cognitive decline and how it creates vulnerabilities to fraud. They really need your knowledge on the subject.

Network, just like most of the fraud fighters mentioned in this book did, and draw upon the tools and talents of your colleagues. You will establish some really wonderful friendships in the process. If you work in the financial sector, hone your counseling skills for when a client or customer appears to be engaged in a fraud-induced transaction and be familiar with company and FINRA rules on placing holds on such transactions. Also if you are in the financial sector, encourage older clients and customers to designate "trusted contacts" who can be consulted if and when it appears that they are being defrauded or financially exploited, and report suspected elder fraud incidents to all appropriate entities (e.g., local Adult Protective Services, FinCEN for suspicious activity reports, local law enforcement for identity theft and face-to-face scams, your state attorney general or Department of Consumer Protection for phone, mail and Internet scams, and the U.S. Postal Inspection Service for mail scams).

Always take care when addressing an older person who is being defrauded. Avoid words, tones of voice, facial expressions or physical gestures that might make them feel chastised or demeaned. That will only drive them deeper into the psychological clutches of the criminals, who are being respectful and nice to them and telling them that they are doing the right thing by spending more money.

Spend more time with friends and relatives who are seniors. Each minute that you spend with them erodes a key vulnerability that the fraud industry exploits: isolation. Make senior scams and the latest solicitations the person has received a regular topic of conversation whenever you visit or call. They receive tons of sketchy solicitations. Be sure to discuss what the people behind those phone calls, emails, letters or door-to-door pitches might really be up to. This will keep them alert for the telltale signs that a pitch is a fraud instead of looking for the signs that it is legitimate—a troublesome tendency that many of us will experience as we age.

The different ways that you can help are limited only by your imagination. The most important thing is this: don't do nothing. That is exactly what the elder fraud industry is counting on.

Thank you for joining the war on elder fraud and best of luck to you.

Chapter Notes

Introduction

1. These first four paragraphs at one time comprised my opening comments when giving presentations on senior fraud in or near my hometown of Chapel Hill, North Carolina. They later formed the initial four paragraphs of a law journal article: Kirkman, D., "Fraud, Vulnerability and Aging—When Criminals Gang Up on Mom and Dad," *The North Carolina State Bar Journal*, Winter 2013, 18[4].

2. Huang, Y., and Lawitz, A., Office of Children and Family Services, *The New York State Cost of Financial Exploitation Study* (2016); Lifespan of Greater Rochester, Inc., et al., *Under the Radar: New York State Elder Abuse Prevalence Study* (2011).

Chapter 3

1. *America Burning*, Report of the National Commission on Fire Prevention and Control, Washington, D.C., May 4, 1973.

Chapter 4

1. *State of North Carolina, ex rel., Michael F. Easley, Attorney General vs. White Associates*, et al., Case No. 95 CVS 03684, Wake County (NC) Superior Court.

2. Pratkanis, A.R., and Shadel, D., *Weapons of Fraud*, AARP Washington, Seattle (2005), pp. 133–38.

Chapter 5

1. N.C. Gen. Stat. § 8C-1, Rules of Evidence, Rule 404(b).

Chapter 13

1. Howe, N., "The Graying of Wealth," *Forbes*, March 16, 2018 (citing statistics from Table 2, p. 13, "Changes in U.S. Family Finances from 2013 to 2016: Evidence from the Survey of Consumer Finances," *The Federal Reserve Bulletin*, September 2017, 103[3]).

2. Templeton, V.H., and Kirkman, D.N., "Fraud, Vulnerability and Aging: Case Studies," *Alzheimer's Care Today*, September 2007.

3. Boyle, P.; Yu, L.; et al., "Scam Awareness Related to Incident Alzheimer Dementia and Mild Cognitive Impairment," *Annals of Internal Medicine*, April 16, 2019

Chapter 18

1. *United States of America v. Robert Marshall House, Sr.,* et al., Case No. 5:96-CR-00174-BR, Eastern District of NC; Indictments filed October 15, 1996.

2. *United States of America v. Anthony F. Mazza, Jr.,* et al., Case No. 3:96-CR-124, Eastern District of Virginia; Indictments filed Nov. 1, 1996.

Chapter 20

1. Titus, R., "The Victimology of Fraud," paper presented to the Restoration of Victims of Crime Conference, Melbourne, Australia, September 1999.

Chapter 25

1. *United States of America v. Anthony F. Mazza,* et al., Case No. 3:96-CR-00124,

Eastern District of VA; Documents 78–80, 82–85.

2. *United States of America v. Gary Anderson Barker*, Case No. 3:96-CR-00141-RLW, Eastern District of VA; Document 12.

3. *United States of America v. Robert Marshall House, Sr.*, et al., Case No. 5:96-CR-00174-BR, Eastern District of NC, Documents 161–64, 166–69.

4. *United States of America v. Robert Marshall House, Sr.*, et al., Case No. 5:97-CR-00011-BR, Eastern District of NC, Document 34.

Chapter 26

1. *United States of America v. Kenneth R. Overton*, et al., Case No. 5:04-CR-2-1, Western District of NC; Document 166.

Chapter 27

1. *Federal Trade Commission and the States of IL, IA, NV, ND, NC, OH and VT vs. Your Money Access, LLC*, et al., Case No. 2:07-cv-05147-ER (E.D. PA).

2. Office of the Comptroller of the Currency Press Release, "OCC Directs Wachovia to Make Restitution to Consumers Harmed by the Bank's Relationships with Telemarketers," April 25, 2008.

3. Office of the Maine Attorney General Press Release, "Maine Joins Agreement with Western Union Over Fraud-Induced Transfers," December 29, 2005.

4. *Consumer Sentinel Network Data Book, January–December 2015*, Federal Trade Commission, February 2016, p. 8; *Consumer Sentinel Network Data Book, January–December 2018*, Federal Trade Commission, February 2019, p. 11.

5. Weiss, G., "The New Currency of Fraud," *AARP Bulletin*, June 2019, 60[8], p. 24.

Chapter 28

1. *United States of America v. Langman*, et al., Case No. 5:98-cr-00009-H (Eastern District of NC), Case Doc. No. 72; Overall sentence reduced to 66 mos. per Rule 35 and $1,713,971.77 restitution order entered on 11/14/01, Case Doc. No. 226.

2. *Id.*, Case Doc. Nos. 73 and 77.

Chapter 31

1. *Carol McPhaul v. John M. Shearer*, Case No. 07 CVS 11377, Wake County (NC) Superior Court, Civil Judgment entered 03/08/10.

2. "Contractor to Pay Nearly $125K in Restitution to Elderly Couple," https://www.wral.com/5onyourside/story/4100028, published 12/08/08.

3. *State of NC v. John Martin Shearer*, Case No. 07 CRS 72638, Wake County (NC) Superior Court, Criminal Judgment entered 12/08/08.

Chapter 34

1. *United States of America vs. Clayton Atkinson*, et al., Case No. 5:08-CR-70-BO, Eastern District of North Carolina.

2. *Id.*, Case document 77, Sentencing Hearing Transcript, March 15, 2012.

3. *Id.*, Case Document 67, Judgment Order, March 15, 2012.

4. *Id.*, Case Document 76, Judgment Order, March 15, 2012.

5. *Id.*, Case Document 117, Sentencing Hearing Transcript, May 9, 2013.

Chapter 36

1. Templeton, V.H., and Kirkman, D.N., "Fraud, Vulnerability and Aging: Case Studies," *Alzheimer's Care Today*, September 2007.

Chapter 37

1. N.C. Gen. Stat. § 14-401(13) (three-day right to cancel off-premises sales).

2. N.C. Gen. Stat. §§ 75-1.1, 15 and 15.1.

3. Hard copies of the extensive pleadings and court orders from this case are found in Wake County Clerk of Court file number 07 CVS 07752. Electronic copies of North Carolina trial court documents are not generally available online.

Chapter 38

1. "Troubleshooter: Paver Banned," https://abc11.com/archive/7483644/, June 7, 2010.

Chapter 40

1. https://www.justice.gov/opa/pr/north-carolina-paving-contractor-sentenced-prison-tax-and-bank-fraud.

Chapter 43

1. *State of North Carolina v. Gary Anderson Barker, Jr.,* North Carolina Court of Appeals file number COA14-774, Record on Appeal.

2. *State v. Barker,* 770 S.E.2d 142 (2015) (Court of Appeals Opinion).

Bibliography

Books, Research Publications

America Burning, Report of the National Commission on Fire Prevention and Control, Washington, D.C., May 4, 1973.

Asp, E., K. Manzel, B. Koestner, C. Cole, N. Denburg, and D. Tranel, "A Neuropsychological Test of Belief and Doubt; Damage to the Ventromedial Prefrontal Cortex Increases Credulity for Misleading Advertising," *Frontiers in Neuroscience*, July 2012.

Boyle, P., L. Yu, et al., "Scam Awareness Related to Incident Alzheimer Dementia and Mild Cognitive Impairment," *Annals of Internal Medicine*, April 16, 2019.

Castle, E., N. Eisenberger, T. Seeman, W. Moons, I. Boggero, M. Grinblatt, and S. Taylor, "Neural and Behavioral Bases of Age Differences in Perceptions of Trust," *Proceedings of the National Academy of Sciences*, October 2012.

Howe, N., "The Graying of Wealth," *Forbes*, March 16, 2018 (citing statistics from Table 2, p. 13, "Changes in U.S. Family Finances from 2013 to 2016: Evidence from the Survey of Consumer Finances," *The Federal Reserve Bulletin*, September 2017, 103[3]).

Kirkman, D., "Fraud, Vulnerability and Aging—When Criminals Gang Up on Mom and Dad," *The North Carolina State Bar Journal*, Winter 2013, 18[4].

Princeton Survey Research Associates, *Telemarketing and Older Americans: An AARP Study*, AARP (1996).

Samanez-Larkin, G.R., C.M. Kuhnen, D.J. Yoo, and B. Knutson, "Variability in Nucleus Accumbens Activity Mediates Age-Related Suboptimal Financial Risk Taking," *Journal of Neuroscience*, 2010, 30[4] 1426–1434.

Templeton, V.H., and D.N. Kirkman, "Fraud, Vulnerability and Aging: Case Studies," *Alzheimer's Care Today*, September 2007.

Titus, R., "The Victimology of Fraud," paper presented to the Restoration of Victims of Crime Conference, Melbourne, Australia, September 1999.

Triebel, K.L., R. Martin, et al., "Declining Financial Capacity and Mild Cognitive Impairment: A 1-Year Longitudinal Study," *Neurology*, September 22, 2009, 73[12] 928–934.

Weiss, G., "The New Currency of Fraud," *AARP Bulletin*, June 2019, 60[8], p. 24.

Widera, E., V. Steenpass, and J. Marson, "Finances in the Older Patient with Cognitive Impairment: 'He Didn't Want Me to Take Over,'" *JAMA*, February 16, 2011.

Newscasts and Press Releases

"Contractor to Pay Nearly $125K in Restitution to Elderly Couple," December 8, 2008, https://www.wral.com/5onyourside/story/4100028.

"Couple Comes 'Home' After Nightmare Remodeling Job," November 12, 2007, https://www.wral.com/5onyourside/story/2033397/.

"Crews Fix Couple's Botched Remodeling Job," August 20, 2007, https://www.wral.com/5onyourside/story/1723387/.

"Man Accused of Botched Remodeling Job in Jail," October 4, 2007, https://www.wral.com/5onyourside/story/1891301/.

"Man Indicted in Botched Remodeling Job," February 12, 2008, https://www.wral.com/5onyourside/story/2428737/.

Office of the Comptroller of the Currency Press Release, "OCC Directs Wachovia to Make Restitution to Consumers Harmed by the Bank's Relationships with Telemarketers," April 25, 2008, https://www.occ.gov/news-issuances/news-releases/2008/nr-occ-2008-48.html

Office of the Maine Attorney General Press Release, "Maine Joins Agreement with Western Union Over Fraud-Induced Transfers," December 29, 2005.

"State Sues Man Over Botched Home-Remodeling Job," July 19, 2007, https://www.wral.com/5onyourside/story/1613112/.

"Troubleshooter: Paver Banned," June 7, 2010, https://abc11.com/archive/7483644/.

U.S. Department of Justice Press Release, April 4 2014, https://www.justice.gov/opa/pr/north-carolina-paving-contractor-sentenced-prison-tax-and-bank-fraud.

"Volunteers to Fix Botched Remodeling Job," July 25, 2007, https://www.wral.com/5onyourside/story/1634633/.

Appellate and Trial Court Orders and Pleadings

Carol McPhaul v. John M. Shearer, Case No. 07 CVS 11377, Wake County (NC) Superior Court, Civil Judgment entered 03/08/10.

Federal Trade Commission and the States of IL, IA, NV, ND, NC, OH and VT vs. Your Money Access, LLC, et al., Case No. 2:07-cv-05147-ER, Eastern District of Pennsylvania.

State of NC v. John Martin Shearer, Case No. 07 CRS 72638, Wake County (NC) Superior Court, Criminal Judgment entered 12/08/08.

State of North Carolina, ex rel., Michael F. Easley, Attorney General vs. White Associates, et al., Case No. 95 CVS 03684, Wake County (NC) Superior Court (civil case commenced April 1995).

State of North Carolina v. Gary Anderson Barker, Jr., North Carolina Court of Appeals file number COA14-774 (Record on Appeal).

State v. Barker, 770 S.E.2d 142 (2015) (Court of Appeals Opinion).

United States of America v. Anthony F. Mazza, et al., Case No. 3:96-CR-00124, Eastern District of VA; Documents 78–80, 82–85.

United States of America v. Anthony F. Mazza, Jr., et al., Case No. 3:96-CR-124, Eastern District of VA; Indictments filed Nov. 1, 1996.

United States of America v. Boaz Moshe Langman, et al., Case No. 5:98-CR-00009-H, Eastern District of NC; Documents 72 and 226 (Judgment and Amended Judgment).

United States of America v. Clayton Atkinson, et al., Case No. 5:08-CR-70-BO, Eastern District of NC; Documents 67, 76, 77 (Judgment, Sentencing Hearing transcript).

United States of America v. Gary Anderson Barker, Case No. 3:96-CR-00141-RLW, Eastern District of VA; Document 12 (Judgment and Sentence).

United States of America v. Kenneth R. Overton, et al., Case No. 5:04-CR-2-1, Western District of NC, Document 166.

United States of America v. Robert Marshall House, Sr., et al., Case No. 5:96-CR-00174-BR, Eastern District of NC, Documents 161–64, 166–69 (Judgments and Sentences).

United States of America v. Robert Marshall House, Sr., et al., Case No. 5:96-CR-00174-BR, Eastern District of NC, Indictments filed October 15, 1996.

United States of America v. Robert Marshall House, Sr., et al., Case No. 5:97-CR-00011-BR, Eastern District of NC, Document 34 (Judgment and Sentence).

Statutes

N.C. Gen. Stat. § 8C-1, Rules of Evidence, Rule 404(b).
N.C. Gen. Stat. § 14-401(13) (three-day right to cancellation in off-premises sales).
N.C. Gen. Stat. §§ 75-1.1, 15 and 15.1 (Unfair Trade Practices—Remedies in cases brought by the Attorney General).

Other

Consumer Sentinel Network Data Book, January–December 2015, Federal Trade Commission, February 2016, p. 8.
Consumer Sentinel Network Data Book, January–December 2018, Federal Trade Commission, February 2019, p. 11.

Index